Fire of the Five Hearts

To The
Women, Men &
Children
of Trinidad
love ~

FIRE OF THE FIVE HEARTS

A Memoir
of Treating Incest

Holly A. Smith

Brunner-Routledge
Taylor & Francis Group

NEW YORK AND HOVE

Published in 2002 by
Brunner-Routledge
29 West 35th Street
New York, NY 10001
www.brunner-routledge.com

Published in Great Britain by
Brunner-Routledge
27 Church Road
Hove, East Sussex
BN3 2FA
www.brunner-routledge.co.uk

Although these stories are based upon real people all names and circumstances
have been changed to protect the identities of those portrayed.

Cover Design: Jen Crisp
Cover Photo: Imagebank

4-25-07

10 9 8 7 6 5 4 3 2 1

Library of Congress Cataloging-in-Publication Data
Smith, Holly, A., 1956–
    Fire of the five hearts : a memoir of treating incest / Holly A. Smith
        p. cm.
        ISBN 1-58391-354-8 (pbk. : alk. paper)
        1. Smith, Holly A., 1956– 2. Psychotherapists—United States—Biography.
    3. Incest victims—Mental health. 4. Incest. I. Title: Fire of the five hearts.
    II. Title.
    RC560.I53 S656 2002
    616.85'836—dc21
                                                            2002005304

To my children, Lily, David, and Olivia—
With more love than I can ever express

For my husband David,
With love and gratitude

CONTENTS

Foreword   **IX**

Acknowledgments   **XIII**

Introduction   **XVII**

Chapter **1**   **Ricky Still Loves Lulu**   **1**

Chapter **2**   **Isabella**   **9**

Chapter **3**   **The Sins of the Father Are Visited upon the Daughters**   **27**

Chapter **4**   **Lying Down with the Offender**   **43**

Chapter **5**   **"To My Haunting Ophelia, Who Brings Me to My Knees—Tie My Hands": On Esthetics, Art, and Spontaneous Weeping**   **63**

Chapter **6**   **On Siblings and Sex**   **75**

Chapter **7**   **The Therapist with Child: Transference and Countertransference Ad Nauseum**   **97**

Chapter **8**   **On Finding a Voice**   **109**

Chapter **9**   **Falling from Grace**   **127**

Chapter **10**   **Spank Me: On Sex and the Unthinkable**   145

Chapter **11**   **From Field to Administration**   159

Chapter **12**   **Pockets of Compassion . . . When
Mine Are Empty**   177

FOREWORD

Fire of the Five Hearts is a unique and groundbreaking book. It provides the reader with a rare glimpse into the world of child sexual abuse written from the perspective of a seasoned caseworker who has dedicated her career to finding and treating incest.

The title of the book is discussed in the first chapter. "Fire of the Five Hearts" is a Chinese medical perspective that holds that the person retains too much heat or distress in their body. This "fire" analogy is applicable to those for whom this book is about—the victims of this type of abuse, the perpetrators, as well as the professionals who work in this field.

Many books have been written about incest from the point of view of the victim—many extraordinary, informative, and insightful books. However, there have not been any books written about this subject from the point of view of the mental health care professional who treats the victims of this abuse, and which explores the affects this type of work has on the professional. This groundbreaking book examines the challenges that come with working in this field and explores the distress of this work experienced by the caseworker. This book perfectly illustrates and documents the challenges of human service professionals as they learn to survive and even thrive laboring in the fields of broken, abused and traumatized children and parents. In essence, the book examines how this "fire of the five hearts" is enflamed, controlled, and extinguished.

The distress on the health care professional who suffers from burnout associated with being emotionally affected by working with victims of crime or other traumatic events has come to be known as *compassion fatigue.* For several years now, Holly

Smith, a veteran caseworker, has become a featured speaker on this topic. In this book she tells a series of stories of child molestation and her personal actions and reactions as a caseworker. These are actual cases with identities disguised. Reading more like a series of short stories than a non-fiction book about a major social problem, Holly Smith has provided a window into her world that is both distressing and inspiring. She allows us to experience what she experiences—fears, joys, disgust, and all. She is our gentle guide. She achieves the perfect balance between storyteller and educator. Simply put: *Fire of the Five Hearts* is a gem.

I first met Holly Smith at a special invitation symposium funded by the U.S. Department of Justice. The purpose of the meeting was to help develop a program to combat a growing problem among those who counseled victims of crime: compassion fatigue. Holly stood out from the rest of us. Although she had more than 17 years of experience working with sexually molested children, she seemed to not be hardened by the work. Rather than simply report on the struggles of both the victim and those who are hired to help, Holly seemed to relate her experiences with extraordinary grace. Holly had a way with words. By the end of the meeting, I urged her to consider writing this book. I believed that it would be an excellent addition to my book series.

Over the next two years Holly wrote the book, she would send me copies of various chapters for my input and suggestions. Most often I only gave her encouragement. Only on occasion did I give her advice on content and only after direct questioning. I knew from the beginning that she would write a profoundly moving and influential book. And here it is.

As Series Editor, I served as the silent partner in this important writing project. Like a patient gardener hovering over a beautiful and unfolding flower, I was there to protect her from the weeds, ensure sufficient sun and moisture. But once the book was completed we all knew (the publisher, Holly, and I) that this flower was meant for a much larger garden. And so this book is being offered to everyone to read, not just specialists and academics (who are the target audience of my series).

Holly Smith became a specialist in incest not because she was ever an incest victim but because there was a job opening for a caseworker. She quickly learned she had a gift for the work. Reading this book is like going on a journey with Holly as a wise guide who mixes beautiful descriptions of life and beauty with the underbelly of child protection work. We learn a lot about her work with incest victims and survivors. In contrast to victims who are helpless, sometimes hapless and are hampered by their victimization, a survivor has overcome these limitations and transformed them into a source of strength and sometimes inspiration. The inspiration is never again to be victimized and sometimes inspired to help others. Thus, someone like Holly not only saves and heals victims but also transforms them into a powerful resource for helping others.

We also learn a lot about the personal toll this kind of work has taken on Holly Smith over the years. The beauty of the book is that it illustrates that through all of the hardships, both personal and professional that Holly Smith endures her steadfast determination to help these young victims always comes through, even when she is closest to burning out. She never gives up—it is as if she knows that if she gives up, then the victims of these horrific crimes will sense that it is ok for them to give up on their lives: This is her calling, and she perseveres with it time and time again.

This book is not only meant to be read by other mental health care professionals who may have experienced similar situations—it is also meant for sexual abuse victims, their families, and for anyone who cares to learn more about this topic. Most importantly though, this book should be required reading of everyone who loves children, especially readers who care about the welfare of children and the welfare of those professionals who care for them and have *fire in the five hearts.*

—Charles R. Figley, Ph.D.
Tallahassee, Florida

ACKNOWLEDGMENTS

Many years ago I visited a well-known astrologist in Boulder. When she opened the door, she was everything I had imagined her to be—ethereal and diaphanous, much like I would imagine a fairy, or an apparition. She did not walk across the room to seat me; she appeared to float. As she unfurled my chart, her fingers, long and sculpted, led me through my many astrological houses, which looked to me like cryptic scrawl.

I had come to visit her out of my desperation to conceive. I wanted her to read my stars and tell me that all would be well, that I would conceive and that I would give birth to a beautiful healthy baby. However, the first thing she presented me with was my very profound penchant for creativity and insight—that this creativity would evolve through the written word—in fact I would write a very important book. Exasperated and impatient I remember thinking to myself: "Yeah whatever! Who cares about a book? I want a baby. I want to know that I will be a mother."

The birthing of a book was the furthest thing from my reality. I tucked her suggestion in a recess of my brain. I went on to have not one, but three beautiful babies. But each time I ventured back to her house of wisdom for yet another pressing life decision, she talked about the book I would write. Each and every time I waved her off—"book schmook!"

I am a firm believer in astrology. Like any other metaphysical art it is the unknown and the power of suggestion that tends to rattle the undiscovered, uncultivated parts of us. I feel the pressing need to go back to see her, to tell her of course, she was right.

Over the last three years I have labored over the writing of

Fire of the Five Hearts. It has truly been a labor of love, and not unlike the pregnancy and birthing of a child. There were times when I was so full of ideas that they were difficult to contain. There were also the bleakest of times, when I wanted to chuck the whole damn thing. The writing of this book has been both painful and exhilarating.

I would like to give thanks to a number of people who helped me to conceive this book, and will no doubt assist me in bringing it into the world, shaping it and forming it, and ultimately sharing it with my readers.

I would like to thank Charles Figley for seeing something in me that piqued his curiosity and interest. He has been my staunch supporter as well as an unfailing guide when my angst and fear eclipsed my expression and ideas. I believe you know, my dear friend, that you have changed my life. I love that you believe in me and have watched as I have pushed through my bounds, sometimes fearless, sometimes paralyzed. You indeed have given me roots and wings in this process. Many thanks and much love.

Huge love to my sister Laurel for reading each and every chapter. You were gracious and gentle in your reactions. We shared a special gift, you and I, in the writing of this book. I was able to show you a piece of myself that has been long hidden, but which I knew you would understand. As sisters, we are only too aware of our history, and the process I believe brought us even closer. I thank you for taking the time out of your life to listen to me mull over thoughts and ideas. I thank you for your encouragement, and wisdom.

To my therapist, Dr. Susan Oliver, what can I say? You know every inch of my mind. Over the last several years I have left a chapter at your office door, and it became the grist for our therapy sessions. I thank you for your ability to bend in this way—for reading each chapter and pushing my mind further, for soothing me when it felt as if I was looming at the edge and afraid that I was too naked in my thoughts. Thank you for reeling me in. I'm sure in the world of psychiatry these sessions were a bit of an anomaly—I could see of no other way to process this creation. You are a gifted healer, and your ability to reach into my heart when it has been most protected, has been truly a gift.

To Linda—thank you so much for your loving friendship.

You created a haven for me in which to birth my ideas. You listened as I wrote paragraphs and read them out loud. You became my other set of ears and eyes when I was weary, or to close to my pain. You created a sense of organization that I will never have—had it not been for your ability to keep me on track, I'd still be writing. We became friends through a profound tragedy—nonetheless, I hope this book has provided you with some solace, and inspiration. Thank you for the exquisite thimbles full of merlot and Beaujolais—they certainly took the edge off the quake, especially when an entire chapter evaporated into the technological ether—you kept my feet to the fire, and always without fail retrieved my lost words.

Many thanks to my editor, Emily Epstein. This was a challenging task to arrive at, midstream. You have been kind and respectful and have guided me well through the publishing of this book. I am very appreciative of your commitment to this book and your ability to navigate all the various terrains. I know that I put you to the test on more than one occasion, and your advocacy was wonderful.

Thank you to Bernadette Capelle, my original connection to Brunner/Routledge. I know that you took a risk in pushing this baby through, I also know that it had a place in your heart—you will not be disappointed.

Thanks to Henry Tobey for his editing savvy, for being a good friend, and unbeknownst to all of us, for being the conduit between Charles and myself. Thank you for inviting me to be part of the Secondary Trauma Resiliency Training—it has been a wonderful learning and an invaluable tool in the writing of this book. Love and thanks to my parents Irving and Josephine Smith for their love and support and their pride in my work.

Finally, a special thanks to my children Lily, David, and Olivia.

Thank you Lily for your beauty and passion and your uncanny ability at such a tender age, of seeing the injustice in the world and giving voice to it—your spirit has been a powerful inspiration for me. You're beautiful being is laced throughout these chapters. I hope your fairy cards come true! To my lovely Olivia, whose questions about the book were marvelously insightful. Your innocence and wide-eyed beauty keep my perspective of all that is sweet in the world. Thank you.

To my son David, with the sweetest soul and the most tender heart. You see beauty and goodness in everything and everyone. In your sensitivity and your reserve, you knew so much about the writing of this book, particularly by the questions you asked in class. I thank you for reminding me always to stop and smell the roses.

Lastly, the biggest thank you to my husband David for taking over the helm and encouraging my voice; for pushing me out the door to finish a chapter when all I wanted to do was curl up in our bed and nap or editing my slang on boy private parts and bodily functions. Thank you for loving me as long as you have, and for knowing me as well as you do. I know I can be a pistol, but that creates the fire, don't you think?

Thank you for being the kind of husband and father that could endure the absence of a wife and mother for such a long duration. You are a gem.

* * * * * * *

The individuals in this book are real and the stories are true. Through great pains and many rewrites I have disguised all identities. All names have been changes to ensure confidentiality, and life circumstances and details have been changed. In some instances I have grafted part of one individual's identity with another. In essence, the individuals in these stories are a composite of many different people and their life circumstances.

Because incest and sexual abuse have uncanny commonalities, the reader may feel that they are reading about themselves or someone they know. The universality of incestuous couplings is vast—the sexual acts, the verbal dialogue, and the coercive dynamics are sadly similar in nature—that in and of itself will bring bittersweet relief and ultimately sadness.

INTRODUCTION

It is a daunting task to write about incest, even more daunting that *Fire of the Five Hearts* is a book in which I choose to expose my panty drawer to the world, longing for its understanding and compassion, knowing full well that I will elicit ire and contempt from some who wish to venture there.

The panty drawer is a beautiful metaphor for secrets. Everyone has a panty drawer. The drawer of my husband's drafting table is analogous to my panty drawer. One's panty drawer is where one nestles one's most secret, precious belongings. My panty drawer has a scent of lavender and houses my most intimate possessions—my gossamer underthings, delicate and light, love letters from my children, locks of the children's hair, a small ceramic box filled with their baby teeth, and—alas—practical cotton underwear and camisoles. Each and every panty drawer is a road map to our being.

It is a rarity to find people who really understand incest. It is a sordid atrocity from which most any human being would turn away. I wonder why it is that I can't, and why I have chosen to stay.

Fire of the Five Hearts is a book about compassion, courage, and pain. It is a story about feeling crazy, yet always, without fail, finding my own resiliency and floating to the surface. It is a book about how to nurture self-love when you feel bereft and alone. It is a story about secrets.

In short, this book was written on a wing and a prayer. Once the invitation was put before me, I dared myself to be utterly honest, to lay out my successes and my failings of the last twenty years, and to say out loud what others might think but were afraid to utter for fear that they might hear themselves and be frightened by their own interiors.

Over the last twenty years I have managed a team that intervenes with and treats incest. It was not a calling that I longingly cultivated; it occurred by happenstance, as most of my life has. Though it has been a long tenure, I never meant it to be. The job was simply a segue between a master's degree and a doctoral degree. Unbeknownst to me, it took on a life of its own. But I believe there is a divine plan and we are meant to fall where we may. This book, then, was an effort to push through my destiny, to reshape it and to liberate me from a venue that has become increasingly unbearable and has tapped a well of sadness I never knew existed. As is told in the last chapter, my pocket of compassion has been zipped shut; I have no more to give. But the looming question is: How do we know when we are done with our calling? How do we know it is time to leave?

Fire of the Five Hearts is a book that speaks to the issue of personal shame, as does the entire dynamic of incest and rupturing the secret. The writing of the book was a vehicle to cleanse my shame. It was a venue that provided me a stage in which to say everything that has been in my head over the last twenty years—exposing not only the horrors of incest but my voyeuristic draw to the field, as well as my superstitious belief that if I continue to unveil these horrific secrets, I could somehow guarantee the safety of my own children. This service to the world would keep myself and my children out of harm's way. But that is never really the case. The shoemaker's children are the last to receive shoes.

To surrender oneself into a healing venue is an evolution that feeds the soul, particularly if you are a person who is fed that way. I am. Although at times I long to bag groceries or sell lipstick at Lord and Taylor, my work with incest, navigating an oftentimes bleak terrain, provides me with an inordinate amount of satisfaction, much of which stems from the need to have a purpose and a definition in the world. This is of utmost importance to me; however, the cost has been, at times, devastating.

The statistics on sexual abuse are shocking—one in four women will be sexually abused before she reaches the age of eighteen. This will be at the hands of someone who is known to her. The statistic for men is one in six. I find these numbers to be horrifying and unbelievable at times. Nonetheless, I am used to saying them and thinking in my mind that the numbers have probably shifted and now are statistically even more staggering. With that in mind, we know that when we are in a room with four or more women, one of those women will have been sexually violated, a thought that brings tremendous sadness and often paralyzes my comprehension.

The writing of this book took on a life of its own; the chapters and their content often came to me in my dreams. There were times when I would find myself meandering, washing a dish or doggedly pursing the mate for a lost sock, and a thought would come to me as though I were being channeled by some obscure metaphysical force. When I tried to capture my feelings or thoughts about an individual or a situation, I was stunned by the clarity with which it returned to my mind's eye. I often felt the memory in my body before the words were put to paper.

I have journaled intermittently over the last twenty years, and my love of the written word has never waned. When I cannot sleep at night (and there is many a night), I write letters in my head. I write them to other people, to myself, and to the world. There are intrusive, perseverating thoughts whose redundancy begins to birth an idea. If I didn't get the thought through, it would permeate the layers of my life. I would be the captor of my own mind—the thoughts were often poisonous.

Clearly, the writing of this book has been a therapeutic vehicle. It has leavened me: I see my motivations with a keener vision, and that in itself is a relief.

A few of my dearest confidants, who read each chapter, were deeply disturbed by what I had written. Much of the distress seemed to come from the reality of incest itself and its prevalence. Some felt as if they were remiss in understanding the depth of my personal pain and the overarching presence of this atrocity in children's lives. But since incest is a secret, how were they to know? The accretion over time of absorbing others' trauma oftentimes goes unnoticed. It is unutterable. So, in the reading of this book, I would like to caution some. It is disturbing, and one may not want to venture there before slumber; but most importantly, it is a message of hope and faith and conviction. There are things in this world that we do have the power to change, although they often seem immutable. I like to leave the reader with a sense of hope, that with tenacity, perseverance, and the courage to speak one's own truth, anything is possible.

From the outset, there has been an ongoing debate as to whether this book would be best received as an academic tool or a tool for life. I would venture a guess that it will serve a dual purpose. While the book is laced with vignettes about incest, we are constantly reminded of the power behind silence and secrets. This book serves both the educator and the student, as well as any of us sailing through life's tribulations. Each chapter houses a unique and special memory— some excruciatingly painful, some joyous and liberating. While the chapters are without citations of research and statistics, it in no way compromises the integrity of the individuals or the author. So much of this writing is stripped and denuded of anything that would serve to distance our hearts from the truth of this atrocity.

The chapter "On Siblings and Sex" is clearly an anomaly. It is the exception that an incestuous relationship renders anything but trauma.* The beauty of the book has to do with the tenured life span that I have chosen to pursue. Much of my observations and feelings are a result of twenty years' absorption of a trauma that never looks the same.

There are times when my experiences are guided from a deep intuition that in many ways has served as an unfailing guide. While the cost to me emotionally, psychologically, and physically has been harrowing, I still believe that this experience has been instrumental in creating the woman that I am today. I would never trade her for anyone else.

The purpose of this book is to share, in an unadulterated form, my experience as a woman, a mother, and a therapist who has treated incest. I want to give voice to the events of the past twenty years and, perhaps more importantly, to my inner response during and after those events. This book speaks the unspeakable, revealing what others think but rarely utter. Working with incest has permeated and shaped every facet of

---

*More often than not, an incestuous sibling coupling is a devastating violation between children. The sibling couple in this chapter seemed to portray something different. Only time will tell. Perhaps it is my own need to see it as different and it is simply packaged neatly to challenge my perceptions.

my life. My path through this landscape, one where most will never venture, continues to be an informed choice. To those women, children, and men who have experienced the violation caused by unwanted touch, I freely lend my heart and my hard-won courage to seek the truth. In sharing this deeply personal chronicle, I have little shame or reservation, and no question of who I am. All that we bring to any calling, all that we experience, whether it nurtures us and keeps us alive and purposeful or fractures us, robs us, and devastates us, is an integral part of our package as healers.

In our strength and our frailty combined, the heart of this work can be found. Incest, like any other trauma, sends us reeling, and ultimately challenges us on a most fundamental level. Our task is to suspend judgment and heal—not to become a victim ourselves or to be ensnared by our individual, family, or work systems. With an unwieldy momentum, incest takes on a life of its own. While abhorrent and inconceivable, incest as a metaphor spans every system, helping us to see when boundaries become perilously blurred.

This book is for those of you who have found a calling in healing the broken, and for whom this path has led you to question your purpose and your meaning. It is for each and every one of us who continually puts our nose into life's challenges and emerges a victor, simply by becoming closer to our truth and, of course, our hearts. It is for survivors, lay people, healers, helping professionals, psychologists, social workers, medical doctors, counselors, rabbis, priests, teachers, mothers, fathers . . . because each and every one of us will be touched by this or know someone who has been. It is my hope that this book will provide you with the tools to navigate this terrain when it seems most bleak, by helping to identify that which nurtures and regenerates you. Use it to recover your heart whenever it feels lost.

CHAPTER 1

Ricky Still Loves Lulu

My preference is to take the back roads, which inevitably spill out onto Interstate 25. I find that this particular winding road is just the distance it takes to settle me in the morning. I am en route to lead a training session. I don't know exactly why I have agreed to do it. This training distresses me. Not its content in particular—rather, it distresses me because it is not mine and it lacks heart. You simply cannot train someone else's work. It's like trying to wear someone else's shoes. The imprint that is left by your toes and the ball of your foot and your heel belong only to you. It will never feel right to anyone else. People work hard to break in their shoes. It's a very personal, intimate thing to anyone else. My favorite shoes are the well-worn, soft, buttery leather ones where, because they are so thin at the sole, you feel like your foot directly meets the earth.

A Chinese doctor once told me that we have five hearts: one in our chest, one in the palm of each hand, and one on the sole of each foot. My malady was called "Fire of the Five Hearts"—too much heat. I am pleased to know that I have five hearts. I want to cry. I will need five hearts to do this work. One is certainly not enough.

My life's calling is to find incest and heal it. No small endeavor. Somehow, somewhere over the years I have honed my senses. I can feel incest in a very deep place in my belly. I can smell it. I can see how people wear it in their bodies. Healing it, however, is a totally different matter.

For the next three days I will be training brand-new caseworkers on how to interview sexually abused children. I will be cooped up in a lavish old hotel in Denver, training in the penthouse, which was converted into a training room. At least I can see the sky. This hotel was the first Playboy Club in Denver; and I am in the penthouse, training on incest. I do not believe in coincidence. This must be the same feeling a family gets when they find out that their home has been built over a cemetery and the spirits have inhabited their dwelling.

This road has become familiar. Its aged, weathered barns lean precariously to the right. The sumptuous, velvety meadows are burgeoning with spring's delights. Over the last 20 years, I find that my eyes are drawn to scenes that are filled with beauty, color, and intrigue. Scenes that are untouched, unassimilated, and slightly wild. Keeping those pictures in my mind's eye will soothe me, particularly before I settle into a training such as this. This road, and what my eyes feast on, has become a ritual, a visual mantra—if I repeat it enough, look at it long enough, it becomes my tranquility. It is my method of calming my system, readying me for my work, which for 20 years has consumed my life.

As I get closer to the overpass, I notice that the sky is a deep rich rose, with a hint of violet. I know this overpass well. It is one of my landmarks—this one lets me know that I have a good hour of driving left. My car is the place where I can actually hear my thoughts. It is one of the only places I am able to think, where I am able to roll around my thoughts about incest and love and myself, and how this work has transformed me. I have had amazing epiphanies in my car. At times, I arrive at my destination having no idea how I got there.

As my windshield dips under the overpass, I read the graffiti on the bridge. It reads RICKY LOVES LULU. I press gently on the brakes as it hits me again, and then one more time before it registers, RICKY LOVES LULU. My heart starts to skip around in my chest, and I immediately think this is a sign. The universe is signaling to me. My Italian mother has always conveyed her superstitions to me. She has many old wives' tales about death. Maybe they're the beliefs told to her as a child. I am thinking that this is one of those signs where God is telling you something, like the heads-up pennies and kissing the dead—if you find a penny heads up, you make a wish, and if you kiss the dead in your dreams, then you are the next to die. I kiss the dead in my dreams all the time.

I think of a Ricky in my life, and my first experience of love, when I was fifteen. I wonder where he is and whom he loves. My mind starts to open. I think of my Lily, my oldest child. Lily is ten, and I often playfully call her "Lulu." I wonder why these two names are up here, Ricky and Lulu. I wonder if she will have sweet, pristine, unadulterated, warm love, like the love I had with Ricky. Those nights when we cut through the bushes on Planting Field Road, stealthily crept up High Hollow, and found our secret nest on Laurel Lane. We kissed until our lips were sore and our mouths ached. When we got under the street lamp, Ricky looked like a clown. His soft pink lips were swollen and glistening. His scent was all over my hair and my face. It was a brisk fall night. You could see your breath in the air. He smelled of corduroy and some sweet body soap.

I am thinking about incest, and love, and these children who don't have a choice with regard to who kisses them first, who touches their sweetness, who makes their bodies hum, whom they lie with in the bushes, and whose scent is left on their bodies. They have no voice in this matter of love. They are launched over their innocence at light's speed. They are touched and fondled by all the wrong people. Once that touch occurs, they are changed forever, their sense of love and intimacy twisted into some perverse knot.

And I am about to spend three days teaching clinicians how to interview these children. How to unveil their deepest ache, their deepest secret. I feel we have no right to delve, and I feel we have all the right. I want to turn back and find the overpass and dream about RICKY LOVES LULU. I am overcome with reverie and sadness. How do I bring this love back? How do I teach people to pry open the souls of these children who have been violated beyond words?

I want to disappear, and yet somehow, I've made this my calling. With incest, you can't just sit down with a child and get him or her to tell all without knowing some of these things—without feeling the pain of no choice, and the loss of the innocent, childlike understanding of love. When these children tell, they turn in their love.

I can see the overpass in my mind, and I think about the first time I felt Ricky's boy-skin against my body. I have been so changed by my work in incest. Sometimes I have no sense of what love is anymore. I am drawn to love only in secret. I don't remember what is sweet and pure anymore.

A May morning, and my window is rolled down. I can smell the color green. It is moist and rich, and the mares have bellies full of babes. I see a fine new foal leaning into her mama's side. Her noodley legs make her look loopy. She is sleek and fresh and breathtakingly beautiful. My eyes drink in the sights.

I try to focus on my training. I need to do a better job today of "transitioning to the target event." On "doing the do," so to speak. I need to bridge the gap between building rapport using the child's words and jumping into the incest. These folks, these baby case-workers, have a difficult time with ejaculation, penetration, and describing the consistency and the color of cum. Should I do the cottage cheese/pee-hole/groan narrative? I am saturated with all this sex stuff. There is no pleasant way to teach this, to soften it, to pretty it up.

These folks will dissect this approach. They will question the hows and the whys. They will focus on open-ended, nonleading questions. They will debate the dialectic of defense attorneys. They will ponder the importance of establishing spatiality and tempo-rality, of receptive versus expressive language. What about se-quencing? What about logical progression? This is all the techni-cal language of interviewing, all the logistics that lack the heart and soul of exploring incest.

Interviewing children who have been incested is a complicated jigsaw to be pieced together. It is an intimate, interpersonal dance that is at some level unteachable. Either you have it or you don't, and all the technical training in the world won't birth this pro-cess. It is part intuitive. It's more about reading your own body and your own mind than it is about language and questioning. It is about sitting in a room with a child, sliding into some comfort, and talking about nothing and talking about everything. You are molding Play-Doh pies with berries rolled up inside and you are gingerly slicing that pie so that the berries stay intact, all the while trying to touch into this little person. You are the conduit—the vehicle for the secret to be eked out, slowly and in snippets.

Sometimes during these trainings, I notice that there is one set of twinkling eyes in the room. And I can see that this person might have it, might have the fever for this work. While I might not be able to really teach the interviewing piece, perhaps I have succeeded in infecting someone with the passion of incest work. To those who get this passion, I can leave a small bag of tools. The rest is theirs, to do with what they wish. I have often asked my trainees if someone would be willing to volunteer to the group, in steamy detail, the description of his or her first sexual encounter" "I was touched here . . . I felt this . . . I did that . . . " There is silence. There is indignation. There is heat. Faces are flushed. There is always a little bit of hissing. Not a soul volunteers. "So," I say, "this is exactly what we are asking these children to do, with a total stranger. Why can't we?"

There is always, without exception, some speculation as to how I got into this work. Folks always assume that I am (or was) a survivor of incest. I have been waiting for twenty years, and that revelation has yet to come. I find myself answering the question in this way: Many years ago, I was rejected from the Ph.D. program at the University of Colorado due to my abysmally low GRE scores. I saw an ad in the paper for an investigator/therapist for the Sexual Abuse Team, and I inquired. I would stay a year and then try my shot at my doctoral degree. And here I am, twenty years later. I talk about putting your nose into things for a reason and getting hooked. There is something about incest work that is totally riveting, totally captivating. It is like being on a lifelong archaeological dig, somewhere in the middle of your soul. I have been looking high and low for some fabulously obscure, intangible essence, and perhaps until I find it, I will not be freed from this quest.

A very dear supervisee of mine once told me that she believed she had taken the job because, in a past life, she had been a perpetrator of incest, and she was here to serve out her karmic penance. Oftentimes on my drive, I feel paralyzed. I wonder if it is really the fear that someday, in the midst of one of my trainings, I am going to have some great dawning, right there, right smack in the middle of the room. I am going to remember having sex with my father, or my uncle, or my brother. And I am going to have a breakdown right in front of all those people I don't even know. I imagine I would lose my speech and just walk out of the room. When I think about this happening, my hands sweat. My heart starts to race. I feel dizzy, and I feel like I am going to die. And I imagine that this is what the children feel when we ask them to speak.

My job is to understand the intricacies of incest and to try and impart those intricacies to those with whom I work. And I really don't know if that can be done, simply because it is so uniquely personal, almost spiritual. I can't *teach* my process; I can only *be* it.

*   *   *   *   *   *   *

Another training, another visual mantra. I have bypassed the mare this morning because my mind is too full. I am anxiously awaiting RICKY LOVES LULU. They will lift me. They will carry me off into some sensual reverie of some love from some other time. As I approach, I am confused because the overpass has no writing on it. I wonder if I got so deep in my mind that I missed it. I get to the next landmark and am further confused. I turn myself around and am absolutely speechless. The proclamation has been wiped clean! Someone washed off RICKY LOVES LULU! I am appalled! I am indignant! Who would have done such a thing? What does this mean? It is a sign! They are done. They are finished. Maybe they never really loved each other. They were not who I thought they were. These bold, ballsy braggarts, telling all of I-25 of their love.

I wonder if my Ricky ever loved me, and if I ever really loved him. What was it that was between us? Was it simply that we grew up in our love together, preparing each other for a deeper, more grown-up type of love?

I think of the fathers and the daughters they secretly touch. I know that the fathers want to be the first to do to their children what they know others will do to them later. They need to be the first because they can't bear the thought of these ever-so-precious, exquisite bodies being received by another's mouth, tongue, or penis. They are so hungry, so ravenous for love, acceptance, and an intimacy so deep. Who are these fathers? Who are these mothers? These brothers? These sisters? These uncles? Who are these people who sexualize their love, their rage, their control, and their emptiness? Has their trust been spirited away by another at some young age, without them even knowing it? I think of ownership of children and the objectification of children. Once a parent-child bond is sexually violated, there is no RICKY LOVES LULU. There is no love possible as we know it. Love as we know it has been redefined. It has new rules. And it takes only one moment of someone not thinking, not imagining the consequences, to step over the threshold and put one's needs, one's grown-up desire before that of their child—to extinguish love, to erase any RICKY LOVES LULU.

My calling is incest. To unravel it. To understand it. And, I hope, to heal it. I have dedicated my life to this demon.

*   *   *   *   *   *   *

June, before dawn, and the day already feels warm. This is my last training for the summer. I am meeting a colleague for breakfast. My eyes feast upon the meadow. I can see the foal, leggy and lean, prancing around with a white-speckled friend. In the summer, children's legs, like foals' legs, grow right before your eyes.

A red-tailed fox scoots across the road. She is in a hurry this morning, on some mission, not to be deterred. Her tail looks like a million plumes, bushy and red.

I am hoping that my incest training will be alive today. I feel lethargic and blue. It is a stunning day, yet I cannot muster myself. These are the days when I am so done, so completely finished with finding and healing incest. These are the days when I can't imagine continuing this work. I am depleted and empty. I have nothing left to give. Sometimes I wonder if the work will be the death of me. My mother used to yell at us kids, saying that we would be the death of her. I have some sense of her meaning. Even though she loved us madly, we took everything from her.

As I approach the overpass, the sky is growing lighter. I am distracted, but I slow down, hoping there had been some cruel mistake. I brake completely, without even looking in my rearview mirror. It is early in the morning, and the interstate is empty. I pull over to the side of the highway. My heart is beating so fast that I can hardly breathe. I feel as if my eyes need to focus. I am stunned! Absolutely and completely astonished! I read the writing on the bridge ever so slowly . . . RICKY STILL LOVES LULU. As I am reading this to myself, out loud, I can see a young man dangling over the bridge finishing the U of Lulu, with one final upward sweep. It is still a bit hard to make out his figure. Up bobs a girl, with a long brown ponytail. I am transfixed. I feel like I am peeping through someone's window. I am the voyeur. Quickly, he grabs her face and kisses her mouth. She receives his kiss with a giggle, breaks away from him, and they duck out of sight.

I sit in my car as if I have been sitting in a drive-in. I stare at the bridge as if it were a huge screen. I am waiting for more. But it is done.

I don't know what to say to myself. I can't believe what I have just seen. And yet—there are no coincidences. I feel I was supposed to be there at that very moment. I was supposed to witness the message, the sign. It was for me. It was for everybody. The gods placed me there, along with the fox, and the foal, and the sky opening up its light. They placed me there just like they placed me twenty years ago. They gave me this calling. They wanted to see what I would do with it. There are no mistakes. There are no coincidences. And Ricky still loves Lulu.

2
CHAPTER

Isabella

At the close of the day when all phone messages have been returned and all crises temporarily quelled, I make office rounds to see who is still here. Who is being verbally assaulted by a disgruntled client, who is observing a visit between a parent and a child, who is finishing up a late report to the court, and who might need a few words of warmth or wisdom to get them through the night, particularly if the day has been demanding and has absorbed every bit of emotional energy and compassion left in their body. I fall exhausted into my chair, thinking about scooping up my children and wondering what to make for dinner. I can taste my martini in my mouth, particularly the salt of the olives.

I sift through my mail and see what looks like an invitation. I like that kind of mail. I'm always curious about who is starting a new practice, who might be hosting a good workshop, or, better, who might be receiving an accolade for a job well done; those, however, are few and far between in this field. People rarely are appreciated or acknowledged for uncovering incest or treating offenders. Glamorous this work is not.

At times I am uneasy about opening this type of mail. I feel jealousy and envy for those who have made the healthy choice to release themselves from this house of pain. I am introspective and always wonder why I am still here, why I can't seem to leave. What is it about my masochistic self? When, dear God, will I be released from this calling? Better yet, when will I release myself? When will I know that I am done?

I grab my keys and my pager and turn out the light. I open the letter on my way out of the building. It is definitely an invitation. It is thick, and inside the outer envelope, I find another. On the inside envelope I read the words, "Holly, you helped make this day possible, thank you." I have no idea who this could be from, and as I open the invitation, a small photo falls out. It is a portrait of a beautiful young woman, whose shoulders are draped by the arm of a lanky young man. Their fingers are entwined. A delicate cluster of diamonds encircles her finger. The face is at first not familiar, but as I look closer, I recognize the smile. I immediately prop myself up against my car. I feel light-headed. I have an amazing feeling of joy coupled with such sadness. It is a confusing mixture of sentiments. I hear myself say out loud, "Oh my God! It's Isabella. She is so lovely."

* * *

As it turns out, this is an engagement announcement from the first child I had on my caseload. I interviewed this child and confirmed that she was being incested by her father, and had been for at least a year prior. I placed her out of her home on that day. She was four and a half years old. Fourteen years had elapsed.

I am sitting in a small housing complex, tucked obscurely on the edge of the county, underneath the foothills. It is stifling, particularly for May. I am looking at Isabella, who is sitting a few feet away from me in a small, plastic toddler's chair. She is sitting at a makeshift table drinking some lemonade with cookies. I am deeply troubled by the fact that her feet don't reach the ground. For some odd reason I fixate on that, even though she is only four and a half and her feet shouldn't touch the ground. I have spent the last three hours interviewing her with a colleague and a detective from the local police jurisdiction. Her father is being Mirandized, and I am looking at her feet not touching the ground. It is Friday, my fifth day on the job.

I am struck by the tidiness of the apartment. It is spartan, with very little color. Isabella lives there alone with her father. She takes me to her room to show me her stuffed bunny. It is soft and pink with drooping ears. There is a small mattress on the floor with a feminine, ruffled quilt. There is a basket of neatly folded clothes in place of a chest of drawers. Other than that, the room is virtually empty and, sadly, anonymous. She busies me to quell her own four-and-a-half-year-old's anxiety. I am aware of her fear as well as her resourcefulness. She is trying to settle me, knowing I am distracted. I am useless. How did I get here?

Isabella told me earlier that afternoon that her father had had her suck his penis until he peed in her mouth. The last time he peed in her mouth, she threw up on her Tweety nightie. This made her sad. When he tried to put his penis in her "private" the night before, she cried. She tells me this like she is afraid I will be angry. She tells me this like she is an old pro. She speaks of this sexual act as if it were a daily ritual, like grooming oneself, like brushing one's teeth; old hat, so to speak. There is a haunting vacancy in this child that is the hallmark of many children who are incested at such an early age. She seems to lack a connection to anyone or anything.

While Isabella and I are talking, I notice a cockroach crawl across the floor. Throughout our conversation I see about four more. My head itches. I can feel the bugs crawling in my hair. I do a quick perusal of my body, then quickly pull a barrette out of my bag and twirl my hair up in a hasty French knot. My skin begins to itch and burn. I am aware that I am looking at this little person, listening to this little person, and I want to scream. I want to leave the room. I don't want to hear any more.

There is an unfamiliar smell in this apartment. It is a smell I will soon learn to associate with incest. It is a musky smell, like a closet that has been sealed tight for a long time. It is a combination of people's scents—their bodies, their hair, their perfumes, their secrets. I have the urge to open all the windows, to invite a cross breeze to freshen and cleanse. I simply want to bring in air that is moving. This air is stagnant and stale.

Isabella's father, Francis, is a slight man, lean and small of stature. He is neatly dressed in black trousers and a starched white shirt. His black hair is slicked back, and he has very dark skin. Francis had the most beautiful straight white teeth that I have ever seen. When he smiles, he lifts his chin, grinning like an impish child.

When we first entered the apartment and I saw Francis, I averted my eyes immediately. I tried to figure out how I could avoid shaking his hand. His condition was frightening, even hideous. I had never quite seen anything like it. His entire body was covered with sores. He had small puss-filled sores all over his face and neck. He had sores covering his scalp. His arms and hands were covered with tumors. When he sat down and crossed his legs, you could see the tumors of puss on his legs where his pant leg rose above his clean white socks. He was completely missing his left hand. There were tumors of puss that nestled in the stump of his limb, like the caps of mushroom heads blanketing a dewy tree trunk on the floor of a forest.

It was apparent that Francis was mildly retarded. He smiled inappropriately and his speech was somewhat sluggish. He desperately tried to minimize the truth of his contact with his daughter, tried to couch it in some crippled distortion, but inevitably admitted to trying to put his penis in her vagina and also to having her fellate him to the point of ejaculation. I was disgusted, yet at the same time I pitied him. I kept thinking about how tidy their home was, how white his shirts were. My mind shifts to an unwanted visual, intrusive and gnawing. Where was he when he had her suck his penis? How were they lying? Was she reclined on a bed, or was she standing up? Did he promise her treats or trinkets in exchange for his pleasure? How did he get her to do it? How did this very docile man with such a seemingly dull mind cajole her? How did he explain it? Did he say that he was sorry? Did Isabella cry?

Inside the dankness of this tiny abode was an exclusive world where we never dare venture, we of the lavish homes, two-car garages, enough food that we never know hunger. We the people who get to go home to our clean, cockroach-free living rooms and slide in between our freshly laundered designer sheets. What did I know of this world? How had I arrived there?

It was my responsibility to collect Isabella's belongings. Several changes of clothing, hairbrush and toothbrush, a few of her stuffed animals, and a doll named Lucy, who was her pride and joy. As we walked through the living room, she shyly approached her father. He kneeled down and wrapped his arms around her. He told her to behave and that he would see her soon. His eyes were filled with tears. He never said he was sorry.

I wanted to weep. I kept wondering whether or not he had open lesions on his penis and how Isabella could fit a grown man's erect penis into her tiny mouth, sores and all. I chastised myself for even letting such a bizarre piece of imagery into my mind's eye, particularly during such a poignant separation.

Her feet did not touch the ground, but she could take a grown man's fully erect penis in her mouth. I felt ill. I felt my hungry mind wanting to understand, to comprehend the sadness and the perversion of everything that I had just witnessed. It overwhelmed my senses at every turn. I could not extinguish the visual.

Isabella pressed her tiny, perspiring palm into mine. I thought of that palm attempting to ward off its intruder. This tiny little hand, powerless to say no. Her grip was tight. We walked across the courtyard, and I was rehearsing in my head what I would say to her, how I would explain to her that she would be living in another home where her safety would be assured, a foster home. And how would I know that this baby would not be thrown into another ill fate? I had heard such horrifying tales. And all these monumental decisions, mine to make. Who the hell was I?

I held my tongue. For a few minutes, as we walked hand in hand, I was silent. I had no words. I didn't know what to say to this little person. I looked at the top of her head as I walked. Our hands were drenched with perspiration. I never let go. I knelt down to buckle her little sandal. When I lifted my head, our eyes were on the same level. I fastened my eyes on hers. I tucked a piece of stray hair into her barrette. I said, "Isabella, I am so sorry." She was confused. She smiled at me in the most vacant manner. She took my hand again, and we walked to the car. I was not sure what I felt most sorry about. The incest? Taking her from her home? The fact that my own sense of clarity and confidence was teetering on some looming edge of uncertainty? That I questioned myself every step of the way, every decision that I was making? That the bottom line was that in the huge, crazy world of incest, it was ultimately just me and my belly making those decisions, a lonely and isolating endeavor? I was sorry for myself that I was there, that I was witness to this devastation. I felt so little, so vulnerable. I was emotionally stripped. I wondered about myself. What might I uncover? As yet, it was an overwhelming sense of incompetence, which I would visit again and again over the next 20 years.

As I lifted Isabella into her seat and buckled her snugly, she asked after Lucy. I tucked Lucy tightly under the seatbelt on Isabella's lap. We arrived back at my office at four-thirty. A home had been secured for her. The family would be there in a few hours. I placed Isabella at my desk with some crayons and paper.

I sat down at my colleague's desk and looked out the window. It was Friday afternoon. I wanted to go home. I hated it there.

The office emptied quickly. I watched Isabella, her feet swinging under the desk, her curly blonde hair matted to her round little head. She wore shorts and a little T-shirt that were in need of laundering. Isabella's skin was very fair, with tiny freckle-type spots covering as much as the eye could see. Her fingernails were dirty, and she had crusted food on the nape of her neck. She had a small pug nose and very dark eyes. One eye in particular was clouded over. It tended to wander. I wondered about the speckles on her skin.

As I watched her I could not escape the sexual images. She was drawing a flower for me, which was pink and blue with green leaves. I told her about the family with whom she would be going and how excited they were to be getting a little girl. She slid out of the chair and climbed into my lap. Her scent was a strange admixture of sweet-smelling food, stale cigarette smoke, and sex. She had a pungent vaginal odor, which I could smell on her hands. She fingered the strand of pearls around my neck and asked if she could come home with me. I could not recall a time when I'd felt such sadness. My throat constricted. I told her that this family would be sad if I took her home. She did not move. Her roving eye was searching my face. Her seeing eye was fixed on my eyes.

Instinctively, I held her tightly. Everything that I hadn't been able to say came barreling out. I told her that I knew that she was scared; that it had been a long, confusing day; that her father was going to be all right; that he was a grown-up and he just wanted her to be safe; that I was so sorry that he had touched her; that she was wise to tell; that it was my job and the judge's job and all the grown-ups' job to keep her protected; that she had done nothing wrong; that her father was wrong to touch her. Her body relaxed as I talked to her. She understood, in part, all that I was saying. She asked what her bed would look like. She wanted to know when she would see me again. "Could Lucy come?" she asked. "Of course Lucy can come," I replied.

I looked long and hard at this sweet child and became momentarily gripped by the thought that perhaps this family would find her distasteful or damaged. Perhaps they would take one look at Isabella and politely say, "No, thank you," as if shopping for some commodity, in this case a little girl. I lifted Isabella up, all the while smelling her child scent, her body with all of its various and sundry flavors, unable to free myself from the pungent odor of sexual juices.

I carried her across the hall to the bathroom and filled the sink with warm water. I removed her clothing, all the while telling her that we needed to get her ready for her new family. She seemed to delight in the fact that I was attempting to make a bubble bath with industrial lavatory soap, in a sink, no less. I plunked her in the sink, letting her legs dangle over the edge. I started at the top of her head, all the while chatting about this and that to keep my own thoughts distracted.

Her hair had that distinct smell of an oily, sweaty scalp. I gently wet her head and massaged in enough lather to shampoo her hair. I rinsed her head with the coffee mug I had used for tea that morning. I washed her little arms and legs. Her back had some unusual bruising. She looked like a little watered-down waif, a sopping pup. She had won my heart. I realized that I had wanted to sell a child who was not as she appeared. On the surface I wanted to polish and shine her, to pretty her up so as to distract from her impurity. I feared that this would be Isabella's lot. In my own sorrow, I knew the world would begin to see Isabella as damaged and disenfranchised. I felt a part of me go away as I busied myself with my task.

Isabella smelled clean—a tad antiseptic, but clean nonetheless. I promptly threw her clothes in the trash and dressed her in clean underclothes with a little pair of coveralls and a T-shirt. I took her back to my office and combed out her short, wild hair. Her seeing eye never left my face. I took the lavender ribbon that held back my hair and tied it around her head with a neat little bow at the top. She wanted to see herself, so I took out a small mirror and held it up so that she could eye her reflection. She was silent. I was suddenly very self-conscious and nervous. She smiled a huge smile. She asked for my pearls. I would have given her everything I owned. I told her that they were my mother's but that I would find her some pearls, and the next day when I came to see her, she would have her very own jewels.

We gathered her belongings and walked out to the parking lot. She held tightly to my hand. As the family drove up, I knelt down and kissed her cheek. I assured her that I would see her soon. In the car was a stuffed bear, bigger than Isabella. The family was kind. Without hesitation, she slid into the car and vanished. She never looked back. She made the leap, a leap of survival and fortitude that would come to be the very essence of who she was.

I am standing in the parking lot. It is a warm May night. I am overcome with exhaustion and an overwhelming sense of loneliness. As I am driving home, I stop at a red light and I begin to cry. I feel an overlap of feelings that are indescribable. I feel a sense of self-sufficiency and reserve. I am at once removed from myself. This was me today who accomplished this feat, yet I feel empty and bereft. I feel puffed up and deflated all at once. I feel false in myself. I wonder who gave me the power or the right to step into the lives of these people and make such profoundly life-altering decisions. I have no children. I have just walked fresh out the door of graduate school. I am a baby. I am humbled. I feel a sense of shame. I feel that I am an imposter, a sham. I never want to be so pompous and self-satisfied that I am consumed by the deed, losing sight of the purpose, the being named Isabella, and all the Isabellas that have yet to come.

As I make it up the hill and turn into the drive, I am aware that it is too cumbersome and too depleting a day to even recap for my husband. The time it will take to put words to my day is more than I can conjure. I am aware that my surface has been punctured, that the nice cool exterior that I presented to the world has been altered—it has a big hole in it and the pain has just begun to ooze out. I collect myself and walk into my home. My husband is not home yet, and I am relieved. I walk upstairs to the bedroom and flop on the bed. This is the most beautiful room in the house. It was the attic of a very old Victorian house that had been refurbished years ago. The room is all windows, and the light in this room changed throughout the day. The shades of the walls turned from a dusty violet to gray. I see the foothills from my bed. There is a remote velvety lush slice that undulates. It always captures my eye. I feel that when I am in my room, I am living in a tree house. It comforts me always to see the sky. I walk to the bathroom, remove my clothes and run a bath. I cannot get the water deep enough or hot enough. I need an ocean. Water, as always in my life, is the element that gives me the most tranquility and contentment. It lulls me.

Years earlier, while in graduate school, I had listened to a keynote speaker at a conference speak about the need to draw a distinct line between one's life as a healer and one's life outside of healing, one's personal life. He talked about habit and ritual. What was the one thing that you did at the close of the workday that distinctly separated you from your role in your life as a healer? Mine has been water, in particular the tub.

I am inundated with feeling. I feel like a pinball machine on tilt. All the buzzers are ringing, lights are flashing, and I am about to fry my circuits. Nothing is coming in, and nothing is going out. I feel electrified. The wires ignited, sparked, and fizzled. I want it all to slow down. I go right to the water to douse my flame.

I immerse myself in the hot water. I want to wash the smells off my body. I can smell Isabella's hair, her breath, and her child vaginal scent. My hair smells of smoke, and I want to wash Francis off me. I wonder if his puss-filled lesions are contagious. I still feel the cockroaches crawling on my scalp. I would like to turn in my skin and change it for a new epidermis. It feels as if I will never be able to rinse the sadness from my soul. All the while I am cognizant of the fact that I am trying to purge myself of my feelings. I start with my shell.

I am in the water for at least an hour. I immerse my head. My long, thick mane is so heavy, but I feel the lightness of my hair as it floats. I can hear my heart beating in my ears. I wonder what would happen if I died in this water. I drain the bathtub and refill it. I scrub my skin until it stings. I still don't feel clean. I close my eyes.

I switch to lying on my back. I gaze at the heavens through the skylight on the ceiling above the tub. I am thinking about Isabella. I am struck by the feeling of uncleanness that I have been immersed in that day. I would imagine that this child feel unclean always, in body and in mind. I am hoping that the sheets in her foster home are snow white and fragrant. I am hoping that she felt safe. I am worried that she is so deeply alone and frightened. I know somewhere deep inside of me that the decisions and choices I made today were sound. I am praying, with eyes glued to the stars, that I will not awaken in the night with my heart beating out of my chest; that I will not be haunted by Francis's diseased body; that I will not perseverate on every nuance of my day—the smells, the cockroaches, the piercing torment of Isabella's unseeing eye, her father's sore-ridden penis penetrating her tiny body. Yet in many ways this is an experience I hope never to forget. The pearls. I must not forget the pearls that I have promised her.

As I lay my head down on my pillow that evening, I try to

recap tiny snippets of my day for my husband. The muscles behind my eyes are throbbing. My shoulders ache. I may as well have been a Sherpa in Nepal that day. I assume that pain is an integral part of their shoulders, hence their being. I have balanced Isabella's anguish on my less than powerful frame.

As I begin to give voice to my day, my throat constricts and closes off the channel for my tears. I am both horrified and intrigued by my day. My husband lazily drapes a leg over my body while propping his head up with his palm. He listens intently. I see the voyeuristic hook, and then just as quickly, I see the curtain come down when his mind needs to censor the graphic detail of my day.

I feel myself drift in my speech, a product of my fatigue. It is blue sleep, reminiscent of the sleepovers I had as a young girl, when we would rally against repose, yakking till the morn, until sleep would inevitably claim us, midsentence. I could not complete my thoughts. I succumbed to slumber. I would dream the dream that would become an episodic, intrusive night demon for years to come.

I am wandering through an enormous house. It is deceptive, as the outside is lovely and inviting. There is a woman inside who tells me that this is going to be my home. "But excuse me, ma'am, I have a home. I love my home! I don't want this home!" I am panicked as I walk through this house. It is like a maze. It is in a state of ruin. All the pipes are exposed. The floor is rotting. There is no heat or electricity. The windows are covered with soot. You cannot see inside or out. The house is enormous, very dark and cold. It has no life. In the center of the living room there is an orb of light that periodically glows brilliantly and exudes bursts of warmth. As I approach the warmth, it dims and goes out. Most disturbing, however, is the floor, which consists entirely of deep marble baths. As I walk closer to the baths I notice that they are filled with excrement. The stench is odious. I am outraged that I have to live in this house. It is falling apart, and it is filled with shit. I am running through the labyrinth of this home trying to find the door. In my mind's eye I can see my beautiful little house, and I want it back. I am trying to figure out how I could renovate this house and make it livable. I am so sad. I just want to go home. I am yelling at the woman, "This house is full of shit! It stinks! I will not live here!" I awaken. I am drenched in sweat.

There is a woman sitting in the waiting room when I arrived

Monday morning. I am told that she was here for me. I greet her. Her name is Irene. She is a teacher at the preschool Isabella attended. She has tracked this child since she was an infant. She has had worries and concerns. She has always found Francis to be kind yet limited. She has worried incessantly for Isabella's welfare. She has served as a teacher and a caregiver.

When Francis worked the graveyard shift, she kept Isabella. Irene's family welcomed him into their home on holidays and Sunday dinners. They made room in the pew every Sunday for he and his daughter. Fully aware that people were frightened by his appearance, they lent a hand and the graciousness of their hearts. It was always for Isabella.

Something gnawed at her. Something unsettled her at night when she thought of this child. She would take her for weeks at a time, when her father's work schedule was erratic. He always brought her clothes in the same little grocery bag. Everything was laundered and folded neatly. He would slip the handles of the bag over the stump of his arm and amble up the walk with his daughter, her tiny hand clutching his.

He took four different buses to reach her home. Irene was always delighted; her own daughters were in college or married and her home lacked the hustle-bustle of children. When Isabella had lost the sight in her eye from a mysterious fall, Francis asked that Irene and her husband care for the baby. They had been granted temporary custody of his daughter until a full investigation had been completed.

When Francis resumed parenting of his daughter, Irene handed her back begrudgingly and with heaviness in her heart. It was at that point that she'd made a pact with herself—she would never lose communication with Francis. She would communicate with him weekly. Somewhere, she felt that Isabella was her child. Something deep inside her being had rankled and distressed her when she handed back this child. She feared she might not see her again. She feared that she was betraying Isabella.

Just the day before in church, Francis had told Irene that Isabella was in a foster home. His body trembled as he told her. It seemed a confession of sorts, and she felt her face blanch and the palms of her hands burn. The police thought that he had tried to have sex with Isabella. Francis vowed to Irene that he had not. Irene had not slept all night. She was beside herself with grief. How had she not seen this? Her eyes were full of tears.

I handed her a tissue. I gently rested my hand over hers. I looked at her face. It was very round. She had beautiful high cheekbones and blue eyes the color of turquoise marbles. They looked transparent. She looked like a pussycat, with those eyes that turn up at the corners. I'd always wanted those kinds of eyes. I had the fleeting thought that this woman was a fraud; that she was testing me around the issue of confidentiality. But then, with certainty, I knew that she was real. I just knew it. She was so distressed that her body was trembling and she could not stop crying. She kept blaming herself. She felt betrayed by Isabella's father. She questioned how any grown man, a parent no less, could violate a child. She was in shock.

I wondered for a moment where people like Irene come from. She had two grown daughters. When she talked about Isabella, her eyes danced. They sparkled. They disappeared into two little crescents when she smiled. This woman believed that she had been put on this earth to assist and guide this child. Irene needed this daughter. She believed that Isabella belonged to her. I listened to her, though very suspicious in that instant of her entitlement. Whose need was she filling? Her need to save this child, so compromised from the moment of her conception?

Within days, Isabella would be brought to Irene. My heart would rest when I saw Isabella fold herself into Irene's body. It would be the first glimmer of attachment I would see. She would remain fixed at Irene's side like a little shadow. Irene's husband sat in his chair in the living room and cried silently. It was his tacit, masculine pain that would remain with me for years to come. He was a man of very few words, but a man with a spacious, inexhaustible heart when it came to this child.

Somewhere in this world, few and far between, there are people like this. There are individuals who will find a moment, a pause, a breath in their lives when there is no hint of a thought, not one piece of cerebral intervention, but simply a vastness of heart, a desire to help, to heal, to love the fractured and disenfranchised—the Isabellas of the world. This family did not pause for a minute. There was no decision. This child would be their collective purpose, for a lifetime.

Irene and her family would inevitably adopt Isabella, and what they would provide for her would be magical, their commitment to her boundless. I would be in contact with this family on and off for the next fourteen years. When Isabella entered kindergarten, Irene sent me a wallet-size school photo of Isabella. Her little shoulders were hunched. One dark eye was vacant and wandering. She wore a pretty blue dress with a white collar. I hung that photo on the board above my desk, where it would remain for years. This child would embody my purpose throughout my career and beyond. Whenever I lost my way, I appealed to her little face to remind me of my intentions.

I would go to school conferences. I would shuttle her to and from therapy. I would supervise visitation between her and her father. I would visit her at Irene's. I would soon be so overwhelmed by all my other cases that, knowing Isabella was safe and loved, I started to drop from sight.

I saw Francis weekly at a therapy meeting for sex offenders. I met with his therapists and evaluators. There was dim hope for rehabilitation. He would, however, remain in her life. Isabella would struggle. She would be friendless. Children would tease her for her handicaps. She would be lonely and saddened. She would rebound and persevere always. She was an inspiration who was a result of her misfortunes. She never gave up. She had Irene, who was an unfaltering advocate, a lioness who would protect her own. Only rarely would Irene call me, dismayed and disheartened. Would I stand behind her? Would I support her and her daughter? There was never a question that my answer would undoubtedly be yes.

As Isabella grew, I dropped further from sight. I wanted her to forget me. I wanted her to have no recollection of her past. This was silly of me. This past was part of who this child was, and no one, including myself, could undo that.

I sit at my dining room table playing with the contents of this invitation, staring at the picture of Isabella, contemplating all the reasons why I will not go, racked by guilt. All the while I am wondering why the suggestion of this reunion has gotten me so twisted in a knot. There must be something in it for me to be so taken—not so much by the idea of walking back through my past, but more with my own interior machinations.

Under any other circumstance I would make my presence known at Isabella's celebration. There would be no hesitation. I would be there in a heartbeat. This celebration comes at a very precipitous juncture in my career. It comes at a time when I desperately need to make my exit. My plate, so to speak, is heaped higher than it has ever been. I have no appetite, no hunger. The frenetic pace that chips away at my body is worrisome to me. I have always spoken to my adult survivors of the unbounding mysteries of the body, of its uncanny ability to hold memory and trauma long before our mind is privy to their presence. I hear myself sing this lament repeatedly. I am now the survivor and need desperately to take heed.

When my twins were not quite a year, my hair began to fall out of my head. After I washed it, the clump of hair that I would pull from the drain was horrifying. I bounced from doctor to doctor. I was given the following diagnoses: stress; postpartum hormonal flux; lupus, where the body's protective mechanisms attack the body itself. I was terribly disturbed by such a hideous prospect. My hair would not stay rooted in my head. My lustrous, thick mane was thinning by the day. My body felt betrayed by its host.

To add insult to injury, I had developed a benign tremor in my hands. My shake was most pronounced in the morning. It eased throughout the day and was least at night. Interestingly enough, however, when there was an immediate maternal need to dislodge a splinter out of my youngest child's finger, my manual dexterity was perfect.

I am aware that my body is screaming. The metaphors of my maladies are all too clear. I am shaken to my roots. From my head to my toe, my body shudders at the thought of taking in more—more pain, more sadness, more trauma.

Ting Zhang, my Chinese doctor, ritualistically plants one needle firmly at the very top midline of my head. I visualize my angst, and all that it embodies, floating out of the top of my head up to the heavens. He will eventually tonify my blood. He will strengthen it so that I too will become fortified. With his long, beautiful fingers he will rub my forehead in attempts to erase the seemingly permanent furrow etched between my brows. After many years he will give up trying to keep my hair from falling out. Instead, he will help me grow new hair. And he does, with compassion, kindness, and wisdom.

So to take my precious Sunday and to share it with a household of people who mean nothing to me is less than desirable. If it were just Isabella and Irene, my pleasure would be theirs. Instead, I just want to be with my babies. I just want to root around in my garden on this marvelous day.

Somewhere my husband knows something that I do not. Somehow after twenty-odd years he can see things that I, because of my own depletion, have no desire to even venture toward or acknowledge. I will fight him all the way. He challenges me to go. "This is exactly what you need. You need to see that this child came full circle and that you played an instrumental part."

"You are full of shit!" I tell him. "Full of shit, like the shit in the marble baths in my dreams." I am expended beyond belief. I have nothing to give.

But I find myself on that glorious afternoon driving to see Isabella, my daughter Olivia strapped safely into her car seat. I am irritable. I am resentful. Once again, I am doing exactly what I don't want to be doing. I am pleasing someone else at the expense of myself. I don't even know whom I am pleasing anymore. I am comforted by my daughter's presence. I know that I will use her as a buffer between the world and myself.

A very fortuitous event occurs on my drive. I will understand its significance in hindsight. This is a route that I have traveled hundreds of times. However, this time I find that I am lost. At the four-way stop, instead of a vast, uninhabited meadow dotted with cows, a sprawling development of opulent homes has sprouted. I have lost my way. I cannot find my bearings, and there are no familiar landmarks. I see this as a divine intervention of sorts. I see this as my out. In turning myself around, I run right smack into Isabella's street. I see a sprawling white limousine with a JUST MARRIED sign penned in lavender glitter and festooned with streamers and ribbons. I collect myself as I walk backward in time.

A young, unfamiliar face opens the door. As I introduce myself I can see Irene bounding toward the door. My body begins to settle as she takes me in her arms. For a split second I wish that she would just keep holding me. I want everyone else to disappear. Irene's eyes are brimming with tears. I kiss her and whisper, "Look what you have done!" The young woman in the photo approaches. I have not seen her in five years. I would not know her except for that luminous smile.

We embrace, and she focuses on my child. Over Isabella's shoulder I see her father sitting sandwiched between two women. He acknowledges me with a nod and begins to walk toward me. Olivia's eyes are fixed on him the way mine were fourteen years ago. She averts her gaze and buries her face into my neck. She starts to cry. She digs her tiny fingers deeper into my back. I receive Francis's hand in mine with the same trepidation I did fourteen years ago, fear and pathos all rolled up into one. He removes his wallet from his jacket. His face is childish and pleased. From his wallet he slowly and deftly pulls out my business card. It is curled at the edges and feels like a swatch of soft fabric. It could fall apart in my hands. I am stunned that he still carries my card. It seems like a memento of sorts, some perverse nostalgia or memorabilia.

To Francis, however, it is something very different. He tells me that he remembers me. He thanks me. His pride and his love of his daughter register on his face. I know his secret. I know his shame. At that moment I feel as if I might faint. I excuse myself and walk outside holding my child closely. I need to breathe and to see the sky. I quietly slip away.

On the drive home I am ashamed of my hasty exit. I study the lines of my daughter's face. I look at the cascade of blond curls that frame her face. They are almost white, and as fine as silk. Her mouth is shaped like a delicate rosebud. I hold her warm little fingers between mine. At this moment, I know of no sweeter place. I am struck. My daughter Olivia is approaching the age that Isabella was when I found her. It is too painful a thought to let in.

I think of Irene. I think of this woman's ability to honor this bond between these two people, Isabella and her father, Francis. Fully aware of Francis's hideous violation of his then four-year-old daughter, she is able to find a place in her heart for understanding and honor. In her infinite compassion she has loved Isabella on her way through life. She has picked up the fragments and pieced them together with her own dignity and grace. She has been the glue. She asks for no applause, no recognition. She simply did what was instinctual to her as a woman and mother. I cannot think of a person whom I respect more.

And Isabella, in her quiet, unassuming beauty . . . the child whom I bathed in the sink, whom I tried to deliver from her own personal hell. I will never fully comprehend the magnitude of her strength or her ability to rise to her challenges and emerge victorious.

As I round the drive I see my other children in my garden. I walk into my husband's open arms and cry from a depth that I never knew existed inside of me. My son's babbling is quieted when he sees my tears. He takes my hand and shows me the mysteries of spring he has unearthed in my garden. He is overjoyed and has me sit on the ground with him as he uncovers all the earthly delights. His eyes are dancing with excitement and joy. He ever so gently places his soft palm on my cheek. I kiss his hand.

I often feel as if my life is strung together like an archipelago of jagged little islands. When I reach an island, I can breathe life back into myself. The waters in between, however, are often murky and uncharted. Occasionally, their color is the deepest of all sapphires—warm and soothing as an outdoor bath.

Isabella is an island in and of herself. She is a sparkling gem that lifted me out of a very deep and dark abyss. My fall had been precipitous. I had temporarily lost my way. In finding Isabella that day, I rediscovered myself and, most importantly, my purpose. She lifted me and reminded me that I find and heal incest because I believe that no child should ever be robbed of his or her heart and soul. Isabella was able to retrieve hers, and in doing so, she offered mine back to me.

The Sins of the Fathers
Are Visited upon the Daughters

As horrid as it is to contemplate, I have come to believe that there are individuals who look for sexual abuse because they need to find it. They dedicate their lives to the pursuit of this lascivious demon. Their dogged determination makes haste to an obsession. They hunt and track, scouring high and low, for any telltale signs in their children. They desperately need to make their children the victims of sexual exploitation. They ritualistically inspect their children's genitals. They comb hampers and dirty-clothes baskets looking for their daughters' panties. Nose in crotch, they sniff like a hound for any suggestion of sexual impropriety. They probe their children like a digital penetrator, looking for the entrance, looking for the opening to their conviction.

I am not quite certain what this is about, but the tenacity with which they pursue their obsession reeks of craziness. It is a train careening out of control, atilt on the summit of a looming precipice. It is a wildly perverse dance where the parents of these children never rest until sexual abuse has been confirmed and they themselves have been vindicated. For these parents, there is a passionate need to find a violator: an ex-spouse, an ex-boyfriend, a current lover. Frenzied desperation is a hallmark of this affliction. And for the practitioner, it is a slippery slope. It is the shilly-shally, self-doubt, and vacillation that force us to intermittently lose our footing. We can never be sure who is telling the truth.

The child? The parent? The alleged offender? The ground beneath our feet is constantly shifting. It requires a Zen practice of surrendering the desire to know. Perhaps there is no knowing in all of this. Perhaps we must live with the fact that incest is an elusive, oily dynamic whose certainty hinges on little less than trust and faith in the utterance of a child and the intuition of the person who suspects its presence.

Individuals who marry themselves to this endeavor unsettle me. Their passion and conviction assume a maniacal posture. Their crusade for the protection of their children is staggering . . . until I realize that they are terribly ill, and my pursuit takes on a vastly different spin. How do I navigate a safer terrain for children? Better yet, how do I teach them to bend with their parent's craziness and love them nonetheless? That's how it was with Ariel Rose. Five years of unraveling the puzzle, and a lifetime of healing the shame ahead of her.

Ariel's pupils are surrounded by a liquidy turquoise. Floating in the turquoise are pentagrams of gold shimmery stars, which hypnotize her audience. Her heart-shaped face is full and flushed. A bouncy blond ponytail shoots out of her head like a waterfall. She is an ethereal wood nymph, and one would place her in a fairy tale, in another dimension, in another time and space. Her six-year-old's guile reels me in like a bedazzled trout, with its dizzy eye fastened to a glittering lure. I am fabulously intrigued by this child, and I am finally, after almost three years, able to get my hands on this little sylph.

As supervisor of the Sexual Abuse Team, I can't recall the last time I saw a child jangle so many professionals. Caseworkers are swirling around this child. The mention of Ariel Rose and her mother, Diana, piques the interest of many. The mother has become a fixture here. A devoted and passionate advocate for her daughter, she is convinced that this child has been brutally violated by her father. Her daughter is exploring her vagina with great passion and zeal. On this very day her mother found her straddled on the arm of the couch, carefully positioning her genitals, riding the furniture frantically. Her downy head was thrown back, her eyes, according to her mother, glazed with rapture. A glistening strand of drool, like a silken thread from a spiderweb, hung from her daughter's mouth.

Ariel came to the attention of the department with a disturbing laundry list of allegations for one so young. Her mother, Diana, comes through my door one afternoon, breathless and agitated. It is smoldering day late in the summer, and the window to my office is open. I have covered up the floor vent that shoots out arctic air-conditioning. This cooling system has given me a grand headache, and I am trying this day to slip out, unnoticed, when the front desk secretary alerts me that there is a "Ms. Rose here to see you."

I question her to see if I can pass her to a fellow social worker. "Not this one," she whispers. Before going out to our waiting room, I swallow two Tylenol. I sit for a moment, looking at a wash of lilac bushes across the street. It is so hot and dry, it looks as if there is steam rising off the top of the blooms. I liken it to the way my head feels. It is pounding and hot. I feel a familiar discomfort that has loomed over the years when I get a walk-in, a person who comes in off the street to ask for services. The fact that this person is asking specifically for me makes me uneasy.

There is no security in our building. It is starting to empty as the working day is ending. I close my eyes for a brief moment; my hands begin to feel clammy as I envision Ms. Rose entering my office, pulling a gun from her handbag, and shooting me in the face. I can see my blood splattering all over my children's artwork, dripping from the photos of them, their smiles obscured by the garnet blast of blood. I see the fragments of my face exploding off my skull. She will rise, leave the office quietly, and shut the door behind her. Who will find me? I try to douse this visual. My headache is starting to make me nauseated. I wonder if the person in the waiting room is someone I have offended. A mother I worked with years ago, whose child I had removed? A woman whose child was violently raped, whose husband walked free? A client I didn't listen to enough? A woman I discounted or ignored? I have entered the lives of hundreds of people. My decisions have been responsible for the destruction of families, no matter how abusive or depraved. The power I seemingly wield is ungodly. I must have many enemies.

I come out of my office and angle my vision so that I can see the waiting room. Ms. Rose is sitting in the chair with both hands resting loosely in her lap. She has the face of an angel. The tingling in my body begins to settle. I ponder my violent musings I am relieved when I see a woman of seemingly innocent stature. I open the door and greet her. I note that she is carrying some papers and her car keys. She does not have a handbag.

Ms. Rose seats herself across from me. I leave my door slightly ajar. I ask her how I can help her. As she begins to speak, I find myself struck by her beauty. She is of Asian descent with fair coloring. She is a feather, lithe and petite. She is wearing a long, flowing, diaphanous sundress. She floats. Her posture is perfectly aligned. An imaginary string is attached to the top of her head and pulls her straight to the heavens. She looks suspended. Her tiny feet are nestled tightly together as if bound by cord. Her face is the shape of a heart, with fine angles, high cheekbones. Her mouth, a neat rosebud. She is Botticelli-like. Her eyes, however, are haunting. A deep navy blue, they are blinkless and never move. She fixes her gaze directly on my eyes and does not shift them during her hour-long narrative. She barely appears to be breathing.

She begins to speak slowly and methodically. She is pleasant, yet gives the impression of carefully cultivated propriety and control. Diana sketches her concerns about her daughter, Ariel, who is a tad under three. Her fund of knowledge and vocabulary suggest to me that this is a very bright woman. I am a bit taken. She has recently read an article about behavioral cues in sexually abused children. She has been watching Ariel of late. Ariel has complained of her "bottom hurting." The child is rubbing herself on the furniture and has had frequent tummyaches. Diana is pointed in her concerns about sexual abuse. Ariel's father, she calmly explains, had sex with a goat. I do not blink an eye.

I am poised in my next question to Diana. "What was your sex life with him like?" I envision the goat tied up to the back of a barn. This is not the first farm animal I have encountered in the last twenty years. It's rarely a dog or a cow; it's often a goat or a sheep. It must be the wool. She is looking for a sign. Her eyes drill into the back of my brain. She is trolling. She is looking for a healthy bite on her line. She does not scan my body, my office, my clothing. She woos me in, slowly and cautiously. I drift, but she has me gripped. She is sure to keep me captivated and reeled in. I want out. I feel myself emptying. I feel my fatigue. My defenses are weary. My sharpness has been dulled. She feels like some perverse sorceress. I am ensnared.

She explains that she lost interest in sex after she had her daughter. She also has a newborn son. Her husband was angered by this and often forced himself on her. When she would not respond, he, of course, turned his love toward Ariel. This is a classic lament. Diana, however, has me engrossed. It is perhaps her intellect and her savvy. Right then and there, I decide to board the train. My intuition tells me that there is some invaluable learning in this case.

She was recently bathing her infant son. She had the childhood memory of her mother bathing her and taking great pains to clean her vagina. She remembers being precisely Ariel's age. She was frightened by this intrusive visual. I simply listen. I am trying to mirror her by not blinking. This is impossible. It dries my eyes.

One afternoon, while changing the diaper of her infant son, she became so overcome by her child's beauty and her love for him that she began to shower him with kisses. She began to kiss his belly and ended up at his groin. She became alarmed by her rapture.

My mind wanders off to my firstborn and how grossly disproportionate her tiny vagina was. As her elfin body took form and shape, its beauty opened like a delicate flower of spring. Such skin I had never felt. Such a distinct fragrance of infant hair, head, hands, and feet. I could not get enough of her. My face was always so close to this beautiful creature. I could sit for hours stroking her downy hair, inhaling the baby scent that nestled itself in the tiny folds of skin behind her neck. The experience was sensual and intoxicating. Had I ever drizzled kisses all over her? Had I ever let my mouth find its way to her pubis? Yes, indeed I had. I have never given it a moment of thought. I was flooded. I was in love all over again. There was never anything sexual about those kisses . . . or was there?

I am thinking about the fineness of the line between absolute, understandable love for a child and placing oneself over the line of acceptable conduct between parent and child. This dialectic has played itself repeatedly in my brain for years. It is not so much my assessment of the parent as the nuggets of gold the parent brings to me. I feel that something happened the day Diana became enraptured as she was changing her son's diaper. A seed was sown, in the form of a thought or perhaps a memory, and a poisonous incantation took root.

Diana's eyes begin to search my face. She is waiting for me to judge her actions and to validate her memory of her own sexual victimization. I, in exchange, feel self-conscious and dust my fingertips over my entire face, thinking that there is perhaps some crumb of food or some microscopic pieces of lint nestled on my brow. I practice her blinklessness. I keep my eyes on hers and truly wonder if she is a witch. I am conscious of all the photos of my children in the office. I wonder if by stealth she has removed an article from my desk, something with which to cast some spell. This woman frightens me. I am aware of the time. I am aware of my solicitous tone. I want her to like me. I don't want her to do voodoo on my children. I am sharpening my manipulation out of fear. I assure her that I will review her whole file and will call her when I decide how to respond to her concerns about Ariel.

There is a volume on Diana, Ariel, and Ariel's father, Munroe. There have been claims and counterclaims over the years. There have been unexplained bruises and markings. There is a paper trail of allegations of sexual abuse by Munroe against his daughter. I find an additional report of sexual misconduct by a parent whose child had attended day care with Ariel. This one I remember clearly. Ariel attended a small day care center where the staff was particularly concerned about her daily complaints about her "daisy" hurting. Ariel continuously related to staff that her father had put his finger in her "daisy." Reports of this behavior were investigated and found to be unsubstantiated, but the staff at the day care center was appalled at what they believed to be incompetence by the sexual abuse team.

The father of another child at day care was fond of Ariel and attracted to Diana. Diana had taken him in as her confidant. One Sunday afternoon, Diana and Ariel invited this father and his son to an outing at a nearby park. After a delightful day, they stopped for dinner, and Ariel asked to use the bathroom. Diana asked the young father if he would supervise Ariel's use of the restroom while she ordered their meal. Then they had their dinner.

It is a breathtaking summer eve, and I have taken a few moments to plant myself on the front porch. The light is superb. The colors of the spruces are an array of greens and dusty blues, deep and rich. The snow on the top of Longs Peak is silvery and reflects the light like a sparkling gem. Across the field, I can see a sleek red mama fox carrying freshly killed prey to her den. I have seen her for the past few weeks. Skillful and determined, she brings home a healthy feast for her babes. Her tail is the rich reddish plume that women of yesteryear draped around their necks.

My reverie is interrupted by a phone call from the on-call worker. She would like to patch me through to an emergency-room doc who has one of our kids. I am puzzled, as it is rare for sexually abused kids to end up in an ER. This is an emergency room at a large Denver city hospital—even more confusing. The doctor is formal and precise on the phone. He has a four-year-old child whose mother has brought her in after hearing from her child that she was digitally penetrated by a friend that very afternoon, in the bathroom of a nearby restaurant. The mother is requesting that the child be sedated in order for there to be a colposcopic exam of the child's cervix. My eyes are still fastened to the fox and her mission as I listen to his description of the mother.

"She seems rather euphoric and calm for a mom whose child has just been penetrated," he explains. "She says that the child was raped by her biological father. The kid is a wreck. What's the history on this?" I explain to him that in her rather brief existence, the child has been to far too many doctors to be examined for incest and sexual abuse. It is like a ritual for this mother. There have been no conclusive findings. I tell him that I think that this is more intrusive to this child's being than if she had been penetrated. I tell him that I believe that this is a debauched form of child abuse. There is silence on the wire, and I want to grab the thoughts that just flew out of my mouth and shove them right back down my throat. Either I have offended him or he gets my gist.

That is a thought I keep solely for myself. It is provocative and holds more intuitive than clinical weight. I feel the hierarchy ticking in our silence. He is a physician, and I am a social worker. He has a child to be examined, and I am doing a hideous job reining in my big fat opinions.

"I defer to you on the medical end. Knowing this mother and her history, I tell you, you can liken her to a junkie shopping around for dope. In this case, her child is her ruse. I would ask you to reconsider both the issue of examining her and certainly that of sedating her. Please."

Again there is a hum in the phone line. A hum and a long sigh. "I don't envy your job," he says. I know that he will heed my wishes. I thank him.

As I hang up the phone, I can see the twinkle of the first evening star, the wishing star. I walk across the road to see if I can get a better look at the red-tailed fox. I hang off the top of the fence, but alas, she is nestled somewhere deep in the field with her babies. I bid her goodnight and walk back to my home. I feel deeply disturbed by this phone call. So disturbed, I can barely let my thoughts seep in. I wonder what Diana is after. I wonder if she is somehow aroused by this attention. I am thankful that this doctor paused long enough to question what was being presented. I am thankful that he listened.

I shudder at the utter terror this child must have experienced in an emergency trauma unit, with yet one more stranger ready to eyeball her vagina. A frightened baby having her legs pried open to look for what? What must her little mind be thinking? She believes that her mother is trying to protect her. She has no voice. She is only four. I find that I am pacing on my porch. I am picking at the cuticles around my fingernails. I am wondering how the fox protects her babies, how she keeps them out of harm's way. Is Ariel's mother offering her up in an effort to purge and cleanse herself? In her valiant efforts to rescue her daughter, is she trying to rescue herself instead? Unknowingly, this child has become a perverse extension of her mother's historical pain. This thought has yet to take shape or form in my mind. I have yet to understand what I am dealing with.

The following morning, the young father from the day care is in the lobby of my office, accompanied by the director of the center. The director is ashen and quiet. The young father has obviously not slept. I usher them back, and he begins to weep. He feels as if his life is ruined. He desperately searches my face and swears he has never touched Ariel. In fact, he waited outside the stall while she went to the bathroom. He thought he was being a support to Ariel and her mother. They had had a wonderful day at the park together. My heart feels heavy for this man. He has been duped. I assure him that I will consult with the police department.

I find myself at an interesting crossroads with the director of the day care center. She has lambasted me in the last year for being nonresponsive to Ariel's outcries. She has been adamant that we arrest the child's father. After all, he had been brutally violating his daughter. We sit in silence. We agree to have daily contact with regard to Ariel's behaviors as well as her parade of allegations. She and I revamp bathroom policy at the day care center. Not much more needs be said. She is slowly yet cautiously boarding the train.

This is a night when I know it is best to not go home. This is a night when I must reach out and find my islands of solace. I am sitting in a beautiful Italian restaurant, Il Fornaio, in Denver. Across from me sits a longtime confidant, a retired judge friend who was on the bench for close to twenty-five years, a man who exited the system because these cases began to invade the crawl spaces of his mind daily, and then again in his dreams. The material was like an extra skin that had attached itself to his entire being. He felt that the decisions he had to make were getting far too cumbersome and far too intrusive. Toward the end of his career as a judge, he told me once that he feared for his life and the lives of his children. He felt that a clinical diagnosis of his mind should certainly include paranoia. For some time he slept with a gun under his pillow. He would be sitting in a legal conference and he would start to sweat. He was sure someone in the room had been hired to kill him. For years he severed the bond between parents and their children. He said there was nothing worse. He would cry after relinquishment hearings. He was sure one of his own children would die of cancer or be murdered. He believed in karmic return. He was certain that he would be punished for all the decisions he had made, especially those that ended families.

I find every comfort in conversing with this man. He is my father confessor. "Tonight," I tell him, "I'm going to cry." I am stabbing my toothpick into my martini glass, chasing the elusive olive. I can feel the liquor begin to loosen me. If I look directly at him, I will cry. He is sitting against the window in a crisp sky-blue oxford shirt. His hair has become so gray it is almost white. As I look at him I notice that his hair nearly matches his shirt. It is silvery blue and thick, very handsome against his dark olive skin.

I begin to tell him the saga of Ariel. I tell him that I don't know what I am doing. "This woman spooks me," I tell him. "I'm afraid she is going to cast a spell on me. I feel crazy." He looks at me and knows that I am serious. I lay my head down on the cool granite tabletop the way a child would lay his head down on the desk after being scolded. I feel his large warm hand rest lightly on my head. The moment I feel his soft, warm hand touch my head, I start to cry.

"I hate my job. I have no one to talk with. This woman thinks her child has been incested. She would be euphoric if I confirmed it for her. I don't know if she is her daughter's protector or if I am nuts. I feel as if I am resisting her with all my might, and I don't know if it's because I think what she is doing to her child is so horribly abusive, or I am in some horrendous power play with her will. It's sick. I'm ineffective. I'm not going to allow one more interview or medical exam or dialogue with this kid about her 'daisy,' or whatever."

I am sobbing now, and his eyes fill with tears. The moment I see him come apart, I stop. I remember his pain. "Old man!" I say. "We can't do this." I squeeze his hand and order another martini.

Here is when I realize that I can't separate. I am having a beautiful dinner, and I am crying into my martini. Am I crying for Ariel? For Diana? For the poor schlub who went to the park with her? He reminds me that the world of incest is a world of uncertainty. But most importantly, it is a universe of listening to and heeding your instinct. He tells me, as he has through the years, that my intuition around incest is finely honed. It is razor sharp.

"Next time there is an outcry, *you* interview her. You need to put your finger on the pulse. You need to see her, to sit with her, to read her. You feel deeply and emotionally. You know that when you are out in the weeds, you always find your way back home— Il Fornaio, a good strong martini, and a veteran friend like me." I wholly agree.

There is nothing quite like a friend who has walked in the same shoes, someone who has an unadulterated sense of self, stripped and unabashed. I feel tremendous relief in showing him my frailties. I feel at times as if I am on my knees asking forgiveness for my blunders—better yet, asking permission to follow my heart and to heed my instinct, to act on my own sensibilities devoid of rational processes. These people are few and far between.

*   *   *   *   *   *   *

Over the years, Ariel came and went. She spent a year in foster care after her mother admitted to leaving a multitude of purplish bruises like fingerprints on both arms. She fared well, and her mother, once medicated for depression, seemed to flourish under intensive therapy and supervised visitation with her daughter. Diana was under the bell jar.

When Ariel returned home, things seemed almost too tranquil and without drama. We held our breath, praying that the litany of sexual abuse allegations had been put to rest. Sadly, the rumblings began again; we all knew Diana was on the warpath, and Ariel's little semblance of normal self would begin to crumble.

In time, Diana is at my door once again. There is a clamor of therapists, teachers, and concerned friends. All have heard the same outcry that last night, while Ariel was at her father's house, he bathed her. In toweling her dry, his fingers traced the perimeter of her labia.

I ask Diana to bring Ariel to the Child and Family Advocacy Center. Her voice over the wire is slightly giddy and euphoric. She quickly contains her zeal and is pragmatic in her questioning. I ask her to please not discuss these allegations with her daughter, knowing full well that is a temptation beyond temptations.

Ariel and I are seated at a child-sized wicker table with matching chairs. Present at the interview is a detective from a local police department. If there is anyone who can help me suss this out, it will be this officer. She misses nothing. I am trying to situate my rear end on this tiny chair so that I find the smallest hint of comfort.

Pinned to Ariel's coveralls is a cloth heart, decorated with pink buttons and shiny white pearls. In the middle of the heart is a crystal ornament. She points out the crystal and likens it to the tiny cluster of diamonds around my ruby wedding ring. We are in agreement that we both love things that sparkle and shimmer. Above the heart is another ornament, a tiny angel dancing on the head of a pin.

Ariel's countenance is eerie. She is tracking my eyes and my speech with great acuity. At one point she asks to see the color of my eyes. She is almost too vigilant for such a young child. I could easily lose control of this interview. She is cunning and savvy, a dichotomous blend for a child so young and seemingly unformed. We begin our conversation about my role as a social worker and seeing if children are safe. When I ask her to tell me what she knows about the phrase "to be safe," her response is that "safe" means when children are not "abused." I tell her that that is a rather grown-up word for a child of six. I ask her where she heard that. She tucks in quickly and says that she cannot remember.

In our dialogue, we enter the realm of truth and lie. We agree to tell each other the truth. At this juncture, she asks the detective to explain her understanding of the difference between truth and lie. She asks the detective if she will agree to tell the truth. I have lost control of this interview. I note that this child is taking what I have said to her and is practicing it on another so that she has the script down. This I am somewhat enthralled with, as it is confirming my suspicions. I am aware that I have never seen this happen in an interview. I ask her if she knows why I am here with her today. Her response is "Because my daddy abused me?" Many of her responses end in a query instead of a statement. I am getting hotter.

Throughout the interview, Ariel's eyes dart between the detective and myself. She is agitated and working very hard to stay on track. When we talk about her father, she tells us that he rubs lotion on her legs and she doesn't like it. Nothing she discloses has even a hint of incest. She says sometimes her dad doesn't clip his fingernails and sometimes he scratches her.

Cautiously yet zealously, she is trying to sell us a disclosure. I commend her creativity and persistence. She punctuates our interview by telling me that I am doing a "good job." I am flabbergasted and captivated. I want to take her farther to see what else I can find. She is tiring, however, and wants her mother.

I meet with Diana after my interview with Ariel. She too is dressed in coveralls with a fabric heart pinned to the front. I am captivated by how twinned these two are. Where does this mother leave off and this child begin? They are a meld. They are an enmeshed admixture of sickness and destruction. For years now this mother has convinced this child that she is a victim of incest or sexual abuse. It's as if she had told Ariel when she reached toddlerhood that her left leg was broken, and ever since, this child has accommodated her mother's wish. Perhaps she limps and favors her stronger leg when she is with Diana. Perhaps while she is away from her mother, she dances and twirls on both healthy legs. Nonetheless, she has lived an illusion, and the very being of this child has been chiseled away. I can only hope that she will one day come to see her mother's illness and be protected from it.

Diana is enraged with the lack of corroborating information to sustain the veracity of her child's allegation. She is maniacal and begins to rant and rave about my transparency and my inability to protect her daughter. She demands a copy of the taped interview and murmurs something about suing me. After all, I am the "expert." "Anyone can see that this child has been raped!" she says, and storms out with Ariel in tow. On her way out the door, both Ariel's heart and her angel somehow become unclipped from her coveralls. I find myself flying down the stairs with her heart and her angel in my hands. I wonder why she is not relieved by this information.

Custody of Ariel is granted to her father, and Diana's ardent supporters are righteously enraged and indignant. I am barraged with hate mail and threats. I have knowingly and purposely returned this child to the hands of her offender.

Over the years, Ariel thrives. She grows like a weed, tall and lean. I see her periodically during her supervised visitation with her mother. The roundness of her little face lengthens and becomes more chiseled. The little girl I remember is now a child of eight. There is never again a referral with regard to sexual abuse. It all comes to a screeching halt, vanishing as if it never really existed in the first place. Ariel's father divorces and remarries. Ariel's stepmother is kind and nurturing. One day I run into her therapist at the grocery store. I ask after Ariel and her new family. "She is a different child. You would never have thought . . . " She stops herself. She told her therapist that she wished she were the baby and that she could start all over again. She does not want to see her mother. She has to be medicated to quell her anxiety before each monthly visit with her mother. The visits are one hour and they are supervised. Ariel is terrified that her mother will abduct her. She understands that her mother is ill. She lovingly embraces her relationship with her dad.

In play therapy, she latches onto a marble, the kind that looks like the eye of a cat. She spends her entire hour hiding the marble in the sand box, daring her therapist to dig deeply and find it. She does this over and over again until the marble cannot be retrieved. It becomes a ritual for the opening and the closure of therapy. She is practicing the art of hiding, of burrowing deeply into the earth.

Munroe Taylor is sitting two rows in front of me in the courtroom. He is a ghoulish-looking man, yet seems tender and caring. He is of small stature, with delicate features. His sand-colored dreadlocks reach the middle of his back. His skin is sallow and wan. He has a long, thin nose with a slight hook on the end. He is dressed in a three-piece navy blue suit that seems to swim on his frame. He reminds me of a butler or an undertaker. He wears shiny black shoes, almost feminine, as his feet are small and delicate, almost like a woman's. He has always been kind to me. His speech is slow and labored. He thinks about everything he says.

I am looking at the back of his head and wondering what it would be like to have sex with a goat. I am trying to picture this in my mind. I cannot quite picture it. The goat would squirm and kick. Would the man have to be on his knees? Or up on all fours? I put my head in my hands and cover my face with shame. I feel exposed, as if everyone can read my deviant thoughts.

I am jarred when I hear my name as I am summoned to the witness stand. I raise my right hand and swear to tell the truth. I catch the heel of my shoe on the hem of my skirt as I slip into my seat. I hear the rip. I pour myself some water and ready myself for the slaughter. Having testified for the last twenty years, I am rarely ruffled. Today, however, Diana is representing herself in an effort to gain custody of her daughter. Ariel's father says that she "lives in constant fear." She and her dad have rehearsed an escape route. Ariel is afraid her mother will come for her in the night. She will whisper "Goddess, goddess, goddess of the moon." She will be coming to find Ariel. Ariel practices sleeping with her eyes wide open.

I am pleasant as she questions me. She is stern and angry and determined to make me her fool. I am reminded of what my father once said to me: "You never know whose shoes you will end up shining." I make an attempt at respectfulness.

As I de-escalate, her rage begins to mount. "Just answer the question, Ms. Smith," she barks at me. I begin to feel irritated and intimidated. She is good. She is damn good, and she has me by the tail. She is in her element. She has waited for years to take me down. I am the expert, and I have failed her child. She begs the court to hold me liable for the loss of her child, for setting this innocent child loose to be repeatedly raped by her offender.

After five years, I realize that she has not moved an inch. At times, I thought she was on the cusp of lucidity, clarity, and understanding. My interview has been reviewed by the judge in chambers, and back in the courtroom she asks me my professional opinion of separating this child from her mother.

"For years, your honor, we have responded to the outcries of this child. We have interviewed her. We have queried her. We have performed repeated medical examinations on her genitals, at times without sensitivity or compassion. We have subjected her to a procession of strangers querying her about being pinched, poked, massaged, and penetrated. Her sense of her body and the sacredness of her innocence have been destroyed. Her foundation of trust and intimacy, in my estimation, is not salvageable. Her mind's understanding of truth and loyalty will always hinge on this experience. I had always suspected that when Ariel hit the ripe old age of seven or eight, she would begin to see the world through her own eyes. She would assert her tiny voice as best she could, and ultimately, your honor, she would tell each and every one of us what she needed. She would exercise her right to choose freely. She would understand in essence what it means to be safe and protected.

"Our system and its intentions have failed this child. Her mother's dogged determination to find incest has served only to chip away at this child's sense of self and reality. I see this entire five-year process as nothing more that a protracted form of child abuse. She must be set free from her mother. She will come back to her when she is ready, but not until then. Let her go, your honor. Give her back her life, sacred and sweet."

Diana's eyes look as if they are twisting around in their sockets. She is ashen. She is leafing frantically through her papers and documentation. She is compelled to keep this going. As I am stepping down from the witness stand, she states in a very clear voice that she hopes that the next child Munroe rapes is my daughter. As I hear these words leave her mouth, I find myself in an involuntary panic. I can't breathe, I feel my chest constrict, and I begin to feel as if I will faint. I sit down and begin to breathe deeply and slowly. I must bring air back into my body. It's as if her words reached around my throat, clutching, squeezing, and constricting my breath, my life, and my heart.

I am in the hallway exiting the Justice Center. I hear someone call my name. I flinch. It is Munroe. He walks slowly toward me and extends his hand in thanks. Cautiously and quickly, I receive his hand in mine. As I look at his long, tapered fingers in my hand, I notice that his nails have been manicured, like a woman's, but one nail looks as if it has been hastily torn. Its edges are jagged and sharp. I retract my hand quickly, as if I have been burned. I excuse myself. I flash on Ariel talking about her father tracing his jagged fingernail around her "daisy." My cinema mind sees her rolling around on the bed, naked, plump, and pristine, with her father's unkempt nails accidentally scratching the virginal folds of her labia. I am gripped with fear. After all these years, have I been mistaken?

Lying Down with the Offender

It is early morning, and as I descend the staircase I can see men emerging from behind bushes and trees. They come closer to the house, peering into the windows. Their faces are pressed against the glass in the entryway, the living room, and the dining room. The face of a man obscures every view outside. Each man is naked—without a shred of clothing. They are whispering and pleading: "Please find us some clothing. We need to cover up. Everyone will see us." They are huddled against the house, underneath the porch. They are like an infestation of insects crawling out from under brush, bramble, and rock.

I am frozen with fear. While I want to help them, I wonder if this is all a ruse. They want to get into my house. They are attempting to exploit my goodness, and I will fall for the deception. Where have they all come from, and why are they here, looking for me?

I dash upstairs and gather up as many articles of my husband's clothing as I can carry. I open the door and attempt to avert my eyes from their genitals, but I cannot. I see that all these men have erections. Willy-nilly, I start to toss articles of clothing out the front door. Shirts. Pants. Jackets. They paw the clothing as if they were starving animals, ravenous for crumbs.

As I begin to close the door, I notice that there are two men left. I run back up to my bedroom and fetch my own summer robe and a single silk tie. As I hand the robe to the first of the two lone men, he pauses and he whispers, "I have very little shame left." I step onto my porch, and as I enshroud him in this cloak of femininity, his erection melts and he bows his head. I hand the remaining man the silk tie. He is indignant. He puffs up his chest, exalted and preening like a fabulous peacock, his erect penis proud and tumescent. "What can I cover with this?"

"Your heart," I reply. With trepidation he lifts the tie from my hands. His eyes begin to water as if he is about to cry. He moans dryly. He vanishes.

Perhaps it has always been my job to cover up things that are perceived as vile and repulsive. Sometimes I have felt the need to call incest something different than its true name. Like an accomplished offender, there are times that I have tried to minimize and deny the true impact to the victim.

In protecting the integrity of a child, I have also felt the pull to soften for the offender his torrential blow. I have rationalized that it will be easier for the child if I suspend judgment and simply minister in my attempt to heal. After all, children love their parents. In my rawest state, I have wanted to do nothing more than make incest disappear, to render it an invisible entity whose path I have never crossed. But indeed, this has been a chosen calling, no matter how loathsome, no matter how intrusive.

When asked why men violate their children, I always draw a blank. I can rattle off with ease all the clinical implications and motivations of incest, but that is of little help to people who crave an understanding of this atrocity. I find that I feel somewhat contaminated by virtue of association—that I myself fail to fully separate the offender from my being, the same way we fail to separate the abuser from his repugnant violations. It is a difficult question to answer. What I can say is this: Incest is the gravest and most destructive atrocity to be thrust upon a child, and yet underneath some incest is a perverted twist of tenderness. It is love gone deeply awry. In the time that it takes my mouth to utter that notion, I am gripped by its unassailable contradiction. Undeniably, and sadly, this is the only way that I have learned to make sense of this heinous violation of body and soul.

For the last 20 years I have dreamed about my offenders. They nuzzle into my night thoughts with greater frequency than their victim children. It is always a dream that is sexually flavored. As my horror and shame have softened over the years, I have come to know these dreams as my rite of passage, a segue to my own healing. It is my way of creating my own connection to their wretched, depraved pathology. In a dreamed sexual liaison with my offender, I can be both the captor and his victim. I am the voyeur and the dreamer. I am righting his wrong by luring him with a grown woman, replacing the innocent child. I can save the child only by saving myself. It is the only way that I can understand the intention of the offense—to lie down with the offender

On Mondays, I take inventory of the week prior. Every incest referral is my burden to review. My workers review cases with me. They identify the cases by the sexual act. "This is the one where the stepfather shaved his stepdaughter's vagina. This is the 'lick butt, suck pee-pee' case. This is the one where the father forced his daughter to wear his wife's black lace thong, then paddled her rear and fucked her. This is the one where the guy stuck the video camera in the heating vent and watched his pubescent daughter's slumber party. This is the one . . . "

I learn where my folks are in the investigative process. I know which arrest warrants are being crafted, who is to be sentenced, and which children have been adjudicated "dependent and neglected." I know which deputy district attorney I am in battle with and learn with which perps I should not be alone in the same room. I know who peed a dirty UA (urinalysis) and which kids are "cheeking" their meds. I know which perpetrator has reoffended and who failed their polygraph.

What I don't know is how I absorb this information, and what my body does to process it. Is there a small deviant compartment of my brain where I store these images? I am strictly a visual being. My people know to present their cases by sex act rather than by name, because that is the way I can retrieve the information when it is needed. I bring up the visual like one would bring up a file on a computer. It is warehoused neatly and precisely. I write very little down. I do this consciously. It is a coping mechanism. If I write it down, I breathe life into it. It becomes real. I don't know if I could bear that. It is a barrage of sensory overload. I will fry my circuits. I am notorious for forgetting superfluous detail. I float longingly down the river Lethe, one of the five rivers of Hades, with the condition of forgetfulness and oblivion. I thank the gods for my malady.

Usually, I merrily roll along, tucking each scenario into its tidy and seemingly remote pocket of my brain. Every now and then, though, along comes a case that knocks the wind from my sails. It renders me inert and dazed. It leaves me unprepared for the deluge of feeling that is about to inhabit my body. There is certainly no stopping it. It has a life of its own and, most importantly, it has its intention. These moments leave me dazzled in some perverse way. My question always to myself is "What is it about this case that has me so gripped? Why here? Why now? What is the teaching in this? Have I not learned enough?" It is always with great trepidation that I lean into this morass. And it always ends up, without a doubt, a jewel in my underworld. The universe has its reasons.

It is a smoldering Friday in June, and I have no more workers to send out on their quest for incest. Every adult who has been sexually inappropriate with a kid in the county today has been found out and turned in. As I turn off my pager and toss it into the bottom of my desk drawer, I am aware that this is my tacit translation to my administration that any more incest that rears its head this afternoon will have to pass into the ether.

That afternoon, upon entering the Advocacy Center, I see a platoon of exhausted social workers, wrapping up interviews and assessing safety plans with families. There is one last child to be brought in, and I listen as the social worker makes her phone call to the mother of the child. She is fingering a freshwater pearl that dangles off her left ear. Her posture is somewhat collapsed and fatigued until the mother answers the phone. I watch as her back straightens and she begins to explain to the mother that we have received a worriesome report on her daughter. She pauses as the woman on the end of the line responds. I lose the content of the conversation. I feel my body recoil as if it were myself on the other end of the phone line, the recipient of such a cryptic, noxious call. I lift my unruly mane of hair, airing the sweat that has pooled at the nape of my neck. The tremor in my hands is distinctly noticeable. I feel my panic response begin in my groin, an unusual place on my body, but not unfamiliar.

I visualize myself in my kitchen. It is late afternoon, and I am washing the morning's dishes left in the sink. The house is still, soon to be filled by children returning from school. I am thinking about dinner and the bottle of Chianti I am about to uncork. The phone rings, and life explodes. It is one call. That one moment when someone whom you have never met makes the suggestion that your husband has been sexual with your child. Not a neighbor telling you about your husband's paramour, not a lover that he's cheating with, but your baby—your child. I taste the putrid reflux of my lunch as it climbs up my throat and slides back again.

I return from my reverie as my social worker places a tight hand over the mouthpiece. "She wants to know what this is about." Her eyes look fatigued.

I pause and collect. "Tell her we have a child protection concern. She needs to retrieve her daughter from the bus stop and bring her right in. No more dialogue." I repeat this mantra to my social worker because it is so very easy to cave into the questioning from a frightened parent. It is a conscious tactic to give as little information as possible so that if incest is indeed happening, the child will not be harangued by the mom, shut down, or diverge from her initial disclosure.

This woman's drive here with her child will be hell. She will rack her mind and quiz her daughter to settle her own hysteria. That is exactly what the mother at the kitchen sink would do. She is every one of us.

My own cerebral meandering intrigues me. Why do I have to try on every scenario as if it were me? I have made that call hundreds of times, and each time feels like the first time. I feel the fear sizzle across the wire. I am powerless to quell the agitation. What never ceases to amaze me is how quickly people respond and the momentum that is created in the response.

I perch myself on a desk behind the two-way mirror so that I can observe the interview. It is hot and stuffy, and this is the fourth interview I have observed this afternoon. My lumbar spine feels noodley, yet if I were to turn the wrong way too suddenly, it might tighten up. It is Friday at five o'clock. The muscles behind my eyes feel lax. It is hard to focus.

Sophie Dornauer is petite, with a toned, athletic build. Today was her graduation from the twelfth grade. She is clad in shorts and a long-sleeved sweatshirt. Her sneakers wear the signature untied laces. She has the look of a prep school lass, unkempt in her loveliness. She has a small turned-up nose that is in complete balance with her teal-colored eyes. They appear iridescent as the light in the room changes. Her self-conscious mouth is crammed full of sparkling orthodontia. A coppery redhead, she has cinched her hair back in a ponytail, with metallic wisps falling in front of her face. She has disclosed to her best friend, on her last day of school, that over the last year, her father enters her room, sits at her bed, and stimulates his penis to erection. He has attempted to penetrate her both vaginally and anally. He covers her mouth with a warm, dry hand. The last time he did this, she bit his palm. Alarmed, he exited her room with a familiar mantra: "What a bitch!"

Sophie has studied violin since the age of seven and is an accomplished violinist. When there is the slightest squeak of uncertainty in her playing, her father will pinch the back of her neck, leaving bruises reminiscent of hickies.

I am listening intently to this child's description of her father. It is not unusual that on the last day of school, children summon up their courage to speak their truth. If they do not, any outside semblance of support will float into the sultry, hot summer ahead, and the child will have no one. Offenders are brilliantly adept at isolating their victims, and the summer is a rich time for incest to breed, when connections with the outside universe are severed.

My senses are aroused and wakened. I watch her body closely as she speaks. She is bright and articulate. I notice neat healed scars on both her shins. They are white against her sun-bronzed skin. As she speaks, she lifts the loose strands of feathery hair away from her face, and the sleeves of her sweatshirt rise. I see the same type of scarring on her wrists. One scar is fresh, with a newly formed scab. It looks as if it has been gnawed at.

I am astonished at what I take in when I observe an interview as opposed to when I am in the room, conducting the interview. In an interview, my mind moves quicker than my mouth to formulate nonleading questions. As an observer, I can scan for innuendo, for nuance, for what is unspoken. I then let it house itself in my body. In the unspoken, the unspeakable core of incest is found. This child has notched her limbs, the way a foolish lover carves his undying proclamation of love on the skin of a newly grown sapling. She consciously tries to hide her assault on her own body.

The detective's queries are beginning to close in on the sexual contact. Like a shark, sniffing around her prey, she waits for the perfect moment to nudge in. When she poses her questions about the father and the unwanted touch, Sophie closes her eyes and jerks her head back. She is pained to answer the questions. Her life hinges on her response, and she knows it. This young woman has rehearsed this disclosure in her mind several times before. It is her prayer, her incantation. Each answer is wrenched out of her. As I watch her body contort and twist, with eyes tightly shut, I envision that this is the very response to her father's approach.

She now talks about her habit of cutting on her body as well as her penchant for saving her blood-soaked menstrual pads. She meticulously burrows them in a hiding place, similar to a squirrel storing acorns in the belly of an oak tree. The monthly letting of blood, and the preservation of this blood, is of great significance to this young woman.

Her phrases are adult and unnerving. There is a stark contrast between her sexual verbiage and her young age. There is a venomous anger attached to the descriptions of her father's ritual sexualizing. She lifts up her sweatshirt and reveals a very recent cut on her tummy. A notch. She keeps score on herself. Another incision on her body to validate her aliveness; another conquest for her father. She wonders out loud if this could be happening. A defense attorney's delight, I muse.

Knowing that survivors of incest are often compelled to self-mutilate, it still sickens my senses. "How does she cut? Scissors? Glass? Razor? Where does she do it? Does she close her eyes and writhe?" Of course, she must tidy up and sponge down any trace of muss. The physical pain of attacking one's body will be exchanged for the emotional pain that it replaces. It often brings children to a place of calm and self-soothing. The jolt to the body temporarily quells the emotional ache.

At the close of her interview, while the social worker is attempting to find hospitalization for this child, I watch the interaction between her and her mother. I know that this interaction will be a diagnostic gem. Her mother is asking Sophie why she didn't tell her. Sophie is by turns crying and soothing her mom. This woman looks as if she has violently collided with her conscience. She is in shock. She sits on the couch with her daughter and holds her. Sophie apologizes. Her mother does nothing to stop the apology. The child speaks to her mother as if she is the adult. In joining with her mother, she makes safe what has always been unsafe. As long as she is the bad one, her mother remains the good mother. The daughter must be skillful. She must not tip the balance.

The mother is rocking her own body back and forth to soothe herself. She encircles herself with her own arms. Her daughter is smoothing her mom's hair and telling her mother how sorry she is. She prays with her mother. Together, they recite the Lord's Prayer. I have watched this scene more times than I would ever like to recount. Her mother looks at her daughter with sorrowful sadness. Sophie holds her mother's face in her hands and speaks softly to her, her mouth close to her mother's mouth. Their boundaries dribble over into a pool of enmeshment.

The mother takes her daughter's head against her breast and cries. Otherwise, she is mute. It reminds me of a child's attempt to cajole a parent out of a drunken stupor or a drug overdose. What child should ever have to be responsible for that? This child has done her best to survive.

I cannot take my eyes off these two women. I am wholly absorbed and engrossed. I am crying as I watch this. I am all too aware of my exhaustion. I feel how perversely tender this exchange is. This is what makes my heart ache so. This child has protected her mother for a long time. I wonder who has parented her, and I feel my rage begin to define itself. Has their survival been dependent on this collusive dynamic, with Mr. Dornauer at the helm? His presence and his perceived omnipotence looms. As I watch this child and her mother, I feel numb.

I distinctly remember a young girl once describing her stepfather to me. He had anally penetrated her every Saturday morning for a year, while her mother worked at the 7-Eleven. It was not the abuse she described in such detail, but the pervasive power he wielded over her and her mother. She was terrified of his anger and was in a constant state of perpetual vigilance. Every waking minute, she was crouched, awaiting his breath, his step, the rattle of his keys in the lock. . . . His physical presence shook her to her core, and I remember her picking her cuticles to a nub as she spoke. I clearly recall my own horror at the prospect of having to confront this man. I feared for my life. I arranged legions of police backup. I was stunned when her stepfather opened the door. I will never forget my response. He was a bespectacled, tiny, wilted nothing of a man, no taller than me. His two front teeth were missing. How could such a man instill such an environment of fear? This was one of the first clues about the power of incest.

Whenever I am about to meet an offender, I play this interesting game in my head. It is a carryover from this girl and her stepfather. I visualize the offender's body, his carriage, his stride, his face, and his mouth. I attempt to visualize the sexual act. I create a vision in my mind and then get to see how far off from reality I reside. With offenders who are tightly lawyered, whom I will never have access to, I can only respond to their outer shell; their interior is too protected. I see them in court. We exchange glances. The depth of that exchange is more piercing and incisive that one could ever imagine. It is gold.

I imagine Mr. Dornauer cutting a striking figure, poised and charming. I envision that he is handsome and fair, with red hair and blue eyes. He is slick and deceptive, cunning and shrewd. He is deft at manipulation. He rules his roost. Twenty years into this work, I should know better. I always paint the perpetrator with a semblance of illusory aplomb. My own denial, I suppose, of my all-too-keen familiarity with these men.

Monday morning, I watch Mr. Dornauer as he rounds the corner of the courthouse hall. There is a bevy of attorneys on his left. His wife allows her hand in his awkwardly, seemingly shy. When I finally see him, I am speechless. I am stunned by my own response. Why do I create the fantasy versions of these men? They are rarely congruent with my reality. Mr. Dornauer is short and stubby. His chest caves inward and his shoulders are hunched. His skin tone is gray. He is bald. He is a nebbish. He carries a briefcase and he is smiling. When I see his puffed-up grin and his brigade of legal counsel, I feel the need to say something. Knowing me as well as she does, the county attorney walking at my side rests a hand on my forearm and admonishes me over her bifocals. She doesn't have to say a word. Her gesture cools the words off my tongue. I watch his flattened rear end as he enters the courtroom. I visualize him naked, stealthily entering his daughter's room, his thumbs and forefingers practicing the rolling of his daughter's nipples, to the point of erection. I take my seat in front of the judge.

Mr. Dornauer and his wife are seated a few rows ahead of me. She acknowledges me with a quick smile. Her husband's hand, like a claw, grips her shoulder. I cannot remove my gaze from that hand. She is turning around and looking at me. My eyes jump from her face to his hand on her and back again. This is not a welcome hand. This is a hand that is meant to keep this woman under its grasp. This is a hand that finds its place and cannot be moved. She watches me and self-consciously moves her shoulder out from underneath his grip. He notices immediately, without interrupting his conversation with his attorney, and resituates his hand back on her shoulder. She smiles sadly, almost apologetically. She squirms. He is hurting her, and his knuckles are white. All of this transpires without a word. From this seemingly small interaction, I attempt to read his intention. Perhaps she has succumbed. Perhaps he is her captor.

In the courtroom, Mr. Dornauer and his wife are pouring over the report from the psychiatrist who examined this child during her hospitalization. The physician's findings are compelling. Somewhere in this child's life, she has experienced an unutterable trauma—none of us is quite clear about the extent of it. This unknown trauma, and my attempt to uncover it, may very well be my nemesis.

I am riveted as I observe them reading. I am damning him under my breath. I am wondering what he is thinking. As they finish the report, there is an obvious blotchy red mottling that forms a collar around Mr. Dornauer's neck. I feel a sense of satisfaction watching this involuntary physical response. Mrs. Dornauer turns around and smiles, almost inappropriately. He immediately follows her gaze and locks his gaze on mine. It is at that moment that I feel a profound sense of terror. It's as if he knows me and on some intimate level can see right into me. I immediately look at the clock and try to figure out where my children are at that moment. I feel an overwhelming loss of control. I excuse myself from the courtroom, as I feel as if I have urinated on myself.

We really know very little about sex offenders. Their essence is profound. They are masters of their trade. The more accomplished an offender, the more skilled he or she is at silence, at assuming an authoritative stance, at grandiosity, and eventually at exercising the power to create and solidify a pathological bond with the victim. They will give us crumbs to satisfy our therapeutic hunger. We will think that we are sated, but it is all a sham. How could we ever entertain that we really have the virtuosity with which to crawl inside their minds, to permeate that silence? We assess and treat offenders with our intuition. It is often our bellies that guide us through the muck and mire of duplicity and bluff, and even then, we have just ruptured the skin of their unutterable debauchery.

After court I am far too angry to venture back to my office, much less home. I plunk myself down in the waiting room of Mr. Dornauer's attorney. I hate it when we are on the opposite sides, as I have known this guy for fifteen years and love him. I love attorneys who wish they were social workers. They capture a degree of emotionality and compassion absent in most pragmatists. I love attorneys who know my work and believe in my integrity. When I sniff out that component, I am sure that we make a better partnership for our clients. We trade places. I lean toward the side of harshness, and they open their hearts.

When Joseph Mattingly opens the door to his office and sees me, his smile is devious and alive. He takes my hand as we meander silently through the maze of offices. He indulges me, as he always has my reversal of roles, and offers me the beautiful aged oxblood leather chair behind his desk. He is seated as the client.

" I want to talk to your client."

"No way in hell," he replies. He starts on this dissertation about his client and the fact that he feels I would take advantage of his very fragile disposition, that the guy is a wreck, and that his life, for all intents and purposes, is over.

"As it should be," I muse to myself.

"Anyway, I think you would annihilate him." He is picking at his Pradas as he is talking to me. I am aware that he is making no gesture toward eye contact. That is a mighty powerful verb he is tossing around.

"*Annihilate*. Let's see." I pick up the dictionary. "'To nullify and render void; to reduce to nonexistence; to vanquish.' Seems to me that that is precisely what your client has done to his child." By this time I have removed my shoes and am spinning around in his chair. There is dead silence. My cynicism is splitting at the seams. I explain to him that I have no way of helping this child if I cannot at least have a conversation with her father. If I cannot speak with her father, all I have is my prurient fantasies of what he has done to her, and my fantasies will simply dry up any scintilla of compassion that exists. I cannot help her without having a dialogue with him.

As I hear myself say this, I know that it is absolutely true. I rely on my human connection to people to help me comprehend their behavior. I am better able to separate offenders from the atrocities they commit if I can sit down with them, face-to-face. I know exactly what the defense will do with this child. They will chew her up and spit her out. They will attempt to bring in experts to prove that she is mentally ill. After all, she slices up her body. Lastly, they will make her crazy. And she, in tenderness of age and vulnerability of mind and spirit, will succumb.

"You are too overinvolved, too angry." His comment singes my foundation. He is right. I am bigger than angry. I am outraged, and I am righteously indignant in my outrage.

I turn the chair toward the window and look at the most stunning undulating curve in the foothills. It is a mossy green that looks like it would be velvet to the touch. "I love that color. I would like a dress made of that color."

He indulges my need to lapse. "Then you shall have it, my dear." He rises and walks toward me. He lifts me out of the chair by the shoulders. I can see his distress, and I take his bearded face in my hands. I question him with my eyes but am indifferent to his next thought. I butt my head against his shoulder like a buck rubbing its antlers against a great pine in the forest.

"If I hear of one more sexual transgression, my mind will explode." My hands cover my face, and like a stoic, I refuse my tears. He is silent. I cannot bear to hear his response. He tells me that he hates this case. He hates it because he is trying to stay neutral for the sake of his client and that his job is to defend him. He thinks the guy probably molested his daughter. He is trying to talk with the couple's son to see if he could shed any light. This is Sophie's twin brother. I feel my body fold as he says those words. I am leaning my cheek against the coolness of the glass windowpane. He begins to tell me about his client coming in early this morning with his wife and that the guy cried. I whip around and say, "He should be crying! He should be weeping a river for what he has done to this child! He is not remorseful. He is only shamed by the fact that he got caught. He has destroyed this child. There is nothing left of her. She refers to herself now as a beautiful red Delicious apple that, when one bites into it, is full of worms and holes. What people see on the outside is lovely and enticing. She is rotten and evil on the inside." I feel the horror of such maladaptation as I utter these last words.

I cannot catch my breath. As I am ranting, he lets me go, like a diseased animal, like a rabid dog. I am tracking the perimeter of his office. He is right. I am nuts. Something in this case has ensnared my best intentions, and I cannot find my ground. I feel as if I am this seventeen-year-old young woman with the mind of a forty-five-year-old. My anger is unraveling. I feel tremendous shame. I place my hands over my mouth. I thank God that Joseph is the receptacle of my lunacy—a trusted comrade, a true friend.

I apologize for my outburst. I concede to his initial response—"no way in hell." He is right on the money. I have temporarily slipped to the edge. I would try to annihilate his client. I am too angry, and it is too fresh. I lie down on the couch in his office as he returns calls. My body feels depleted and used up. I marvel that after 20 years I have an uncanny sense of where to go to fall apart. I know my safe havens. I know where I will not be judged. I await the moment when my anger melts to sadness. It is in close proximity. I am thankful for my anger. I am grateful for my aliveness. When my passion gives way to numbness, I know that I will be done.

Before my exhausted mind drifts off to rest, Joseph leans down and kisses my forehead. He tells me to remember Henri Chabot, another sex offender we worked with years ago. "Were it not for the grace and humility of Henri Chabot, neither you or I would be here doing this type of work. Remember, he redefined our whole purpose and opened our hearts." I rest.

Twenty years ago, it seems, incest offenders were more apt to admit to their offenses. The laws were not as tight, the sentences not as stringent, the humiliation not as public nor as visible. Incest was quieter, and there seemed to be less to lose. Over the span of my career, the movement that has spearheaded the protection of children has championed this cause with great fervency and passion. The shame attached to this outrage destroys the child who has been violated as well has the family that has harbored the secret. Our systems revictimize the victim, and oftentimes our community's affluence makes us feel immune and entitled to our duplicity, to our hypocrisy, and mostly to our denial.

Henri Chabot was an anomaly, an exception to the rule. A man of much reserve, he turned my skewed notion of incest offenders on its head. It was the first and the only time in my twenty-year history that a man walked into my office and shattered the myth of secrecy. He self-reported. He turned himself in.

When the secretary at the front desk rings me to tell me there is a man in the waiting room to see me, I try my best to avoid her. It is the magical hour; four-thirty in the afternoon, when the curtain comes down on the day and we can all go home. I know that if I open my door for this man, my evening will evaporate into the winter sky. It is bitter outside and the condensation in the corner of my window is beginning to form ice crystals on the inside. I float down the hall to see who else is still in the building, as I can feel the fear tingling at the tips of my fingers. All catastrophes seem to cluster at the close of the day and find my listlessness and fatigue. My distress is exacerbated by a nearly empty building and, of course, the unknown. People are tidying up and closing down their day. I feel ashamed of my vigilance and paranoia. I call home and leave word for my husband that I will be late. "If I am not home in a few hours, come find me." I dramatize my thought, leaving it dangling. He knows what I am thinking.

It only took me a year or so to come to trust my level of discomfort when I was alone in my building at the end of the day. At times I feared the janitor more than the client I was sequestered with. But slowly, I learned to trust the humming in my head and the knot in my gut. I learned to tell someone where I was and what I was doing. Being distrustful of everything and everyone, I lived in a constant state of watchfulness. My startle response had me skittering like a jumping bean. The more strung out my body was with sleep deprivation, the worse off I was. As the perpetrator isolates his victim, the isolation of incest kept me in a perpetual state of aloneness.

As I exit my office, and before I open the door to the waiting room, I say a prayer for personal safety and protection. I envision myself rounding the bend up the gravel drive and seeing the porch light glistening. For a millisecond, it quells my distress.

There is a tall, slender man sitting there in an expensive suit, with a loosened tie dangling off his collar. His head is in his hands, and I cannot see his face. It is rare to see anyone other than an attorney in such attire, particularly in my place of business. I can see his long, tapered fingers as they rake through his hair. I approach him and introduce myself. He lifts his head and attempts a smile. He is at least six feet tall, with a striking face. Handsome, dark features, full yet crooked mouth. I am cautious. I lead him back to my office and leave the door wide open. He introduces himself. I can hear a hint of a French accent as he begins to speak, and for reasons unknown, this settles me. He has gotten my name from a friend. He apologizes for not scheduling an appointment with me, but he feared that if he did, he would not have shown. He has been trying to get here for the past few days but has been frightened. All the while he is twisting a band of gold—a wedding ring, I would assume—around his finger. His thick black hair, in need of a trim, periodically falls over his forehead. This man is so agitated that my intrigue begins to melt my fear.

"What can I do to help you, Mr. Chabot?" His response seems to be jammed in his throat. His eyes scan my face with an intensity that unnerves me. For a moment I think that perhaps he has been guided to the wrong person. I quickly surmise that he was incested as a child and is here for a therapeutic referral. He is anguished and is now slipping the ring off and on his finger. His wife, perhaps? Is something wrong with his wife? I speak quietly and gently and tell him that whatever he is here for, perhaps he would like to give it some thought and come back. It is not unusual for people to come into this office and twist and turn. They expose a sliver of their intention and then seem to recoil. I am tired and will not indulge him. If I were shored up, I would carefully nudge his secret. At this moment, all I want to do is go home. This man feels like a ticking bomb, incendiary and ready to explode. I am in no position to pick up the pieces, and his agitation feels like a contagion.

"No." He is barely audible. "I have done a horrible thing." I am gripped, and I stop him. My mind is swimming, and I am wondering what he is about to confess and if I will be able to hear it, much less contain my own anxiety. While I have been the recipient of a vast array of lurid secrets, I feel the force of my resistance. I do not want to hear what this man is going to say. I have shut the door on his confession, but he is determined to keep it open. He pushes against my denial. Before I can buttress it he blurts out, "I have touched my daughter. I have touched her in a sexual way, and I have ruined her."

As I register his confession, I feel an odd wave of relief. I am stunned. This was not what I was expecting to hear. Why is it that I feel relieved? Finally, for the first time in my career, an offender is offering up his sins, his secrets. He is placing them in my hands, a memento of love gone awry. This is what we wait for. This is what we pry and prod and cajole and beg for. Here it is in my lap, and I find that I want to give it back. Consumed by my own distress, I watch as he drops his head in his hand. He begins to cry.

While this man just unravels, I find myself in a similar heap. In my exhaustion, I am fearful that I will lose my boundary. It is difficult for me to stay planted in my chair and not respond physically. I feel the need to put a hand on his arm and to soothe him. I want to hold this man and let him weep. Perhaps it is I who longs for an embrace. At this moment I feel nothing but compassion. I wonder what my colleagues would think. I somehow feel disgrace and embarrassment for opening my heart. I have never had a man come into my office and admit to a sexual relationship with his child. There is a part of this exchange that feels unreal. I chastise myself for allying with this man, who has defiled his daughter. It feels as if I have crossed a line. In feeling compassion for him, I have betrayed his child. I have betrayed all children who have been violated by a parent. I feel sullied and corrupt. I am seduced by his ability to expose the truth, and yet it is in that revelation that I garner hope for his child. Somewhere in my confusion I find the presence of mind to find both an attorney and a detective to assist me in my obligations.

Henri Chabot sits with his eyes closed and his head resting against the wall of my office. I explain to him that before he launches into any more detail of his disclosure, he must have an attorney and I must talk with his little girl. He is in a state. His dark eyes are shadowed by sleeplessness. They are swollen and puffy. I don't recall a time when I have seen a man cry so deeply and for such a duration. He echoes into the air that he is so ashamed and that I must think him evil. I tell him that I have never had someone come forth the way that he has. I admit to him that his motivation will help to heal his child, that most fathers deny their children's truths about incest. He seems piqued by this, yet only momentarily. His body collapses. He asks about his child and if he can be with her, speak with her. He is racked with guilt and wants desperately to apologize to her. I assure him that there will be time for that. I tell him that I must interview his daughter. In the meantime, he must surrender himself. He is met by a police officer and is escorted out of the building.

As I wriggle up the winding alleys that encircle the University of Colorado, my efforts to find Henri Chabot's house are fruitless. It allows me time alone with my mind. So many of the pieces of the puzzle are amiss. What about his spouse? His daughter, Claire, is with Henri's sister, Yvette. How do I explain this disclosure to this child? I feel as if I am doing things in reverse.

Yvette Chabot opens the door to a small yet lovely home. Little Claire enthusiastically pushes her lithe body toward the front door. She is clad in a soft pink nightgown with satin ribbons laced through the bodice. On her feet are little embroidered woolen socks that look European. She has her father's striking darkness, her face as round as a full moon. Her cheeks are flushed from the warmth of a crackling fire, which illuminates the room. The house looks like an academic's house, with floor-to-ceiling books and a beautiful baby grand piano that takes up almost an entire room. Claire looks at me quizzically and asks her aunt a question, speaking fluent French. "She wants to know if you are her mother." I take in a breath with this question as Yvette leads me into the child's room. On her nightstand is a small framed black-and-white photo of a young woman holding a toddler. The woman has an uncanny resemblance to myself. It is in fact eerie. Her delicate features are defined. She is laughing with an open mouth with perfect white teeth. Her hair is dark, curly, and wild. Claire is chattering to her aunt in French. Yvette is explaining to her that I have come to talk with her. She draws back and tucks herself into her aunt's hip. She is disappointed that I am not her mother. I, on the other hand, feel I have walked into a potential nightmare. I feel a deep sadness for all these young children who are unmothered.

Yvette is a beautiful woman. She looks almost a twin to her brother. She is wary of my presence, and for a fleeting moment I let my mind wander to her relationship with Henri. Might it have been sexual? I have nothing to hinge this on other than my belly and my confabulation, brought on by exhaustion.

Claire brings me to her room and introduces me to her animals, which are placed side by side against her down pillow. Claude, a rich auburn-colored bear, polices the entire menagerie. He is the papa. She asks me with disarming directness where her papa is. She looks worried. She tells me that she has no mama. This child has a keenness and persistence that call for a genuine response—no fluff, no hedging. I explain to Claire that her papa came to see me today and that he was very sad about something that he had done to her that may have made her feel confused. "Ah," she exclaimed, her eyes bright and intent. "Papa kissed my pee-pee this morning, after my bath!" Yvette, who is standing at the door, covers her mouth in horror and vanishes. "I told him, 'No, Papa! It tickles and it smells of pee-pee.'" She giggles and turns back to Claude, her bear. She peers at me from behind the bear.

I ask if it has ever happened before. She is clear. "No." She is unusually sanguine for a child. Her shame, if it is present, is tucked neatly away. Someone has done well parenting this child. Claire fixes me pretend tea and tucks a doily under my chin in the event that I should spill. She moves her body closer to mine, and I feel her huge black eyes with their fanning lashes take in my face. I can smell her sweet little-girl breath. She wears two exquisite French braids that swish against her tiny waist. "Who fixes those beautiful braids, Claire?" I assume she will tell me it is Yvette.

"Papa, of course!"

In my mind's eye I can see his long, dexterous fingers plaiting her silky auburn locks as she chatters to him. One could see this as grooming. One could see this as braiding his daughter's hair, an intimate and nurturing gesture. He is her anchor, in light of an absent mother. Should I separate this father and his daughter? Is he inclined to violate her tiny body again?

Claire's mother left her father when she was a toddler. Just vanished one night, tearing asunder the foundation of her world. Her father, taking a teaching position in the States, moved his three-year-old daughter, finding the best preschools and after-school care for her. With his heart heavy with loss, he felt that he had failed this beautiful child, and he was overwhelmed with the responsibility of her care. As Claire grew, he immersed himself further into his work. His teaching and his daughter were his life. She loved him the way no other had loved him, unconditionally and with great depth. She filled a hole in him left by the absence of his wife. He felt his love for her changing into a more erotic fantasy, forgetting at times that she was a child, only a child of seven. She had quietly slipped into the role of his intimate, his confidant, and his *amour*.

The morning that he put his mouth on her genitals, he stood her on the bathroom countertop to dry her off, his face directly in front of her vagina. She had her hands on the top of his head, stroking his hair, when in a split instant he kissed her. He cannot remember what was coursing through his mind. He fell to his knees, fearing that his action would forever damage his daughter. He was beside himself, leaving her with Yvette that day. He did not show up for work and ended up in my office, where he confessed with powerful remorse his despicable act.

I have never had another Henri Chabot cross my path. Sometimes it feels as if he was invented in my mind to give me hope, to strive for what I believe will liberate incested children from their captors, the captors who must also save their children with their honesty and apology. Henri Chabot's empathy and compassion for his young daughter enabled, after many years, a relationship built on reciprocity and respect, though always laced with an element of distrust.

I realize something: In my dream, it was Henri Chabot who allowed me to wrap him in my feminine gossamer robe, while a self-satisfied and prideful Mr. Dornauer begrudgingly accepted the silk tie.

There are times when I actually forget what it is that I am warring against. Is it the atrocities committed against children, or is it my own eroded perspective, my self-important presumptions that I can change the power of denial into empathy and compassion? I will never change a David Dornauer. He has destroyed his child. And in an effort to preserve his image of himself, he must annihilate her being, rendering her nonexistent.

She has betrayed him. He could not keep her in captivity. Somewhere in this child's fragmented and inauthentic reality, she found a tiny pocket of herself to honor. She told. She gave voice to her own devastation and violation because no one else chose to see it or acknowledge it. This betrayal will follow our children always, and the saddest piece for me is that the truth of love and intimacy may never be a part of their lives. This by far is the basest form of human disgrace and degradation—the absence of love.

"To My Haunting Ophelia, Who Brings Me to My Knees— Tie My Hands": On Esthetics, Art, and Spontaneous Weeping

Joyfulness has eluded me of late. It has been replaced by sadness and sorrow. I can't recall the exact moment in my life when I lost my capacity to feel joy. My ability to delight in earthly pleasures has been temporarily obscured. Contented friends are but an intrusive annoyance. I am envious of those who are unfettered and spontaneous. I feel my own ache of constriction and isolation, one that is self-imposed and has crept up on me in an insidious, stealthy manner over the years. My sorrow has eroded and devoured my spirit. Its new embodiment comes to me in the form of tears. They begin at the smooth, soft hollow at the base of my throat. I feel the constriction, and with that narrowing comes an immediate bitter taste of bile and an obstruction of air. It rises with great fury up my throat, and I cannot speak. The tears collect underneath my bottom lid and pool there, refusing to erupt and stream down my cheeks. My lower lip quivers and then is stilled. The tears evaporate, never evolving into a satisfying, cathartic weep.

For years, I have listened to and observed the suffering of children and families who have been caught in the incestuous tryst. I can't recall a moment when I have listened to a child and not felt the urge to weep. Instead, I have bitten a permanent hole in the inside of my left cheek. If I slide my tongue along that velvety, warm skin, it will find its slippery little furrow, without fail. I bite down so hard that I will not cry. I mutilate my interior in secret. It is habit. Such sorrow is unbearable. I must constantly steel myself against my own emotions, keeping everything within its tidy compartment—professional, aloof, and well guarded. I am an accomplished "nonemotive" when duty calls. I can pull families and children together with tremendous skill, with supreme foresight and acumen. I can navigate them through the muddiest of waters, all the while juggling crazed collateral agencies and a mammoth judicial system. I am a semblance of competence and aplomb.

I realize how labile my emotions are one evening when I head into a packed auditorium and seat myself alone in the last row to listen to my children's winter concert. They are about to raise their voices in song, celebrating Mother Earth and the preservation of her environment. The audience settles as an eight-year-old boy walks to the center of the stage. He is a plump little guy with a beautiful round face as shiny as a penny. His hands are nestled deep in his pockets. His hair is pasted down with a goopy, shimmery gel. The din is silenced by his presence. He begins to sing. Moments before he even opens his mouth, my throat begins to close and my eyes brim with tears. My body begins to heave, and the torrents of tears are uncontrollable. I push through to the cold air outside, attempting to still my staccato breathing. I feel such shame at my reaction. I feel my craziness.

This little person's tenderness and vulnerability touch me in a part of my body that I cannot even identify. This is a normal, happy, sweet child who walked out in front of hundreds of people, raised his face to the heavens, and sang. What would be to most people a moment of preciousness and joy renders me an inconsolable river of tears. Where has my sorrow been hiding all these years? I believe it has been in the same little burrow, right beside my joy.

A therapist friend in another state is dying of ovarian cancer. She whispers over the wire with sisterly foreboding, "Get out now. It will kill you." She believes that her work in incest for the last twenty-five years has devoured her body; that over the years tiny droplets of pain and suffering have housed themselves in the crawl spaces of her body and nudged it into surrender. Her sadness has poisoned the well of her life source. She is convinced. She devoted her life to unveiling this insidious violation, and now her cells have gone haywire, silently invading her fortitude and her belief. She is besieged. She has thrust her weary bones into submission. She has been the protectress of thousands of children. "Who protected us?" she muses. I listen. With fear and angst coursing throughout my body, I want to lie down and weep.

Fear of death has always been my nemesis, my internal goddess of retributive justice and vengeance. If I stay in this work, it will kill me. If I leave this work, I will die. This fear has left a gaping wound in my existence. It has paralyzed my being, yet out of that wound my creativity has been birthed. A dual-edged sword has never glistened so brightly.

* * * * * * *

Splattered across the bridge of Antonio Petrocelli's nose is a constellation of freckles that look as if they have been randomly sprayed by a painter's brush. Minute, flesh-colored speckles anoint his tiny patrician seven-year-old nose, while a wild, unruly cowlick juts up from his head. His anxiety permeates the room as his eyes dart from wall to wall, and he constantly wipes his clammy palms against his corduroy trousers.

We are situated across from one another at a child-sized table. My knees could flip the surface if I made a sudden move. I rest my chin in my hands as we start on a journey punctuated by resistance and fear. Under the table, I notice that his socks have slipped deeply into the heel of his shoes and his laces are untied. We are both drawing pictures of our families. Antonio loves to draw and would like to become a famous painter. On his paper he draws his mother, his stepfather, and his stepsister. In a separate drawing, he sketches a faceless picture of his father with a gargantuan protrusion sprouting from his groin.

A year ago, on a visit to his father's home in Bethel, Maine, Antonio Petrocelli's father fondled his son's penis every morning after bathing his son. He would stroke Antonio's penis until it stuck straight up. His dad's penis would spring to the ceiling until, of course, he peed, sometimes on Antonio. The boy returned home replete with a stutter and an involuntary gag response. He would dissolve into a puddle at the drop of a hat. He would not sleep alone, and he wet his pants. Because his father resided in another state, the district attorney conveniently let the case slide into oblivion and refused to return my phone calls. With gentle therapeutic intervention, Antonio began a long, arduous journey to understand his separation from his father and his reversion into toddlerhood.

Of late, the stutter has reared its ugly head and the phantom gagging has returned. This morning at breakfast, Antonio's mother could see that her child's agitation was spiraling. He chucked his cereal bowl against the sink, cupping his ears as it shattered. Holding her son in her arms and gently probing as to his increased distress, Antonio told his mother that his older cousin Andrew tried to suck his penis.

Antonio's mother is in an inconsolable heap, and I find that I myself am equally as disturbed. This little boy's fragility is the texture of freshly blown glass. Knowing as I do that certain children are repeatedly victimized, I also know that this child cannot withstand another inquiry, much less the knowledge that he must start healing all over again.

His picture of his stepfamily is beautifully detailed. He pens his cousin in the picture, then quickly erases him from the scene, again wiping his sweaty paws so that the marker stays in his grip. His mother is smiling and holding his hand. Her dress is a soft pink with delicate detailed flowers, purple with yellow centers. Her hair flows down to her waist, though in reality it is short and neatly cropped. His chocolate Lab, Jake, sits obediently at her side. In his meticulous rendition of life on paper, Antonio Petrocelli's existence is one of sweetness. In reality, the pubic protrusion is a haunting demon that snakes itself around the paper. Needing to be exorcised and decimated, its enormity has infiltrated this little boy's body and soul.

As we are talking about our day, I feel the heaviness in my own chest. I cannot bear to hear this child's disclosure. I feel his fear as if it were my own. I notice the tiny cowlick on his head tremble as if it had a life of its own, as if the terror and panic were afire on the tip of his head and a magnetic field involuntarily were lifting the downy hairs. I look at his grubby little nails as his fingers encircle the marker, and I think only of my son, the same age and seemingly as sensitive and delicate. His scent is even similar— sweat and sweetness and little-boy grime.

At times I am fully cognizant of how to shut down a disclosure and not elicit the information that I need. I feel the heaviness of my heart. I don't want this to be a reality for this child. Not again . . . not a second time. Knowing that he cannot contain his own fear, I feel the palms of my hands sweat sympathetically as I begin my inquiry. While Antonio is drawing, I ask him about Andrew. His round green eyes take hold of mine. As his pupils are swallowed by terror, his eyes begin to fill with tears, and without restraint or cognition his head slams against his drawing with a thud. He is weeping and laments his internal shame. "I can't tell you! I can't! It's not fair! Not again. Not me. Why does everyone do this to me?"

His head is flat against the table. I can see the tears spilling onto the paper. The images that he has drawn lose their definition and the edges of color ooze into one another. His warm tears puddle into his ears. His body flutters with each sob, and I can hear his sadness, like the droning echo in the depth of a damp cave. I leave my chair and kneel besides him. I place my hand on his head and stroke his hair. I can smell the wetness of his tears. When I kiss the cheeks of my own crying children, I always taste the salt of their tears.

Years ago I would have waited for this child to collect himself and then continued my questioning. Today, I know better. My heart is my guide, and this child is broken. Stroking his head, I tell him that he can go. I tell him that when he is ready to tell me, then we can talk again. My head is close to his as I am speaking to him. I do not want this to be picked up on tape. I do not want the world to hear this exchange. I want this child to acknowledge his pain only when he is ready.

As the tone of my voice approaches a whisper, he lifts his little head. We dry eyes and blow noses. My eyes are misty. "You are sad," he says.

"I am," I whisper. "But you know, I need to be sad. I don't like it when people hurt children."

He is scanning my face. His eyes are tracing along my forehead, my hairline. They settle on my mouth. "What are you thinking?" I ask.

He is silent and still. I touch his cowlick. His gaze is uneasy yet inquisitive. "Will you die from your sadness?"

I am riveted, and my eyes open wide. Innocent and fey, he reaches out his hand to the pendant hanging from my neck. He fiddles with it while he awaits my response. I falter. My throat narrows. I feel his warm little fingers barely brush against my skin. I am clearly gripped by this question coming from this child, as if he knows something. I cannot find my voice. Antonio Petrocelli's question burrows itself so deeply under my skin that the very suggestiveness is like a harbinger, and feels haunting.

That question from this tiny tortured mind hangs around my being for the rest of the day. I have met other children like this—otherworldly, seemingly clairvoyant with some visionary power. They spook and unnerve me. Their line into me is often jarring. I muse about my transparency, about my vulnerability and isolation. It is curious to me that this child, whose life I have barely overlapped, shares such an intimacy with me. It frightens me that my sadness is so surfaced and observable. I believe incest is like dying. A part of a child's spirit is extinguished with that touch, never to be retrieved. I wonder if my absorption of this suffering is slowly asphyxiating my being.

After this exchange I need air and sky. I feel as if I am suffocating. My earlier buoyancy flutters downward towards a predictable dark abyss as I perseverate on my imminent demise. As I hit the sunlight I walk toward my roots—wonderful Italian fare. I can smell *pomodore* and garlic as I round the corner. I poke my head into a quaint framing shop to ask what time it is. Against the east wall of the shop is a dark painting. I feel my body melt as I take in this vision.

Rarely drawn to the Romantic, pre-Raphaelite period, I am piqued. The painting is encased in a heavy gilt frame, which adds to its aura of antiquity and grace. The painting is almost as tall as me and is easily five feet across. It is a painting of a young girl floating in a body of water. Her face is luminescent in the moonlight. I am aware of the sensation in my body more so than the painting. I feel mysteriously drawn, like the earth is pulling me toward the floor. My extremities feel like ice, yet at the same time, I feel warmth in my loins. The crushing sensation in my chest traps my air so that I can't find my speech.

The woman who owns the shop asks me if I am all right. Never really replying to her question, I begin to ask about the painting. She explains that a woman who just returned from Paris saw the painting in the Louvre and fell in love with it. She was able to find the print and brought it in to be framed. "It's very beautiful, don't you think? But it's too sad," she laments as she looks at the print. I ask if I could just sit for a few minutes. My legs are wobbly and unstable. I feel as if I could fall to my knees like some religious zealot, chanting and praying to my wailing wall. The young woman on the canvas is a vision, a vision in the sense of indescribable beauty, but even more than that. I have seen her somewhere before.

She looks like a fallen angel. The shop owner looks up at me over thick tinted spectacles. I wonder for an instant if she thinks I am a nut. I wonder if people ever come into her shop and fall to their knees because they are enrapt by the sheer exquisite symmetry that flows from an artist's mind through his hand and onto the medium, whatever it is. "I believe it is Ophelia," she pronounces, rather aloof and distracted. "Hamlet's Ophelia."

I don't know what it is about this painting that fills me with such rapture. It has jolted me from a previous existence, only hours before. Fabulously eerie, the sky is bluish black, and a huge, unseen, pregnant moon reflects on the water. The drapery of the woman's gown, while appearing heavy, floats like gossamer—sheer, delicate, even tenuous. Her long tendrils of reddish gold hair appear to be undulating with the silent ripple of the water. Her hands and waist are bound by cord. A halo hovers beside her head as though, on her descent down from the heavens, it has slipped from her silken locks, landing exactly where it should—beside the frame of her delicate face. It is relucent. The colors of the canvas are pale white, cream, and an opalescent green. Both the halo and the moon illuminate her face. She is fairylike, angelic, and chaste. She should feel cold to me, suspended by the current of midnight water. Instead, she is radiant, resplendent in her death. Her aura is luminous.

Upon leaving the shop I am quite certain that this image feels oddly akin, like some foreboding inhabitant. I think of Antonio Petrocelli's query about sadness and death, and my dying comrade and companion. There is never coincidence in life. Looking for someone to tell me the time, I found an apparition that has so consumed me that I must find her. I must feast upon her and see why it is that she has come to me in this serendipitous fashion.

I hear the words I say when I train other clinicians about incest: "When you work in this particularly sad and hideous venue, you will see things that people will never see. It will shatter your spirit and it will break your heart."

After several days of dogged persistence, I find my Ophelia in a tiny gallery north of San Francisco. The owner knows very little about the painting or the artist. "It's very morose," he utters hesitantly. "Where will you hang this?"

I feel my shame. "I'm not certain," I reply.

I wonder if I am morose. I wonder if I am going to die soon. I wonder why I see such intoxicating rapture in something so utterly sad. I think sadness is a state of being for me. I feel more identified with a spirit of melancholy and blue than any other emotion. I think I stuff it. I think I rename it. I think that if I let myself feel it, I will never emerge intact—I will implode. My entire being will capsize. I feel what the children and adults I work with must feel. Insularity is an illusion. One carries the pain always. It is an integral part of one's being. I think in slow motion of Antonio Petrocelli's head hitting the table with such a thud, he could not even register the physical pain. How hard he cried. How deeply his pain has taken root in his little-boy frame. If I let him say his pain, than I too would have to feel it . . . and I couldn't bear it. Some aspect of this suffering seems to liven me, to breathe into me a very precious secret that I have yet to comprehend.

When the print finally arrives, I haul it up the three stories to my therapist's office. I explain the events that led up to my finding the painting. I unroll the print and set it in front of her. I am kneeling on the floor. My chin, like a child's, rests on my knee. "Doesn't she take your breath away?" She is silent. Interminable, that silence has no beginning or end. It exists outside of time. How could she not love this? How could she not be moved by its sheer beauty, its holiness? It is divine. She asks me a therapy question. "Tell me what you see."

I begin my dissertation with great intention and zeal. I am gingerly unearthing all the beauty in this horror. "She is dead. She has been drowned. Her hands are tied. I found that when I laid eyes on this painting, I awoke with a jolt, like being thunderstruck. I wanted to fall to the earth and cry. I can't remember the last time I felt this way. I can't remember a piece of art moving me this way. I feel alive."

I am quiet as I wait for an approving response. There is pause. These are the times in my life when I feel most maniacal. I sink my teeth into a conviction, a cause, a crusade, and I am a polemicist.

"I feel like her. I feel like at one time in my life I was an angel. I have fallen from grace. All my sins are exposed. This is the death of my innocence. I began this work when I was twenty-four. I was a spirited, sassy thing, unformed, full of bravado, sensual, playful, and provocative. I had the world by the tail. I walked into this work, and my whole foundation was turned on its head. . . . I saw things in life that I never expected to see. My whole take on life has been altered. I see the dark when it is light. I won't tap into my joy. I'm terrified of it. I don't know how to be light. I want my sass back. I want my pristine, unadulterated self, back. I hate this shit! It's going to kill me. I'm going to get some hideous cancer and shrivel up into nothing. And for what?"

I hear the next question before it even hits the ground, before it flies out of her mouth. It's the "How does this make you feel?" question. It's the one where I flop back against the couch and don't know how I feel. But this time I do know how I feel, and I'm frightened of what will fly out of my mouth if I try to say it. I feel my body begin to itch, my palms, my tummy . . . like I want to crawl out of my skin. My beating heart begins a slow descent to its baseline. I can feel my sorrow the way Antonio Petrocelli felt his sorrow when I asked him about Andrew.

"This painting is about every child who has seen incest. It is the death of their innocence. They come to this world like angels, each and every one of them, stunning in their nakedness and purity. They are reproachless, sinless, chaste. Their world is unedited, unsullied. And then there is this act, this violation, this touch, this unspeakable atrocity—nothing that they have ever asked for. The ground underneath their feet shifts. Their hearts and their minds shift. And it's permanent. It shapes their external and internal terrain for eternity. Neither I nor anyone else can undo that. When we fall to this earth, we are bound by the confines of humanity, by compassion and by suffering."

I gently smooth out the print with my palm. I feel the depletion of my entire body, as if its energy has been slowly drawn off. I am left feeling somewhat dreamy and content. I have some clarity, yet my mind still hungers. It has been in the sorrowful demise of this young woman that I have found a semblance of tranquility and repose.

At a small frame shop on Fifteenth Street, I place my rolled-up print on the framing table in front of one of the owners. He unrolls it while I hide my eyes behind dark sunglasses. "Ah . . . Delaroche." He is silent. I want to fall though a trap door. I balance my glasses on the top of my head. "Finally, someone has brought in a painting of true elegance. It is exquisite."

I feel the inside of my heart flap wildly. "You are the first person who has said this to me. . . . Everyone thinks it's so sad, so morose."

"It *is* sad!" he states with much confidence. "Life is sad—so what of it?" I am loving his irreverence and defiance. "It is in sorrow that we find our true appreciation of art and beauty. I am so sick of this artsy-fartsy stuff in Boulder. Everything is always so perfect. This, my dear lady, is art." I could fall in love with this guy for sharing my sentiments. We select a beautiful frame. We talk about how not to frighten my children with this painting, and where to hang it. He tells me about the painting and the artist.

Painted in the mid-1800s, the title of the painting is actually "The Young Christian Martyr." The artist, Paul Delaroche, completed it as his last painting. The vision came to him as a dream during a fevered illness. It was the saddest and holiest of paintings that he had ever painted. I listen like a child would listen to a fairy tale. The painting shows the tearful fate of a young Christian girl at the time of Diocletian who, because she was unwilling to sacrifice herself to pagan gods, was cruelly condemned to die by being drowned in the Tiber.[1]

"So she is not a fallen angel?" I ask.

"She is of sorts," he replies. "She is art. She is anything you want her to be. She is you!" Shocked, I look at him with horror as though he has been in my head all this time, and I don't even know this man.

"People choose art like they choose lovers. It's a reflection of who they are, or who they wish they could be." He is writing up my receipt for the frame and the labor. He has the same quality as little Antonio Petrocelli. My heart is on my sleeve.

I leave my print with this man and walk out into the crisp dusk, with its clarity and briskness. I feel an unbelievable lightness, like thistledown or a bubble ascending through the ether. Something is very clear. My spirit is leavened.

Feigning illness, the following day I drive myself up to the mountains to my favorite ice skating spot. It is midweek, and the place is empty.

Skating is a secret love of mine. It has the quality of floating on

---

1. Norman D. Ziff, *Paul Delaroche: A Study in Nineteenth Century French History Painting*. New York: Garland (1977), pp. 250–251.

air. It is peaceful and redundant. Its repetition is like music. The lake is virtually empty, with only one skater other than myself. I at first do not notice him, as I am in my own rhythmic world, pretending that I am some ice maiden whose birth took place in an arctic region, and ice is like breathing. I am sitting on a bench to warm my paws. I watch this skater. I would guess him to be as old as my father, somewhere in his eighties. His agility and grace are astounding. He is waltzing with himself as "The Blue Danube" pipes over the lake. His eyes are closed and he holds tightly to an imageless apparition, a spirit made of air. His lithe body glides and dips at a miraculous speed. My palms sweat as I watch him; I am horrified that he might fall. I am falling in love with his symmetry and elegance. The sun splashes on the ice, forming a rainbow of shimmery crystals. This moment could never be so sweet. Like a girl at a prom, I am praying that he will come over and ask me to dance.

I rise and begin my predictable loop around the ice. I trace the periphery, rarely venturing to the middle. I keep my eye on the other skater until I am following his endless track. I pick up my speed with a fury until I have caught up to him. "Sir," I shout. "Can you show me how to waltz on the ice?"

He is delighted at my invitation. We both remark at how empty and beautiful the ice is. He is eighty-three and has skated since he was about five. He instructs me how to angle my blades. He pulls my back snugly into his chest, placing one hand on my waist and raising my other arm loosely to the heavens. He tells me to close my eyes and let the music guide me. "Trust me," he says. "If we fall, we go down together." I never ask his name. As he pushes off, I let my torso relax into his and put trust into my legs. The strength of his lean, limber body floats me along the ice as if I had wings on my heels. I am laughing and crying all at the same time. I am exuberant.

6
CHAPTER

On Siblings and Sex

When I first began gathering my material on siblings and sex, I was not quite sure what it was I was after. Something lured me into this sinuously forbidden hotbed of erotic love between siblings. Sibling sexual bonds occurred with more frequency than any other incestuous coupling. But the children kept emerging with their stories, and while those stories were disparate and qualitatively unique, I was compelled by a seeming overlap and commonality in themes and lifelong impact. I found these children captivating. For some, underneath this visceral, mystical connection there was an impenetrable bubble that they had created, womblike and warm. Their fusion was profoundly complicated and mysterious. Others related heinous sibling violations that destroyed the tissue of their lives—atrocities of such a violent sadistic nature that the fragments of their selves seemed tattered, unsalvageable. The divergence had my mind reeling and my interest piqued.

Of course, my intrigue nipped at the heels of my own very personal exploration into my beloved familial constellation, attempting to make sense of the intricacies assigned only to its players. It is always most powerful and humbling when we are working on the very same issues as our clients.

As I crawled deeper into my calling I passed dizzily through a revolving door of sexual deviance and violation that for my very new and innocent self seemed unfathomable—an assault to my very being. The deeper I delved, the flimsier my own sexuality seemed to me, and the more frightened I was of merging with the souls of the very people I was here to treat. The murkiness of my own, sometimes boundaryless sexual self was in need of some reining in and some self-repair. I deeply hungered for an understanding of how sexuality emerges in a family and how this powerful potion pulls at the spirits of its young.

The children in my study talked at different levels about the emotional and physical unavailability of their parents. Their language ranged from the words of a five-year-old all the way to that of a seventeen-year-old, but the message always seemed the same. The children appeared like misguided little planets whirling out in space, uprooted and so alone—like orphaned urchins looking for a lap to rest their weary heads. Their fear of abandonment or virtual invisibility propelled them toward their siblings not only as ballast but also as comrades in a secret sanctuary, warring against inadequacy and a lack of warmth and nurturance from their parents.

The sexual climate in these families slid along a spectrum from rigidly restrictive to loose and ill-defined. As the sexual temperature sailed from cool to tepid to hot, these children were left to simmer in their own confusion and to decipher a language both cryptic and foreign.

Most striking, however, was the pervasive sense of sadness and potential loss of a family constantly suspended on the precipitous edge of dissolution. Exquisitely attuned to their parents' lack of interest, to their philandering and paramours, my little siblings in the incest bond simply mirrored what was unspoken but deeply absorbed. These children were trying desperately to mimic a secret that they could barely articulate, much less comprehend.

In my own family we poked and prodded, exposing our genitals with both shame and titillation. Some of our play blurred the lines of exploration and fell into the realm of questionable sexualizing. But whom else would we practice on? Didn't it make the most sense to try out our newly formed sexual awakenings on those with whom we lived? With whom we were closest? The question, of course, gnawed over time, and the more I looked at my own cases, the more dissonant my experiences seemed.

In my family, talk of sex was strictly suggestion and innuendo.

My mother's very puritanical mores trickled out with religious overtones. She condemned masturbation and premarital sex, yet her presentation to the outside world conveyed a very different message. A lustrous Italian beauty whose voluptuousness was obvious to every eye, she was hated and envied by all her so-called friends on the block; the men however, tripped over their feet to have a simple moment with her. My experience of her sexuality as her second daughter was one of intrigue and confusion. I lay on her bathroom floor as I watched her pour her womanly body into a snug black silk dress, plunging and revealing. Her tacit sensuality oozed out of her being, as if she possessed two variant selves. I learned early on, through my beautiful and precocious sister who paved the way, to do in secret everything my mother would not approve of.

My father, on the other hand, believed himself a ladies' man, though his woo, I'm afraid, was simply his ability to charm intellectually. He idolized the women of haute couture and fashioned himself as an expert on clothing design and the way in which women should be swathed. Charming and complex, his sensuality was more a marriage to his own narcissism. My parents' love was quiet and distant, with conflict that burbled under the surface—a breakdown of a smoothly flowing current that directions off, one to the north, the other to the south. They always seemed to find one another again, but their conflict and distance seemed more a result of innate beliefs and values which were always at odds with each other.

My parents were both covert and overt in their sexual messages, and I found what was unspoken to be a powerful vehicle that shaped my sexual yearnings, beginning in my own home and then spilling out into the world when I became more confident and defined.

As an adult, ravenous to understand the origins of sibling incest, I needed to go no further than my own neighbor's house; and so I did, with great trepidation and a pounding heart.

*   *   *   *   *   *   *

Lying across Marisa Murrow's bed, I cannot help but wonder who picked out the furnishings for this child's room. Every swatch of fabric, every piece of ornamentation, and every detail, down to the rose-colored flecks in the berber carpet, are in complete and utter harmony. There are conspicuous hints of adolescence in this room; the decor, however, smacks of nouveau riche. I am sprawled on my belly with my knees bent and my ankles locked together, slowly and rhythmically crossing and uncrossing my feet. I am not even aware that I am doing it until I lose my grip on one of my clogs and it lands heavily on my rear end.

This posture is nostalgic, somewhat refreshing. I can feel my illusory knee socks crinkling at my ankles. It surprises me that my body still invites this type of girlhood contortion. Marisa is seated at her French provincial desk, painting her nubby little nails a bilious green. I remind myself to comment on her creative color choice. Draped from post to post on her bed is a swag of brightly colored fabric, impeccably matched with the duvet cover and pillow shams. I muse that when I was an adolescent, this room would have caused me to swoon with envy.

Against the south wall rests her tennis racquet, a soccer ball, and a fine pair of ice skates hanging from a hook. She is chattering about her friend Abby and how she has been talking behind Marisa's back to her other confidants. I am half listening as I am perusing an article in *Seventeen* magazine about sexually transmitted diseases. Next to it is an ad for some new luscious lip goop from Revlon. The side-by-side layout for these two items seems counterintuitive.

Every Friday afternoon for the past six months I have come to see Marisa. Daily, after the school bus empties them into the cul du sac adjacent to their house, she and her younger brother, Evan, let themselves into this enormous, sprawling home. Rarely is a parent home to greet them, to inquire about their day, or to fix them a snack. It is an ambiance of emptiness and lassitude, tied up with a pretty bow.

I look forward to these Fridays. It brings closure to my week and gives me a place to disappear to. I have learned with great agility and finesse how to vaporize in midafternoon to avoid the possibility of a Friday-evening nightmare of incest. I love simply hanging out. My requirement as a caseworker is to have monthly contact with all the kids on my caseload. Marisa is an exception. I feel her loneliness and fragility—the potential for her ego to collapse and deconstruct. She is tremendously intriguing to me. I will learn something about myself from this young lady. She is my first female sex offender. At the ripe old age of twelve, she is my first case of sibling incest.

Watching Marisa at her desk reminds me of my own adolescent awkwardness—how desperately I wanted to be liked, to be unique and special. My long, leggy rail-thinness was a constant reminder of how I did not fit in. My ethnic coloring was my bane. She, on the other hand, is everything that I wanted to be in physical appearance—athletic and saucy, with bronze-colored skin and a thick mane of straight flaxen hair unusually laced through with stands of auburn and chestnut and pulled back in a haphazard ponytail. She blows puffs of her warm breath straight up the bridge of her nose, up her forehead, to keep the feathery loose strands from adhering to her freshly painted nails. The contrast of the shocking pink ribbon tied around her multicolored locks and the bilious nails is so Marisa.

As she gingerly adorns her final pinkie with green lacquer, she turns her chair toward me. Crossing her white-sock-clad feet, she drops her head back against the chair. "Anything in that magazine about stopping the sexy feeling?"

I look up, confounded. "What do you mean, 'the sexy feeling'?"

"Do you ever have a feeling in your body where you want to do sexy things?"

I flip onto my side, propping my body up on my left elbow. I am balancing my clog on the tip of my toes, contemplating a response. I know exactly what Marisa is referring to. As I open my mouth to form my response, she is quicker, and pinks up my already windburned cheeks with her query.

"Do you ever touch your soft spot?" Her almondy eyes, with their sooty smudged rims, are locked directly on mine. Her lashes, like fans, come down to half-mast. I think for a split second about her directness, about her need to know that what she feels in her body is not unusual or bad. She is offering a running commentary on her eroticism, on her sensuality, on that tingly sensation that hums in her body—her evolution into a sexual being.

Her path, however, has taken a precipitous jog, hence her ability to trust her feelings is jangled. Both Marisa and I know about what happened between her and Evan. We skate around the specifics, as her shame and humiliation ooze out of her being like pus from a wound. This child is forthright and curious in her inquiry about sex and sexuality. It is an opening that I seize upon like a pearly, shimmery shell being whisked off by the tide. I am constantly chasing Marisa's innuendo.

Today is different. Could there be a more revealing, intimate dish to be served? She is asking me if I ever touch my "soft spot." I want to respond like the adolescent I feel like in her presence, when we are leafing through girlfriend magazines and lounging on her bed. Instead I feel my social-worker façade slide down like a suffocating mask. I try to calculate her mother's response. I hear my therapist in my head about my own sexual boundaries. Yet here is a child who over a period of a year engaged in a sexual relationship with her nine-year-old brother. Not sexual play, not sexual exploration, but an intimate and secretive sexual liaison— touching, kissing, rubbing, simulating intercourse.

Marisa feels my evasion. I feel my familiar sexual bravado wilt. My light, playful, brazen verbiage sputters, grinding to a halt. I feel all of a sudden somewhat shy, coy, and a bit guarded. She has yet to take her eyes off of me.

"Stop staring at me!" I say, startling her. She grins. I feel naked. I feel as if the hierarchy between client and therapist collapses with my own ineptitude.

"What have you and your mom talked about with regard to your soft spot?" There is a moment of silence, and then she lets out a howl, a deep bellyful of laughter, to the point of almost tipping her chair backward. I can't tell whether she is laughing at my ludicrous suggestion or because her mother actually told her something warranting such a response.

"My mom pretends that she doesn't even hear me when I try to talk with her about sex." I now easily translate her laughter. How outrageous a suggestion. How sad she looks at this very moment, as if tears will rupture through her wall of laughter. Her impeccably painted nails cover her face with splayed fingers.

"Marisa. Come here." I pat the bed. "Bring your brush and I will braid your hair." She dutifully rises, grabs her brush from her bureau, and sits Indian-style in front of me. She undoes her ponytail and shakes loose a mane of breathtakingly beautiful tresses. Her hair smells of a citrusy, fruity shampoo. This child melts when she has her hair brushed. Her shoulders relax and her breathing steadies. Such a primitive, simple gesture will allow us this diatribe on sexy feelings and soft spots. It will be easier for me to busy my hands and talk to the back of her head about sex and masturbation.

"I remember sitting cross-legged in front of the TV when I was about eight or nine. I had the heel of my foot underneath my crotch, and I was so entranced by what I was watching that I started rocking back and forth on my heel. All of a sudden I felt this warm, tingling sensation—it was caused by the pressure on my soft spot, and it felt great. I tried to do it again, but I was too self-conscious, and I was afraid my mother was on to me. That's the very first time I found my soft spot! I was thrilled at what my body could do!"

With one braid near completion, Marisa turns around. Her face is within inches of mine. "Did you ever try to find it after that?" Her eyes are impatiently imploring me to validate her, to tell her that this is normal.

"Of course!" I hold my breath waiting for her response. Who is validating whom? I wondered. With my proclamation, she throws her arms around me, like we were long-lost sisters. I give her a tight squeeze and lace together the strands of her second braid.

On Fridays, when I have the opportunity to sit with Marisa and Evan, I am intrigued by what I see. Today when they got off the bus, Marisa knelt down and zipped up Evan's jacket, as the chill was biting. When they came into the house, Marisa asked Evan what he would like for a snack, and fixed him three Oreos with a tall glass of chocolate milk. After his snack he showed her a puncture wound where he almost stapled his thumb while hanging a picture today. She gently took his thumb in her hand and inspected the wound. He leaned his delicate frame against her body. Their knees touched.

They were unaware of my presence. I watched how closely their faces came together, her stunning bronze coloring and his curly chestnut locks in need of a trim. I wondered whether, when they lay together, they kissed. I wondered if they were completely naked. I mused about her tenderness with him. She fusses over him like a hen. He is trusting of his guardian. She is his sentinel; he is dutiful and obsequious.

Marisa took him over to the sink, got out the first-aid kit and began running warm water to clean his wound. When he let out a wail that he was afraid it was going to sting, she stopped and brushed a big brown curl from his forehead. "Let's sing 'You Are My Sunshine' so that you won't think about the sting, okay? We have to clean this out so it won't get infected."

She started to sing and he squeezed his eyes tight and sang with her. Before he knew it, she was done. She put an antibiotic ointment on and let him select a special Band-Aid with big blue stars on it. She wiped away a few little tears and then bent down and kissed his thumb. He smiled at her, a big warm smile, and then ran into the family room, where we could hear a tub of Lincoln Logs being overturned. He is in love with her and she with him. An obscure love, a secret love, a visceral, mystical love. Have I had a taste of this kind of love?

While Marisa is putting some morning dishes in the dishwasher, I am thinking that six months earlier this little girl came close to being arrested for fondling her brother's penis and having him rub her vagina. Yet what I observe between the two of them— her zipping his jacket, fixing him a snack, cleaning his cut—has everything to do with the incest. She is like a mother to him. How is it that the nurturance that I observe becomes eroticized? One might observe their union as hierarchical coercion, surreptitious and clandestine. Others may experience it as a secret sanctuary amidst an ocean of hopelessly vacant familial ties. I am so accustomed to seeing adults sexualize with children that children with children has a distinctly different flavor. There can be a tenderness in the bonding that is both nurturing and sexualized. There can be hideous sexual violation that scars a life time.

The day that I met the Murrows, Evan had told a friend at recess that he was having sex with his sister. The friend told the teacher, and the teacher in turn told the principal. When the principal called to report, he was having trouble trying to spit out the details. "This is such a nice family," he said.

"I'm sure they're nice, Mr. Andrews, but what exactly did Evan Murrow say?" I hear the insolence in my tone.

His malaise bumbles across the wire. "He said that his sister um, touches his, um . . . "

It feels like an eternity for him to say *penis*, but I refuse to say it for him. I wait in silence. "Touches what, Mr. Andrews?" The word *penis* is hardly audible.

Late that afternoon, I come out to interview both Evan and Marisa. When Evan is brought into the room to be interviewed, I am struck by how tiny and vulnerable he seems. He has a mop of auburn ringlets that encircle his delicate features like a halo. His dark, rounded eyes move abruptly from my face to the door. His lashes are tipped with a reddish hue, as if they have been professionally tinted. His tiny mouth houses teeth too large for his delicate jaw.

He sits next to me on the couch and laces his fingers together.

There is the beginning of a hole in the knee of his trousers. He begins to pick at the fabric while I make idle conversation with him. I can observe the subtle activation of his senses as he begins to understand why he is there. His breathing is shallow and somewhat stridulous. I note that he has taken his place next to me, which I find quite unusual.

"Evan, I'm here because someone had a worry about you, and I wonder if you might know what that worry is?"

He begins to rock back and forth, wiping his sweaty paws on his pant legs. "I hope Marisa is not worried . . . I love my sister, and she takes good care of me."

His response causes me to lose my sense of what he said. I am unsure if he said something about his mother or about Marisa. At that moment I think about my own baby brother, whom I looked after as if he were my own. I adored him. I relished his admiration and dependency on me. It removed me from the distress of relating to my own peers. He filled me with an indescribable sense of importance in a world where I felt a huge gulf of loneliness. I ran home after school every day just to be with him. In the second grade I brought him in for show-and-tell.

It appears to me that Evan's anchor, his ballast, is his sister. Odd, I muse, but not so odd. He will protect her with all his being. There is something in this sibling tryst that serves a very specific purpose, but where are the parents in all of this?

Evan lumbers through his disclosure. I listen attentively in an effort to pick up the nuance of this bond. Since he was seven, he and Marisa have been showing each other their private parts. She would fondle his penis and he would open her labia, touching the "bud" inside. Sometimes at night when he was frightened or could not sleep, he would crawl into her bed. She would hold his hand and tell him a story. He would finally fall asleep. He says that Marisa's bed smells like her—like flowers. He loves the smell of her hair. When he was feeling really sad or lonely, he would ask her if he could take one whiff of her ponytail. She would always say yes. When I ask him why he has told someone now, he responds by saying that he was embarrassed and his friends would tease him. He hopes that Marisa would not be mad.

At this juncture in our conversation, there is a sizable hole in the knee of Evan's pants. Not once have I heard him refer to his mother or his father. These children feel like Hansel and Gretel. I see them meandering through the forest leaving bread crumbs, hoping to find their way back to a different home, to a stronger, more present constellation.

When questioned about his mom and dad, he tells me that his mom has a boyfriend and his dad works all the time. He and Marisa take care of themselves. I instantaneously take note of the "boyfriend." I will be intrigued to query his sister. I assure Evan that he is not in any trouble, that I will speak with Marisa as well as his mom and his dad.

His expression changes from one of relief to panic. "Where will I go when I cannot fall asleep? Where will I go?" He falls into a puddle of tears. He allows me to hold his heaving little frame as he weeps. Somewhere this unformed little boy knows that the permanence of his sanctuary is coming to a close. Somewhere his heart is shattered.

Stunned at my own response, I too feel his loss, his grief. I am an interloper. I am destroying a tender yet corrupt intimacy, which because of its corruptness needs to end.

I find it uncanny when I come upon a client who echoes my deepest sentiments. There is always a child or an adult that galvanizes my subterranean memory. Somewhere, somehow, Evan was destined to cross my path. This aching little boy, whose sister has become his solace, his sanctum, his nurturance, and his replacement for a mother, is soon to be redefined and cleansed of impropriety. I question my each and every move. Part of me wants to let them be. Part of me wants to roll back in time and forget that I ever came here. I feel such ambivalence about stopping this incest. I am ashamed.

When Marisa Murrow is Mirandized, I want to leave the room. This little girl has her hair in two long braids with red ribbons tied in perfect bows. Her Top-Siders are unlaced and her knee socks are drooping. There is a doodle of a heart penned in the palm of her hand. I have to blink to readjust my vision. This cannot be! If the sexes were reversed, I know my bias would kick in like nobody's business.

I am quiet as the detective explains to her Evan's allegations. She is so agitated that she begins to stutter and cannot string together any expression. I feel the squeeze at the back of my throat. I know that I will cry. I ask that the detective dismiss himself so that I can talk with her alone. Although I have rankled him with my suggestion, he begrudgingly complies.

I am aware when my gender is inhibiting an individual from

their honest disclosure. I have only to set aside my ego so that an investigation proceeds with greater ease and less anxiety. As soon as he leaves, Marisa is better able to focus. She has a sweetness beyond words and a kindness that defies her act. I want this all to be a sham. This child appears as if she is in agony.

"I am so em-em-em-barrassed," she stutters. "I feel terrible that I-I-I may have screwed up my brother for life." She swallows the word *screwed* as if she will gag and regurgitate it. Marisa makes no eye contact. She picks at the rubber trim around her Top-Siders. "Look," she implores, "my parents are never around. I can't re-re-re-remember the last time anyone hel-hel-helped me with my homework or cooked a dinner. I'm like Evan's mom and it got out of hand."

This statement is unleashed with anger and indignation. It erupts from her mouth with ease and fluidity. And then she begins to stutter uncontrollably. She is so shamed by this involuntary quirk that she gets up and starts to pace the room. At one point she rests her cheek against the cool glass window in the room. She places both palms against the window, then wipes away the condensation created by her hands. To relieve her tension, I start to talk—it is truly my own anxiety.

I tell her that I have talked to her brother and that I think that I understand what happened, and that if she could help me to better understand, we may be able to help her.

Her statements are punctuated by elongated stutters. She describes a high-achieving family with little time for children. She feels as if she has raised herself. She has everything that money can buy, but this is a home devoid of warmth or love. Her parents hate each other. Her mother has a boyfriend; her father angles around a bullish stock market or reads *Penthouse*. The only thing they enjoy together as a family is skiing. She is traversing the room and sucking on the end of one of her braids. Her agitation and her anger are spiraling up by the minute. She asks me if I think she is a freak.

"I think that you are sad. I think that you have had too much responsibility and too little time to be a kid." I have not answered her question. She cuts me off. She utters what I dare not utter out of my need to protect her and to protect myself.

"But I tried to have sex with my baby brother!" She sits down on the floor and digs her nails into the ankles of her socks. "I tried to be his mom, and then it all got funny." The pupils of her eyes are dilated. "Nobody will ever love me—not my mom, or my dad, or any other boy."

My heartbeat quickens. I realize that she does not need protection. She needs someone to be straight and direct.

"I don't want to feel these feelings with Evan anymore! It's sick!" She collapses into a heap, a replica of her brother only moments before. She is brittle. She has navigated this bleak terrain for far too long. I feel intense rage at her parents. She will not be held or touched. She recoils like some odious creature, undeserving of kindness or compassion. Between sobs I hear her lament, "Where will we go, what will we do?"

There is a sense of imminent abandonment with both these children. They have sought refuge and solace in each other. An unspeakable dynamic in this family has brought these children into a union of survival. I am fascinated by what I see. I hark back once again to my own siblings. There are some startling similarities.

Daniel and Elaine Murrow are seated in the waiting room with a chair in between them. They do not look old enough to have these children. They both smack of an advertisement from Brooks Brothers, in their camel's hair and blue oxford cloth. Her leg flutters and vibrates spasmodically. His face is buried deeply in the *Wall Street Journal.* She has a sorority loveliness—tanned with streaked hair and a small turned-up nose. Her body is long, lean, and graceful. He has a look similar to his wife's, youthful, agile, and handsome.

They exude an aura of tightness, fixed and unbending. A gulf of tremulous tides flows between them, much like an undertow. The moment I open the door to invite them into my office, in unison they scan me from head to toe and then smile. I have passed a test. What test that is, I have yet to comprehend. It has something to do with presence and exterior. It gives me a leg up. I must meticulously traverse the sexual issue with a certain permissiveness. If they feel admonished or judged, I will lose my toehold.

I introduce myself and explain my role. Daniel Murrow is a financial analyst. I can read his arrogance in a millisecond. He exudes an air of authority and control. I feel an instant dislike and then something analogous to pity. I am cognizant that I am presumptuous and judgmental. So be it.

Elaine is a lovely backdrop. She appears concerned yet remote.

Daniel Murrow has rolled his *Wall Street Journal* so tightly that it looks like a bat he would take to someone's head—mine, I am thinking. He keeps slamming the rolled-up paper against the palm of his hand as he speaks. I am thinking about the doodle of the heart in Marisa's palm. Elaine opens nothing more than the top button of her camel's hair coat. She keeps her Weejuned feet perfectly paralleled as if there were magnets joining her ankles.

I begin to tell them about the concerns that were reported today. As I open my mouth, Daniel begins to pontificate on the rearing of his children. He assumes that the allegations have something to do with Marisa. "She lies!" he snaps. "She will not focus on her schoolwork. She was on the tennis team and . . . "

I put my hand up, as if I were a crossing guard. He turns a bit pink at my gesture and tucks his tail. "Let's not make this solely about Marisa. There is something that is happening in this family that may be contributing to your children's behavior."

This father's snarling protestations reek. I am captured by Daniel Murrow's eagerness to profess his child's failings, yet none of his own. He is righteous in his portrayal of his daughter's deficits. My heart freezes when he begins to talk about her lying. He is critical of her grades, her proficiency as an athlete. "And she can't get a goddamn word out of her mouth without stuttering!"

"What do you make of the stutter?" I ask rather sheepishly. I don't listen to his answer. I watch Elaine, and I have a visual of him fondling Marisa. The thought flutters across my brain, and I take note of it. I also take note of the fact that I think this guy is a shit. I think he is mean and does not like his daughter. I think that if I were Marisa, I'd be looking for a place to get out from underneath this man's condemnation. I might very well lie down with my brother. There is a refuge in Evan. Daniel Murrow has gobbled up any semblance of his daughter's being. Any last remaining crumbs of her emerging self have been devoured.

My thought quickly collides with a profound emotional kick in my tummy. Evan is the coveted child, the male child. She has sullied the prince. Her sexual act is the big "fuck you" to her father, perhaps to her mother. As if, without a voice, she is conveying her displeasure, her need, and a poignant and deeply etched pain.

While he is talking to me, his wife is quiet. She nervously twirls her diamond ring around her finger. She turns the gem to the inside of her palm and closes her fist. Daniel Murrow pummels his palm with the rolled-up paper as he looks at my breasts. For a moment I look down to see if there is a spot or a spill. Noticing the chill in my office, I can feel that my nipples have tightened and that this man is trying to unnerve me. I fold my arms over my chest and gaze at his heavily garmented wife.

I am intrigued by the first twenty minutes of this interview. There are nuggets here. My mind goes back to the faces of their children, and I muse to myself that their unadulterated honesty is compelling juxtaposed with the finger-pointing, pigeon-holing father and this vacant, voiceless mother.

The Murrows resist the sexual implications of their children's behavior. They attempt to explain it away as play, exploration, curiosity—anything but sexual. Sexual. If I were them, I believe I would be desperate to see it as anything but its reality.

I make the suggestion of couples therapy and individual work for both children. I instruct them how to approach this situation. I turn to Elaine and tell her in front of her husband that we need not shame either child. What we need to do is to understand what brought them together. They must be supervised at all times. I assure them that I will be out to the home tomorrow to see how everything went.

Daniel begins to squirm and questions the necessity of a home visit. This man knows exactly what I am after. What he is not familiar with is my tenacity. I explain to both of them that until the dust settles and therapy has begun, I will have frequent contact with the family. I see his litigious cogs gyrating. I get some pleasure from this.

As they exit my office, I walk them out to the waiting room. I notice only then that Elaine Murrow is several inches taller than her husband. The gulf that exists is vast. It also pulses with an interesting sexual tension.

Back in my office, I smell their scents. Usually I open the window and air out the smells that my clients leave—somewhat of an exorcism. I want my own smell back. Theirs is an interesting admixture—musky and camphorous with a tinge of lily of the valley. I feel like an animal tracking an odor, trying to find my answer.

I put my feet up on my desk, turn off my phone, and close my eyes. My mind is spinning out because I have taken so much in. The spirit under the dialogue was less interesting than the nuance, the power differential, and the mother's muted voice. I think she has a lot to say. What about the boyfriend? Her husband must feel so betrayed, so emasculated. Yet it all feels so juicy, so rich. Secrets spawn secrets. It is not as much about Evan and Marisa as it is about Elaine and Daniel. I am eager for tomorrow to come.

I am early to arrive at the Murrows. Marisa and Evan are both snacking when Elaine opens the door. She is tentative yet kind. Evan recognizes me and greets me warmly. Marisa wants to show me her room. As we wind up the stairs, I am struck by how everything seems so without life or character. I ask Marisa if she is okay. She assures me that she is, but it reels out with a stutter.

There is a sense of urgency in Elaine Murrow. She takes me into the study, and we slide into the soft leather couch. On the coffee table is a copy of *Penthouse*, with a sumptuous, bosomy young woman in stiletto heels perched on top of a glistening baby grand Steinway. She is the epitome of erotic consumption, with her thighs open to the world.

I pause to see if Elaine will move it. She does not. It is obviously a fixture in this room. I ask Elaine how everything went last night, and she starts to cry. I rise and close the door to the study. She explains through her tears that she thinks this is all her fault. What topples out after this is unbelievable. She has had a lover for the last two years. Her children know this man, and they had to keep it a secret from Daniel. When Daniel found out, he too took a lover, and they decided to divorce. Since then, both paramours have gone, and they have decided, because of the children, that they should stay together.

"My husband is a pig! All he wants to do is have sex, and I can't bear the thought of him. The kids used to hide in the closet when we made love. He knew they were there, and he loved the exhibitionistic thrill. When he was in college, his mother was an alcoholic and used to go to bed with all his friends when he brought them home for the holidays."

I am silent for a few moments while she collects her thoughts. "Who does the *Penthouse* belong to?" I ask.

"It's his." She says this in such a way that I feel her sense of powerlessness. I watch the pulse in the hollow of her neck as she speaks. She wears a pair of khakis and a snug-fitting sweater. She does not seem as guarded about her body as the day she was in my office. I wonder about her sexuality. She seems oppressed and terribly unhappy. I picture her in my mind's eye lying with her husband. She is still and nonemotive. He pumps away in his own narcissistic bubble. There is no connection, no passion, no playfulness. She is a receptacle, and she allows herself to be one.

Elaine looks at me in the way women look at other women when they long for camaraderie, frightened of admonishment or reproach. "I was molested by my father when I was a bit younger than Marisa."

More than her statement, I sadly acknowledge that this is the first time that I have heard this mother use her daughter's name. It is as if they are strangers, unrelated.

"When Marisa was six, we went to visit my parents. One afternoon I was looking frantically for her. I couldn't find her, and I was going crazy with fear. My folks live at the edge of a wood, and we were scanning the periphery of the property with hounds. It was over an hour."

I am watching Elaine speak, gesticulating with her hands as her knee shakes wildly with the story. It's as if she is reliving it while she is recapturing her horror. Her face is flushed and her hands are clammy as she rubs them against the elbows of her sweater.

"I went into the kitchen to the pantry to see if I had left my jacket in there, and the pantry door was locked."

There is a silence that seems eternal. I know exactly what she is about to say. It is sadly predictable, and I ache for all that I know.

"When the door was unlocked, Marisa came scampering out, and my father was behind her zipping his trousers, sputtering some feeble excuse. He was intoxicated." She begins to cry again. This time her fists clench and her jaw tightens. "I never asked my daughter what happened. I made believe that everything was fine. I gave her a bath. I scrubbed her vagina so hard I made her bleed. I fed her and I put her to bed. From that day on I wanted nothing to do with her. I rejected her. I left her in the dark. She was dirty, she was rotten, and she was me."

Elaine Murrow is slumped on the couch, holding her mouth as if she will vomit. There are beads of perspiration clinging to her upper lip. Her entire body is trembling. I cling to the visual of this mother scrubbing the demons from her daughter's genitals. My mind splinters. I hear my voice whispering, "I am so sorry. I am so sorry."

For a split second, the voice does not sound as if it belongs to me. I pull the damp hair away from her forehead. Her mascara streaks down her cheeks like a charcoal drawing left in the rain.

I fold her into my arms, and she just weeps for what seems like forever but is simply some minutes. I bite the inside of my cheek between my teeth so that I will not cry. It is a futile attempt, and I cry with her. I smell the lily of the valley scent clinging to the strands of her hair.

She weeps uncontrollably for the pain of her own misguided past and her regret at her invisibility with her daughter. She barely knows Marisa. She checked out emotionally when Marisa was six—the girl was too excruciating a reminder of her own quiet violation.

As I gaze down at her crumpled body, I see her loveliness. I see her daughter's profile etched in her tiny nose and delicate jaw. I find that my own mind is frozen. There is something in her memory that, while graphic and compelling, leaves me paralyzed with fear. I can feel my own agitation—angst that comes when something is too close to my interior, something is too warm.

I can see Daniel Murrow as he rounds the drive. I feel a sense of urgency to clean up his wife and reassemble her so that it appears as if nothing has transpired. It is futile on my part. She is lying on the couch in an exhausted state. She is clearly somewhat in shock. I feel like a little girl who dropped Mommy and Daddy's prized porcelain figurine. I am scurrying and scampering about, trying to piece it back together. I am terrified that Daniel Murrow will walk through his front door and explode. I know his family secrets. I think of the rolled-up paper. I regret not being kinder to him.

I hear his key in the door and feel a sense of shame and panic— as if I have come into his home with a time bomb. I have set off the explosion, and the family is shattered. I feel as if it is my responsibility to piece it all back together. He enters his study. He sees Elaine, and he approaches me as if he is going to throttle me. I step toward him and quickly recap my conversation with Elaine. Compassion immediately replaces anger. He kneels down next to his wife and strokes her hair. Her eyes are closed, and she looks close to sleep. He covers her with a beautiful cashmere throw.

He walks aimlessly into the kitchen and pulls out a chair. He rests his head in the palm of his hands and is very still. I feel the inclination to place my palm on his back, but I refrain. He looks up at me, and the first words that come tumbling out of my mouth are "This all makes so much sense now—Evan and Marisa." He nods. His eyes are filled to the brim with tears.

Marisa comes into the room and is frightened by her father's presence. He holds out his hand toward her. She is suspicious and tentative. She steps toward him, and he takes her hand. She looks at me for acknowledgment and protection. I nod. I can see her whole body begin to decompress. He holds her hand tightly and begins to cry. Then he says the words that I am always waiting to hear. He tells her that he is so sorry. It is barely audible. He says it again until she can hear him. "I am so sorry for what has happened to you. I am so sorry that I have not been here for you."

She responds tentatively, by inching closer. She sits down on her daddy's knee, and he brings her close to his body. She folds, she melts. She rests her cheek on the shoulder of his overcoat, and it's as if she is inhaling his scent. Her eyes are closed. He is rocking her like a baby. He is stroking the tangled tresses. She is crying, and he is comforting her. When was the last time he held her like a father who loves his daughter?

What I see moves me beyond words. I feel that it is time for me to go. I leave the kitchen, check on the sleeping Elaine, and amble up the stairs to where Evan is sprawled across his parents' bed watching cartoons. I tell him that his mom is resting and his dad has just gotten home. He pulls me down on the floor to show me an intricate cabin of Lincoln Logs that he has constructed. His eyes are sparkling and attentive. He asks when I am coming back. "Soon," I say. "Soon."

I wonder, on my drive home, what will happen to this family. Marisa and Evan's love unleashed a torrent of secrets. They ruptured through a system on the verge of dismantling itself. It is all unraveling. I drive past the exit that will take me home. I feel such sorrow, such melancholy, so blue. I feel as if I came late to the party. There is very little that I can do. This family needs desperately to reorganize, to reconstruct its foundation.

Daniel Murrow's outstretched hand held little promise. I could not forget his rage at his daughter's deficiencies, which seemed to be blanketed underneath his rage at his spouse and, most profoundly, himself. And then there is his voiceless wife, paralyzed by her own secret exploitation. Their preoccupation with themselves seemed merely a product of the faltering machinery of their own marriage. They needed only to look at the holes in their own love, so long denied, in such disrepair. In those frailties, they would find the fusion of their children, searching desperately for a presence, for a mooring, endlessly hoping for what every child wants—a family that is warm and loving, where intimacy and nurturance are the rule, not the exception.

Years later, Daniel Murrow's firm transferred him, and the family moved to a suburb outside of Seattle. The last time I saw Marisa, we took a walk on a stretch of open space behind their property. She had matured over the years, and we stood nose to nose. Her stutter was barely noticeable, and she tended toward her jagged speech only when she was excited. When we said our goodbyes, we both teared up. She handed me an envelope and told me not to open it until I got home. I gave her the tightest hug with a heavy heart. Halfway home I opened the envelope. It was her school picture. On the back, inside a frilly pink heart, were the words "You helped me so much. I love you."

"I love you back," I said to the picture. I kissed her smiling face and placed the photo back in the envelope.

Some time after that, as my gloved hand reached to turn out the light in my office one afternoon, the phone rang. Expecting it to be a return call from my husband, I answered. There was a pleasant woman across the wire asking me if I could provide her with some information on "a Marisa Murrow."

Feeling my heart take a leap, I naively cried, "Oh, how is she?" The frigid silence across the wire caused my knees to fold into my chair. The woman identified herself as a psychiatrist at a private hospital outside of Seattle. Marisa had tried to take her life. She had made a significant gash to one of her wrists. Prior to doing it, she cut off all her hair. I felt ill. My whole body felt hot. I could feel her satiny tresses in my hands. I could smell her. I hung up the phone and cried.

* * * * * * *

I am seated at a stunning oblong walnut conference table with members of the editorial board for an international journal. I am twenty-eight years old. I can see my reflection in the finish of the table. I am drenched in sweat and can feel the moisture underneath the mass of my hair at the nape of my neck. I am here to review my research article on sibling incest with the board. They have rejected it twice, and I have done two rewrites. The editor in chief has asked that I present my findings, as the board is not quite sure of its relevance. I know its relevance. I can taste its relevance.

I believe that I have uncovered something that is different, or perhaps it is simply that I see it differently. I just want people to hear what I have to say. I scan the room and see the face that I have been looking for. He acknowledges me with a warm nod. He has been my mentor, my friend—the man that I began to consult with about the Murrow family. I told him that I thought I had found something unique in this family; that when I put together all the characteristics, it was truly fascinating. I predicted I could find it in many sibling incest families. So little had been written on sibling incest, and he firmly believed it should come off the front line. He celebrated my instinct and my intuition. Unrelentingly, I had tracked this family. I had turned down every bedsheet, opened every closet door. All my cases were predicated on what the Murrows had taught me. The next twenty families had uncanny commonalities, distinctive in their characteristics yet seemingly similar.

"We think that your observations are quite interesting, Miss Smith. However, we feel that they lack clinical applicability. This is an empirical study, Miss Smith—one that is derived solely from observation. There is no theory; there are no control groups . . . "

He continues his diatribe, and I feel myself go away. I am tired. I am weary and worn out. I wonder about my need to convey what I see and feel to the world. Why is that so important to me? Other than Dr. Jacobs, the editorial board is present as a matter of course—perhaps to indulge me. He wants them to listen. He sees that I have departed, and he knows that I am merely minutes from respectfully excusing myself from this dialogue.

As he begins to speak, I can feel the tremor in my hands start to subside. I think about the first time I spoke with him over the phone. A visiting psychiatrist from Europe, he had a stellar reputation. I called and introduced myself. He listened to my thoughts about sibling incest and suggested that we meet. I listened to his voice, his choice of words, and his articulation—so liquidy and delicious. I fell in love with him right then and there on the phone. Mostly it was because he believed in me.

I begin to tell the board the story of Marisa and Evan and how the research came to be. There is a woman sitting directly across from me. Conservative yet acknowledging, she straightens her body and attends to me. I tell the story about Marisa and the soft spot. I talk about the tenderness between her and her brother. How I stumbled upon a love, the way in which we have all, at one time or another, opened the door on a secret in progress and what power that secret might hold. The majority of sibling incest cases have had dynamics that involve coercion, force, and violent, heinous acts—the inherent power differential between an older sibling and a younger sibling has created a forum for horrendous sibling exploitation. But this family presented with a different twist. Here is an important hallmark of sibling incest.

"Eros is alive in the family. In the next ten years I predict that we will see the burgeoning sexuality of our youth go sorely awry. We will see more youth violating younger children; we will see adolescent and latency-age victims violating their siblings and their peers. Love in the family is not what we believe it to be, and the fine-tuning of our hypervigilant children, and all the unspoken, simmering libidinous energy that they absorb, will certainly rear its head in a sexualized manner."

The people around the table are listening to me, trying to decipher my evangelical zealousness. I have nothing to lose.

"We cannot afford to keep this material buried. It needs to come alive so that we as clinicians have the tools to enter a family where incest is occurring and see it and dismantle it. I understand that this is empirical. I understand that it is not theoretical. But I see this every day. I see it, I smell it, and I taste it. I get the opportunity to hold the hands of the children whose lives are forever detoured by this tragedy. I eat at their tables. I drive them to therapy. I fix them their snacks. We have all, as clinicians, become parents to these children, whose parents are absent and vacant and whose own lives have been touched by childhood incest."

Dr. Jacobs is nodding. He gives me a wink. I realize at this juncture that I am having fun. I feel lightness. I believe in myself. Chemistry is ephemeral. I toss the outcome of this meeting up to the heavens. I am proud that I have done this. I understand at this moment that we must be able to carve out an island in each and every family. There must be a nonerotic haven in a world of simmering eroticism. It is our jumping-off point—a nonerotic sanctuary where love and intimacy can be expressed without a looming sense of seduction or violation.

In my mind's eye, I can see Marisa's impish grin as she tips back precariously on her desk chair, the world in a delicate balance, and prods me inquisitively about my "soft spot." There is quiet warmth in my heart, and I realize that this writing is a tribute to Marisa—for her candor, her humility, and her sadness. Her sadness was deeper than we had all imagined.

7
CHAPTER

The Therapist with Child: Transference and Countertransference Ad Nauseum

I had what I kindly refer to as my nervous breakdown when my older daughter was about eighteen months old. When I speak about it now, it's as if I am referring to an old friend. The fear that was once attached to this time in my life has softened somewhat. Its evanescent, vaporlike memory visits every now and then, like a gentle ghostly reminder. This was not a break with reality, not even an abyss of depression. This was a phantom malady—simply a shattering of my mind. The substance that had once oiled my heart and my brain had somehow evaporated. My logic was elliptical. My circuits were misfiring, and I was almost too fatigued to notice. My vision of the world had been stood on its head. I felt as if I was dying.

I remember the day with great clarity. It was a blustery Friday afternoon, and I had taken a call from an attorney at around four-thirty. The office was almost completely empty except for a supervised visit that was just beginning down the hall from me. Before I closed the light and picked up my keys, I ambled down the hall to peek in on the visit. On the floor with his back facing the two-way mirror sat a rather delicate-looking child. He was deftly running a little Brio train along the figure eight of a wooden train track. Judging from his fine motor skills and his delicate frame, I put him at about two or two and a half.

My presence startled the caseworker when she came into the outer room. She had just brought the mother of the child into the room where the little boy was playing. I watched as the child turned to his mom and scrambled up in her arms. As he pulled his face away from hers, I felt my heart flutter inside my chest cavity with a jolt. The left side of his cheek sagged off the skeletal frame of his face like the wax of a melted candle that has hardened. The skin on his neck and his tiny forehead had the texture of phyllo dough, as if you could peel back and flake the membranous tissue. His facial disfigurement was hideous. His left eye socket housed the remains of an eyelid naked of any lashes.

"What happened to him?" The utterance from the back of my throat cascades out in such a flurry that my own voice sounds foreign to me.

"His mother got so angry after he accidentally peed on her new couch that she threw a pan of boiling grease at him." She scans the visit through the glass and scribbles on her notepad at the same time. "That's not even the half of it," she whispers. "You should see his penis." My hand covers my mouth so quickly that she backs up her chair, fearing that I will vomit on her. I am paralyzed. I have no words.

She stands up and opens the door. "Go home, Holly. You look exhausted." She is practically pushing my frozen frame through the door. My eyes are glued to the mother and her son as she smoothes back the birdlike spikes of feathery hair, which have survived his dousing. The expression on my face must be fearful. "Go!" she commands. Not only does she have to observe this mother and child scene with the eye of an eagle, but also she has to sweep the remains of my half-blown mind out the door.

Once alone in my car, I notice that the tips of my fingers are numb. I rub them together thinking that they are cold, but the feeling does not resume. I begin to spiral out in my mind. I also can feel the numbness in the left side of my face. I have felt this before. I decide on my drive up the hill to my home that I am dying. I cannot get the visual of this child's face out of my mind . . . so grotesque and distorted. Over and over I see his droopy eye drinking in his mother's face. Dauntless and seem-ingly enrapt, the child acted as if this unutterable assault had never taken place. It will not compute in my mind. This mother nearly killed her baby, yet he loves her. I feel my chest begin to close and my breathing quicken. My numb cheek begins to tingle, and I cannot get up the hill fast enough. It is the last such visual of a physically abused or sexually violated child that I can absorb. For weeks I am absent from work. I shuttle myself from doctor to doctor with my symptoms. They give me Valium to sleep. They scan my face with sympathy as I wait for an explanation, some sort of diagnosis. I sense that they speculate about the fragile machinery of my mind. No one says a word aloud. They look at their feet, fingering their stethoscopes. They are anxious to leave my neurosis at the door. My numbness and tingling cannot be explained.

At night I pace the floors, listening to my daughter's rhythmic breathing. My husband is fearful of leaving me alone. My mind dances with thoughts of death—my own, my child's. What if she dies? What if her nanny hurts her? What if her nanny touches her vagina? How will I know? What if I die? Who will love her? I am obsessed and consumed. I cannot eat or sleep. I cannot look at another incested child. The little boy with the waxen face wafts through my mind. I see his languid, saggy eye in my dreams. I have lost my grip.

In the morning, when I nurse my baby, I rock methodically, like a madwoman, in the chair. Her beautiful green eyes roll back into her head with the intoxication of satiation and bliss. I peruse her nursery as if to memorize its colorful, pristine gaiety—simple, yet such a haven of warmth. I can bask in the presence of nur-ture. While I am rocking, the visuals come into my head again, and I gaze down at a tiny pair of soft patent leather Mary Janes. They are delicate and doll-like. I look at them and feel an over-whelming sense of sadness. While she sleeps in my arms, I weep. I am overcome by the opening of such emotion. I am overcome by my own feeling of madness.

Many nights the same dream comes to me. I am walking around the perimeter of a glistening pool of aqua water. I can feel my fear building by the second. Suddenly, the place is filled with people, and I am screaming my baby's name. I can see her in my mind's eye, crawling near the edge of the pool. As I near the deepest part of the pool, I can see her tiny body floating motionless on the undulating water. Her face is down. People are milling around, but no one will help me. I kneel by the edge of the water and pull her out. Her body is stiff and weighty. I am hysterical. I am screaming, and people are still milling. I place her pewter-colored body on a towel. I put my lips on her open mouth. Ever so gently, I begin to blow tiny puffs of air into her mouth. Her lips are icy and shriveled. They are the color of lilacs. My hot tears are falling onto her freezing face, and suddenly, with each breath I blow into her mouth, the temperature of her body begins to warm, and she pinks up. Before long, her little legs are gyrating and her lashes have opened. She is cooing and raising her tiny arms, pulling at my soaking hair. As if I have pulled off a miraculous feat that could be reversed at any second, I flee.

I awaken from this dream, and my nightgown is soaked in sweat. My body temperature will not modulate. Quietly, I swing my legs around and feel the balls of my feet hit the chilly floor. It is like clockwork. I go into the bathroom and change my gown. I grab a towel to lie over the pool of wetness I have made in my sheets. I walk to the crib and listen for my baby's living breath. Somewhat eased, I pull the rocker next to my slumbering child and rock myself to sleep. If I could put her back into my womb, I would. Somehow, I believe she would be safer there—out of harm's way and safe from the craziness of her suffering mother. I have seen the atrocities committed against children. I am at a loss as to how to protect my own. I know too much.

I read a story once about octopuses. After a female octopus lays her eggs, she stops eating. She focuses her life force on blowing highly oxygenated water over her eggs to keep them from dying. When the eggs finally hatch, the mother dies from exhaustion

It is the dream! After I have dreamed this dream one billion times, after my third child, I realize this. It is me. I am blowing life back into myself. I am dying, and with each breath, the life inside me is restored. Each breath seems a willful reminder of my purpose, my place, my intention. Each burst of air is simply bringing life back into a depleted enervated soul.

I remember once attending a lecture by a renowned geneticist. Her specialty had to do with pediatric anomalies. Extremely pregnant, she paced the floor as she spoke, her left hand systematically stroking her distended belly. As I gazed, that hand never left her belly. Not once did she remove it. She just stroked this heavenly being as if to cover its ears and protect this child from the horrors of all that she had seen and treated. As I watched her, I could feel the tiny hairs on the back of my neck rise. I knew her conundrum. I knew it well. Her calling, her pediatric anomalies, was slowly being absorbed into her system. As she spoke, she could not help but think of her own child, soon to enter this world. And what if, just what if, she had to face a child who was handicapped or marred?

When I carried all my babies, I could not dispel the thought that I would lose one of these children—that somehow my work with incest was preparing me to rear a child who might very well be violated sexually or, even more frighteningly, a child who could violate another child. Perhaps I would have a child who would become a sex offender. All my knowledge and expertise would be for naught. This is where I lost my control.

Moving from clinician to mother and then back to clinician was a passage I was totally unprepared for. I feel acute sensitivity and compassion for any woman who makes this transition. After we have made our babies and have nuzzled into our euphoric nests, returning to the world of incest is like stepping out into a blast of arctic air, having forgotten our coats and mittens. Our nerve endings are frozen by tiny ice formations, rendering us no longer immune and protected. We stumble through our days without buffer or cushion. These could be our children. These could be our babies whose vaginal openings or anuses have been torn. Any comforting distance of objectivity is soon punctured by the perception that life's pain is random and nobody escapes tragedy and sorrow.

Becoming a mother during my career in the protection of incested children tapped a reservoir of apprehension and empathy. In some ways, it forced me to operate from my heart as opposed to my head. My reactivity and indignation were the fire inside my spirit. It would also be my bane, and intermittently it would eclipse sound judgment.

*   *   *   *   *   *   *

Mia Antonelli's wail is so high-pitched, it is reminiscent of the cry of a sheep or a goat. In an instant her bleat is silenced. Her cry, as if in a dream, is mute. I observe the lines of complete and utter anguish crescent at the corners of her mouth. Her head is wrenched back, and I gaze at her tiny, perfectly spaced teeth and the pink of her tongue. Tears are streaming down her face, pooling delicately into her mouth as she consumes her sorrow. I am gingerly attempting to peel back her thick little fingers, like tentacles, from around the throat of her mother's long, swanlike neck. Her tiny digits are adhered. Her diminutive nails still house flecks of pearly pink nail enamel with a splash of glitter.

As I attempt to strip back her fingers the way one would skin an orange, her nails embed into the skin of her mother's neck. Her mother weeps quietly, loosening her daughter's grip, yet simultaneously clutching her small rigid body closely, with the fierceness of her will. Mia's tenaciousness is exactly as it should be for a four-year-old child soon to be separated from her mother, from her lifeline.

When I gently tell her that we need to leave, the child turns fully toward me and swiftly slaps my cheek with a crack that echoes in the narrow of my ear canal. I feel a bitter sting in the side of my jaw. It leaves me flushed. It leaves me humiliated and chagrined. There is a deluge of tears about to rupture from my throat. Her mother puffs up her chest with righteous indignation and hubris. Her daughter has simply brought to fruition her mother's secret intentions. Fists in round clenched mounds, the mother, Maria Antonelli, would love to pummel me. On some level I wish she would. Right here, right now, in front of all the security people, in front of my staff who peer out from behind the security of their offices to observe the commotion. They are glad it is happening to me and not them. Everyone shares that thought, and I know it. I have had that same thought a thousand times before, when I have observed someone in the fray, and I bustle past the tortured inhumanity, late for a lunch date or an appointment. It is commonplace. It is the nature of this beast. If the mother decked me, there would be a flurry of commotion, and she could abscond with her babe. In my death wish, I welcome a good bust in the chops. How is it that we get to judge the mothering of this child? Perhaps someone will come and judge me someday.

As Mia succumbs and crawls unwittingly into the grasp of me, her abductor, her arms are outstretched to her mommy. It is as if that gesture, in her child's mind, will miraculously elongate her limbs so that she can wrap herself once again in the warm embrace of her mother. I am on the verge of crying. As I exit the building, she weeps quietly. I walk toward a parked vehicle that will whisk her away to an unknown home, with foreign smells and foreign faces and no mommy. She pulls back her little round mug and cries to me, "My hands smell like Mommy's rosy perfumey. Here, smell my mommy on me. Please give me back to my mommy!" She holds her thick little fingers underneath my nose, and I inhale her four-year-old's scent with a distinct aroma of gardenia. I feel as if I am carrying my shame and ambivalence in my arms. My legs begin to fold underneath my frame, and I head toward a bench underneath the canopy of a linden tree.

I wonder what scent my children carry of me on their tiny fingers, in their hair, on the soft fold of their necks where I nestle my goodbye kisses. I distinctly remember my own mother's smell. I sit Mia on my lap. She has transferred her death grip from her mother's neck to mine. She asks if I will bring her home. She is worn to the bone from her fight. Her flaccid little legs and her ruddy checks are streaked with the soil of her tears and her saliva. I feel the sickness well up inside my body. This is a despicable, cruel component of my work in protecting children. When it is done reactively, it appears self-serving and inhumane. By removing this child from her mother, I decimate a core piece of her tiny being. I hurl her into the thin ether with no mooring. She is like a vessel adrift. Rudderless, she steers herself by the scent of her mother's skin.

I open the curtain for a millisecond on my own horror. What if someone took my child from me? I would be insane with murderous fantasies. It is the one situation in which I believe I could take another's life. I have removed children countless times over the years. This one I cannot do. The intrusive visual of my own children's screaming faces collide with my instinct. My body is gyrating with apprehension and misgiving. I can feel the beads of sweat forming on the back of my neck and behind my knees.

Across the street I spy a young doe emerge from someone's vegetable garden, a splash of green dangling from its mug. I turn Mia's body so that she can see this sight. Her round little frame engages with the scene. She is fearful that a car will hit the deer. She turns her face to mine. It is as if I am levitated by an ethereal, impalpable essence.

I scoop her up in my arms and walk back into the building, where I search for her mother. I can see her in the courtyard, sitting with her eyes closed, facing the sun. Her cheeks appear marbleized from the wetness of her tears. Mia is confused. Arms outstretched once again, she navigates my course directly to her mother. No sound emanates from her mouth. I can feel her heart flapping wildly, like a captured baby bird inside her chest. We are like the force that exists between two electrically charged moving particles. I am at the point of no return. I approach Maria, and as her eyes open, she lets out a yelp. I place her daughter back into her arms. I apologize and tell her I have made a terrible mistake. Before I can complete my lament, she has vanished.

The judge is flapping her arms in her robe as she paces her chambers. She looks like an enormous magpie with a long, sharp beak as she pecks out her admonition. She chastises me for violating an order of the court. She feels that I have been purposefully duplicitous and calculating. I presented a heinous scenario in the morning, and by late afternoon I have overtly violated her order. She spreads her voluminous wing as she gesticulates her displeasure with me. She informs me that she can jail me for contempt.

I stop listening. I feel the panic rise up inside me as I think about being separated from my children. It is not the thought of going to jail; it is what their little minds might do with that information. I begin to hear their pleadings: "Where is my mommy?" What utter despair and horror a child must feel when she does not understand a separation from a parent . . . such an unformed, vulnerable being. I can feel my daughter Olivia's little fingers on my palms. When she is frightened, her hands and feet sweat—a moist, slippery, salty slick envelops her extremities. I never have to ask—the perspiration that seeps from her skin at a time of fear or panic is like a weather front rolling in. Like smelling the first snow, or the suggestion of rain—you can simply feel it.

I bow my head like a child being scolded. When the judge takes off her robe and takes a seat at her desk, I am captured by how delicate her body is. She is petite and almost frail. She is simply a woman. Nonetheless, I have displeased her by pushing against her power and capriciously changing my assessment.

"You are a mother, for God's sake! Of all people, you should know that we must err on the side of caution in protecting children, especially in families where there is incest—indeed, sibling incest!" I feel it best to be silent and listen. She looks at me, waiting for a response. Her eyes look a little cockeyed and maniacal.

She reminds me of my second-grade teacher, the clip of whose high-heeled shoes by my desk sent me into a tailspin of terror.

I have never before violated an order of the court. I did plead this hideous case of sibling sexual abuse to the judge earlier that morning—five children involved in various and sundry sexual liaisons, stopping short of four-year-old Mia. "This mother cannot supervise these children," I professed with much adamancy. Now I have broken my own rule. I could not do it. I could not bear to watch this child lose her mother. I folded. I succumbed. My heart split; my mind cracked open. I watched the deer. She was my guide. I crumbled. I took leave of my senses.

*   *   *   *   *   *   *

When I lost my first pregnancy to a miscarriage, I was alone that afternoon in my bedroom. I watched as the life oozed down my thighs. I held on to my body, trying to put everything back into its nest. It was beyond me. I was mad with sorrow. My body could not hold the life within me. Alone, I lay on the floor of the closet in my bedroom, weeping into a beautiful tailored tweed jacket belonging to my husband. I cried into the lining of the coat. I cried with such depth, I could not hear my sobs. I could smell his hair and the very male scent of his body, faint but distinct. I wept into that jacket the way a child would weep into a blanket or a warm lap. I believed with all my being that I was being punished by God. I believed that he was taking from me all the children that I had so cavalierly taken from every mother over the years. The fact that my body would not host the union that my husband and I had created was proof. The universe would deny me.

As I lay on the floor of the closet that afternoon, I could visualize with such clarity the sheer hatred and contempt that these parents had for me. I could hear the shrill and piercing howl of every child whose spirit I had shattered. I could feel in the hollow of my belly every time I had literally removed one flailing body from another. I could see the eyes of the mother who damned me to hell, cursed my nonexistent child, and wished that each and every one of my children should die a hideous death. And it is with such visceral memory that I can remember the smell of her spit as it splattered across my face and hung in my hair. A scent of cigarette smoke and vomit. As I removed her child from the front door of her home, I saw her bend over in a corner and vomit on the carpet. Such repulsion and rancor I had never before received.

I did not begin to think about the impact of taking a child from his or her parent until, of course, I had my own children. Attachment and separation were merely clinical terms. I am forever haunted by my nonchalance and my ignorance.

It is a sparkly morning in late July. My twin babies are perched in their bouncy seats on the dining room table. Every parent knows that this is forbidden, and every parent I have known tempts fate every now and then with the safety of their children. I am no more than ten feet away from my babies, attempting to brush out my hair and tie it in a twist at the top of my head. I can already smell the heat of the day as it floats through the window screen, and the aroma of cedar from the deck is distinct.

My three-year-old toddles over to the bouncies to greet her six-week-old brother and sister. I watch her as she climbs up on a chair and kisses the toes of each baby. I warn her not to nudge the seats. As if in slow motion, I watch my infant daughter's seat slide off the table and flip in the air before her head, the size of a grapefruit, meets the hard oak floor. I hear her muted howl as my older daughter scampers down, and I scream for my husband. In all the commotion, I remember to move my son's seat from the table and put it on the floor. My breath is lodged in my solar plexus, and I cannot breathe. Holding this tiny infant in my arms, I can see the pink knot as it swells on her head. I find that it is unbelievable how we are able to mobilize our resources when crisis hits.

I wrap her in a blanket and drive her directly to the emergency room. As I find the first nurse, I can hear the panic in my voice as I try to recap this event. She takes the baby from me so that her head can be scanned to see if there is a bleed. I plead to be with my baby, and she consents. As I watch this tiny bundle be swallowed into this cave of machinery, my panic descends and I break out into a drenching sweat. I want to go in there with her. She sleeps throughout, and I am afraid that she is dead. As I begin to crawl onto the table with her, a technician gingerly takes my arm. She leads me out of the imaging room the way someone would escort a crazy person to an asylum. I look at her face blankly. I am in shock.

Sitting alone in the waiting room, I look down at my feet and realize that I never even put on shoes, and I am still in my robe. I am appalled at my appearance. The doctor comes in and explains that my daughter has a hairline fracture. She will need to be monitored for the next forty-eight hours. He asks me to explain the entire chain of events. I can feel the coolness of the tile floor beneath my feet. I smooth my wild hair so that I don't look as crazy as I feel.

As I am retelling my tale, a police officer enters the room. I am waiting for the doctor to tell him that he is in the wrong room. He says nothing. I feel the pace of my heart begin to race. My mind has yet to catch up with my body. As he begins to introduce the officer, I hear an unfamiliar cry emerge from my throat. The officer takes out a pad of paper, and I realize with sudden horror that these two men believe that I intentionally inflicted this fracture to my baby's head. I am speechless. I don't know how to defend my position. I don't know how to impart my honesty. It is not anger or indignation I feel. It is utter fear.

I explain to the officer the same thing that I explained to the doctor. He asks few questions and writes very little down. They both excuse themselves. I am sitting in a sterile medical room, with no shoes on, in my robe. My baby has a fracture in her skull, and they think that I inflicted it. I am alone. I weep.

I have my other baby brought to me that evening. I spend the night in a mostly empty pediatric ward, watching the nurses come in every hour on the hour to check my daughter's pupils. Outside my window is a street that I must drive up and down every day. The summer heat has dried the tips of the zinnias in the garden below. I feel my exhaustion. My body smells of fear.

I pray that night on my hands and knees. I pray that my baby's head will mend and that she will be healthy. Her brother snoozes nearby, and I can see the crown of his beautiful white-blond hair nestled deep in his swaddling blankets. I pray to understand what happened to my children this morning. I want to know why this is here for me, in my life. My pediatrician spends several hours with me. I lay on my left side, my heart side, while he listens to my lament. I should never have put those babies on a table. My older daughter is so angry at me for having those babies. What have I done? He sits at the foot of my makeshift cot as I hammer my being into the ground. I tell him that I feel like all the mothers who have ever risked losing their children. I tell him that I am no different, although I think I am. I can feel the fear electrify my body the same way it did only twelve hours prior. He watches me pad across the cool floor to touch my sleeping children. I know that he worries after my mind.

"Perhaps this happened today so that you can think about your relationship with your children." I interrupt him, as I know that he is being kindly cryptic and that he is also hitting something very deep and something very known. He has watched me grow as a mother with my three-year-old. He has commented before on my protectiveness, my unending worry, and my obsession with safety. He has suggested that the work has compromised my ability to parent—that with this calling come all the trappings of a clinician who has seen far too much and who feels too deeply the pain of others, as if it were her own. He has suggested that the work will indirectly impact my children. I can feel the guilt as if it were present in every cell.

His eyes take in my face. He and I have known each other for years. He is the pediatrician to whom I have sent every fractured child. He has celebrated my devotion and my commitment many times over the years. He gives me a long, loving embrace and assures me that my baby will heal beautifully—as will her mother, he quips.

I do not sleep that night. I will not close my eyes. I listen to each and every tandem breath of those babies. I envision my three-year-old's frightened green eyes as the baby fell in slow motion toward the floor. There is an ache in my heart, and my body startles at the image of that moment.

There is not enough Arsenicum Album to quell my lifelong relationship to fear. A powerful homeopathic remedy that treats like with like, over the years it has been my mainstay. Somewhere in my life, fear crept so deeply into my being that on a cellular level it is, quite simply, who I am.

I see my work with incested children and their families as a sort of homeopathic remedy that will help me become a healthier mother for my children. It does not leave my parenting bereft and stripped; rather, it fills me with appreciation and joy at healing children and families, including my own.

In homeopathy, the symptom is the gem. It is the glistening nugget of gold that the sage homeopath yearns for. It is not so much eradicating the ache of our distressed minds and hearts as it is cultivating the balance of a seeming polarity that brings wisdom, grace, and healing.

CHAPTER 8

On Finding a Voice

At an angle I can see the fullness of this child's face, round and billowing, her cheeks crescent like a harvest moon. Her stocky little body appears robust and healthy. Her shorn tresses are like those of a crazy person, hastily chopped and asymmetrical. Seated behind her, my breath is precariously suspended. I am careful not to disturb her play. I am present to observe. I have spent years as a mindful, heedful servant to these children. My attempts at invisibility are often for naught. They know that I am there to watch them; they know that I am looking for something.

Emma's compact body is thick and sturdy. From behind, she would meld into the mix with her four-year-old peers. It is her erratic paroxysms and her intermittent twiddling that give her away. Busily absorbed, she methodically lays out her dolls side by side. She is preparing a scenario for me. I watch her head jerk spasmodically to the left. She is focused and concentrated, which is an anomaly for Emma. Spikes of oily hair jut from her unkempt scalp. She is clad in faded tan pinwale corduroy coveralls and an uncomely blouse that is too large for her frame. It is terribly soiled around the cuffs. It is winter, and she wears holey canvas shoes with no socks.

According to her parents, Emma lost her capacity for language at around the age of three. She simply stopped talking. Words were replaced by bizarre gestures, and peculiar utterances burst forth from her lips like a bleating sheep, pained yet indifferent. They are convinced that she had a severe reaction to a strep infection and a wildly high fever. It was at that moment that Emma's world grew silent. After this sickness, she was agitated and was unable to be soothed.

The teachers at her school have grown increasingly more agitated at the themes in her play, violent and sexualized. And I, the consummate voyeur, am here once again to watch.

As I sit in my silence, I feel forlorn and desolate. Her little behind sways rhythmically to an internal melody. She is busying herself with the repetitive task of covering and uncovering the three naked dolls. They are a malleable plastic material, pudgy and well nourished for inanimate babies. She inspects the glass eyeballs of each doll, opening and closing them by pinching the bristly lashes.

I have been here before with Emma. I am a master at controlling my breath, as the slightest jarring move will send her spiraling into some unfathomable orbit. She will allow me into this room, but I must situate myself at a safe distance from her body. When I am in a room with Emma, I feel ill at ease and unauthentic. Perched and tentative, I feel the same way I do when I am cooped up with a dog that is unfamiliar to me—a dog that can be quirky and unpredictable. My jaw tightens involuntarily; my spine, straight as a rod, suggests vigilance and preparation for a hasty retreat. My rear end barely touches the chair. Looking down at my feet, I am certain to place them firmly on the ground, as I feel the potential for my foundation to shift and erupt at any moment.

I get heady around Emma. I take a lot of cerebral notes. I do not know where else to go. Her mind is closed off from me, and the only way that I can absorb her is through watching. As I contemplate a shift in my chair, I pick obsessively at my cuticles, gingerly pressing back the skin that has grown over the pale white moons at the base of my nails. Self-manicured, I temporarily forget my purpose and myself. A feral growl jolts my absorption. I look up and Emma ambles toward me. She has the gait of an inebriated clown. I feel my interior respond as my heart picks up speed. In a melodic voice I hear myself say, "Hello."

This is not a child whom you would like to scoop up in your arms and stroke and kiss. This is not a child who invites cooing and enrapture. Captivated by most children, I fawn over and inhale their vernal spirits. With Emma, I am unbowed, with a sheepish revulsion. She does not invite tenderness, although that is exactly what I believe is absent. I think of parenting a child who is unable to attach and bond. I feel a vacancy and despondence. I wonder to myself what type of touch she would respond to, if any.

As she approaches my physical space, I feel my neck recoil, the way a turtle tucks into its shell. I feel the need to protect my face, particularly my eyes. Emma begins to sniff me, first each and every finger. She halts abruptly at the trillion rubies in my wedding band. She stares at them and brings her nose down to my finger to smell the gems. I lapse into the thought of how lovely it would be if diamonds and rubies had a scent. Incongruously, I get a waft of the rank odor of her head. Her stubby little fingers are warm and uncommonly soft. I feel my body begin to melt as I envision myself lifting her into my lap. But I dare not.

She moves swiftly from my hands to my head. She takes strands of my hair and buries her nose in them. I can hear the beating of my heart in my ears. Her eyes tightly shut, lashes fluttering, she is a sight to behold. Through the lucent delicate lid of her musteline-colored eyes, I can almost see the outline of her pupils, fixed and thinking. She begins to nuzzle her nose into my neck, and suddenly she stops, frozen. I can feel her heart against my breast, and she is still. Attempting to muffle my own breathing, I am unsure whether she will sink her teeth into the side of my neak, or whether she smells something that pleases her. She scours my skin until she finds the secret spot where in ritual I dab an essence of exotic flowers every morning. She finds it and rests. I feel her musty breath as she pants underneath the heaviness of my hair. Astonished, I feel her warm little lips seal a soft wispy kiss on my neck.

As always, my resistance to Emma's volatility softens. I have made contact. She turns and heads back to her babies. I rise from my chair and kneel at her side. She slides her body over. I can feel her corduroy brush against my thigh. She methodically begins blanketing her dollies as I narrate her gestures. My sentences and thoughts are edited. I begin to breathe life into these anonymous puppets.

I ask Emma who these babies are. She ignores my questioning. She is ready to tell me something. She lifts up the first doll and rips off the arms and the head. I sit back on my heels, knowing that I must move my physical space. With her right hand, she takes the doll and batters it against the table. Her eyes are closed. Spreading her feet apart, she rocks side to side and she moans. She gazes down at the limbless, faceless torso and throws back her head. Her body goes rigid, and her eyes emit tears without a sound. She places the baby back on the table and covers it. She uncovers the next baby and spreads open the doll's legs. Her tongue unfurls from her mouth like a python as it laps up the interior of the thighs with relish. She turns and faces me square on. She is able to roll her eyes back into their sockets. I instinctually pull my head back. I fear that she will spit fire. The last of her babies she holds closely against her heart. She then methodically unscrews the head and spits down the orifice of the doll's neck. She places the doll's face between her legs and rubs it sensuously against her clothed vaginal area. Her eyes are tightly shut; her lashes flit in a restless fashion. She soothes herself.

I am riveted; the rancid flavor in my mouth feels like death. I am a fish out of water. What is this child telling me? What has she seen? Where has she been? Emma's body is more fluid than I have seen it all morning. She is entranced, yet persistent in her communication. Intermittently she twiddles, moving her fingers rapidly in front of her eyes, as if she is signing to herself. Her frenzied hand gestures seem demonic and wild. Her foot taps incessantly at the floor like a horse's hoof, tapping a groove into the earth.

Emma begins to rub her eyes. She is done with her babies and makes certain that each and every one is covered. She switches off the light and leaves the room. I am invisible again.

The teachers, hungry for answers, attempt to read my face. I tell them I have no thoughts just yet. This is a lie. I have many musings, but my mind and my body need to absorb what it has just observed. Sometimes my thoughts explode into a torrent of feeling, and I am useless. I feel their sense of urgency and disappointment. I feel my own. I am spooked and constrained. Being with Emma is at times like being with a haunted soul.

It is somewhere in the middle of the night. Unable to close my eyes, I quietly let myself out of the front door and stretch my legs out on my porch swing. It is a dry summer night, and I can feel pockets of warm air interspersed with cool air as I sway back and forth. My sheer summer gown is moist between my breasts, where it has absorbed my anxious sweat. The evening sky is milky and twinkles with a canopy of lustrous stars. I make no attempt to locate the constellations. My mind is galloping. I yearn for a cigarette.

I do not know what to do with my thoughts of Emma. They tug at my interior the way that all of my confusion does. It is omnipresent and spills into most of my thoughts. It nudges me to a state of vigilance and consternation. When I closed my eyes to sleep tonight, I could see her crazy fingers dancing in front of her eyes. What is that, and what does it mean to her? It's almost as if she needs to see her fingers move in front of her to validate her existence. She is in pieces like her babies, dismembered, limbless, and faceless. With closed eyes I see body parts float across the sky, Dali-esque and surreal. I think about her sexual gestures to her dolls.

I think about suggestibility and overinterpretation. I feel my terror as it shoots up my spine. I think that Emma has experienced and seen hideous ritualistic sexual violation. My pathos and my horror are wadded up into a clump of timidity and dread. I can only use my own fragile interior to navigate hers. Emma's being has been witness and subject to the unutterable, her words singed off her tongue. Someone, somewhere has pissed on this child's soul. Something or some hideous being has extinguished her spirit. It is a thought too painful to let in. I sway in that swing until the sky turns tangerine.

With trepidation I walk up the front steps of the house the next day. My head is logy and pounding, as if my body is trying to shed the toxins of post inebriation. The sun scalds my sleepless eyes; fear turns my legs into jelly.

The house is rundown; a piece of gutter dangles from the roof. The curtains are drawn tight. There is an enormous pale blue lilac whose scent is sickeningly sweet. I marvel at the strength of the lilac. No matter how, no matter where, these gorgeous bushes will thrive despite dryness or lack of sustenance. It is a sign I muse upon. There is a BEWARE OF DOG warning at the front door. I think of turning around and getting back in my car. I think of the moment in time when one decides to move forward into the unknown, trusting that somehow, somewhere there is an angel with a wing thrown over one's shoulder, offering protection from all that is evil. I think of my naiveté.

Trying to soothe my mind, I pray to God for safety and protection. I pray that someone doesn't blow my face off, like Emma's doll. I ring the bell.

All I see is a flash and floating particles of light when the door opens. Stepping backward, I miss the bottom step. Losing my balance, I fall backward. I am swift to cover my exposed thighs and lacy panties under my sundress. I want to cry. Emma's father stands at the entrance with an enormous drooling Doberman, counting the seconds before he can rip out the Polaroid. I am speechless.

Nonplussed, I obsequiously extend my hand to greet this schmuck. He is a bit older than I had imagined, with a crinkly face and a pronounced nose; he is small and stocky. Cigarette smoke wafts through the front door. His pelvis protrudes, and I can see the outline of his penis though the thin fabric of his trousers. He tells me that he must photograph and document every person who comes through his door. He can catalogue his solicitors. Barely taking in his rambling, I am able to string together that I have come to talk with him about his daughter, Emma. Camera in hand, he invites me in.

I am sure that I will die. I am more than sure that he is crazy. I keep myself situated in the entryway. I present in detail what I have observed with his daughter. He explains that he has a pending lawsuit with the child's pediatrician for missing the telltale signs of a fairly common strep infection. He believes that her prolonged high fever of 104 degrees Fahrenheit made her crazy. I listen. They are firm believers in nudity, and he is sure that Emma is quite comfortable with their practices. He asks me if I would like to see her room or would like a tour of his home.

As I peer in the front door, I see that the house is spartan and orderly. A wall of smoke hangs in the entryway, creating an ocherous hue. He and his wife occupy the basement, and Emma and her sister live upstairs. I decline a tour of this hellhole, leaving him my card and a time to meet with me in my office. He assures me that Emma is fine. He tells me that he is working on a very sensitive biomedical project. "Top secret."

"Hmmm," I say. I cannot conjure a speedier exit.

The Doberman is pacing in the doorway. He approaches me and juts his sleek snout into my crotch. Emma's father watches as I try to maneuver my groin away from the dog's nose. In an instant I can visualize the dog lapping away at Emma's vagina, with the father looking on. "He just loves women," he says with a leering smile. Excusing myself swiftly, I hear the click of the camera and feel the flash of light at my posterior like some perverse X ray that sees every contour and nuance of my body.

He disappears into his house, and I think that he will masturbate to the tune of my fear and humiliation, to my sundress twisted around my waist and my exposed panties. In the car, I lift my dress up so that I can see what it was that he saw. Shamed and enraged, I sit by the side of the road and cry.

Eclipsed by a sense of disgrace, my emotions feel momentarily stifled and disconnected. Instead of anger, I feel dishonored and exposed. I cannot even formulate my thoughts, much less speak them. My integrity and my humility have been violated. I have only my indignation to spur me. I do know this: Emma will become an obsession of sorts. She will become my mission. Over the years, she will be a child I will visit and revisit. I will watch her grow and evolve, like a damaged, unruly weed that tenaciously ruptures the barren earth without water or sunlight. Despite the seasonal poisoning and uprooting, she will not die. She will stay with me until I find her, years later, a child with the clarity of a shaman.

It is at times when I feel that I have nothing that the gem lies in the palm of my hand. I can only surmise that Emma's disability came at a primitive age of fragility and vulnerability. Something or someone came along and shocked her tender being, leaving her dazed and stupefied, without discourse or speech. Inside her little person lives a loving heart and a lyrical soul—waiting, waiting patiently, to be unfettered and unmuzzled. I could hear the song inside of her. I would try to be her voice.

In the half hour I spent with Emma's father that day, he unknowingly gave me the key. He awakened a piece of rage in me. It would feed a boundless reserve of passion and indignation. I tucked my newfound knowledge away in my pocket for years, until the time came when I could begin to unleash her from her demons.

*   *   *   *   *   *   *

When Meredith McConnaughay asked her daughter, Eva, what she wanted for Christmas, she signed, spelling out d-i-l-d-o. Meredith asked again, sure that this was simply a mistake. Eva signed it again. Meredith's fingers nervously twirl the crucifix around her ivory neck. Tears swallow the verdant patina of her kohl-etched eyes. Hearing her story, I move my chair closer to her. Her contained hysteria makes my chest hurt. Her body is heaving, punctuated by apologies. I feel myself tear up. I hate when this happens. I pinch the palm of my left hand. The tears evaporate. I did this as a kid. I would pinch myself really hard if I needed to reroute a thought or emotion in my head.

Meredith is a striking woman, impeccably dressed, with a shock of auburn hair and skin the color of cream. Her long, slender legs are twisted like a vine. Her hands cover her face, exposing an emerald-cut sapphire the size of a sugar cube. Her nails are bitten to the quick, and her lavender veins swell off her hands like a slender mountain range on a relief map.

Wiping her streaked face and her very flushed nose, she attempts to explain her daughter's diagnosis of pervasive developmental disorder—similar to autism. Emma comes to mind. This past summer, Eva mysteriously stopped talking. Although her language was somewhat delayed, she has been able to string together words enough to express her needs and wants. But a few months ago, out of nowhere, her words vanished. She seemed to regress and draw into herself more than ever. Though Eva had been completely potty trained at an early age, of late she has been urinating and defecating in her panties, and hiding them around the house—the last pair was found in the pantry. Meredith pauses before she continues. She must be reading something familiar on my face that she reads with others—horror, sympathy, and dissonance.

Eva is implicating her teacher at Sunday school. She told her mother that he loves her and that she is his girlfriend. She can describe oral sex. She can describe a grown man's penis in her mouth, only she refers to it as a "prick." I listen intently. She cries again. She is articulate and passionate. Her anger begins to whip around my little cubicle as if one could see it. It slams against the cinder block like a wasp trying to escape. Eva sticks her finger into her anus and licks it. I cannot see Meredith's face at this point. It is practically in her lap. I find myself captured by her. Her anger seems to burble right under the surface. She is a warrior. She fights for the rights of her daughter. This is clear.

She asks me if she looks like a wreck. There is a juncture of tenderness. I tell her that she is lovely and has every right to look like a wreck. She lets out a little-girl giggle whose transience dissolves quickly to tears. It is when she asks me if I can help her daughter that my sentence gets wedged in my throat. I explain a bit about Emma. That I have been suspended for years watching a three-year-old who is now an adolescent, who I believe has been hideously violated. I explain the difficulty in children who have no words. I tell her it is like pushing a river. I try to explain the difficulty in prosecuting cases such as these. She is an environmental attorney by trade, and her expression is at first vacant. Her pupils dart from my mouth back to my eyes. They are intent and probing, almost eerie, and will not leave my face.

Meredith McConnaughay can read a face. She can decipher something that I cannot. She closes her eyes. I can see the gentle flutter of her lashes. The tears seep from under her eyelids like the juice out of an orange, as if they will never end. I give her my word that I will advocate for her daughter.

When she exits my office, I close my door so that I can hear my thoughts. I have failed so far with Emma. I have found no one to listen to my concerns. I pick off the dead leaves of the dracaena that has found its home in my office for the last six years. Neglected, it sits over an air vent, which fries its roots in the winter and freezes them in the summer. I feed it the dregs of my herbal tea every morning. It refuses to do anything but grow, always giving forth a new shoot or unfurling a new leaf. It is determined and persistent, and I would be devastated if it withered. It reminds me of my own self-neglect, and it reminds me of my doggedness.

The day of Eva's interview, I decide at the eleventh hour to bow out of the actual interview. I feel fragile. I want to watch. I am certain that I will learn something. In truth, I cannot bear to fail another child without a voice.

I am sitting behind a two-way mirror when Eva McConnaughay is brought into the interviewing room. When I see her, my eyes betray my response. I feel myself breathe in deeply and hold onto my breath. If an imaginary set of hands could cover my gaping mouth, they would. Roosting on the side of her head like a plume is a beautiful periwinkle satin bow. Similar to the bows worn by Shirley Temple, it is a feminine adornment that serves to detract from her severely compromising disorder. Her hair is the color of rich molasses, hanging down in ringlets to the middle of her back. She is clad in a little navy jumper and tights. Her femininity is startling. She is a truly beautiful child. Her eyes are the color of her mother's, a sage green, and she has a tiny pixie nose and a sensuous full mouth. She paces the room like a bound animal. She flicks the light switch on and off. She moves from the door to the window and back again. What is most evident is that Eva's mouth is agape at all times. She reminds one of a baby chick awaiting a droplet of water or a crumb of food. Her breathing is loud and labored. She is moving at all times. She does not engage the interviewer but hears and comprehends everything that is said.

Sitting behind the mirror, I feel hot and confined. There are teachers and translators with expertise with children like Eva, translating her behaviors. They understand the stress that this child is under. I am thinking about Meredith. I feel a deep sense of appreciation for this mother. There is something strangely burlesque about viewing this. I feel an urgency to leave. I keep myself in my place. I made a commitment to this mother.

Eva cannot sit for more than a minute. She clutches a little stuffed unicorn with long pinkish fur. The unicorn, a fabled creature symbolic of virginity. When she is asked about being touched, her unique form of signing is interpreted by her teacher. Before she signs, she places her forearm up to her elbow, over her eyes. She signs with her right hand and taps with her entire left hand on the table. Intermittently, she twiddles in front of her eyes, the way Emma did. When I watch her twiddle, I begin to cry. It is unbearable.

The amount of adrenaline coursing through these two rooms, between the mirror and Eva, could rock the foundation of the building. I can smell the agitation. I can smell the sweat leaching out through people's skin. I can smell the fear on my own tongue. I can see Eva's anxiety as she is gently questioned.

She signs p-u-s-s-y, gently covering her vaginal area. Six years old, with a pert satin bow and eyes the color of a green ribbon of ocean. My head is in my hands as I listen to the interviewer utter the word and ask her what it means. I think of every child with words and the capacity for expression, and I am seared by what we will never know about this child. In the room where I am sitting, I can hear my mantra over and over again—"Oh my God! What has happened to this baby?"

After close to an hour, Eva is taken out of the room for a break. She has opened and closed the window shades at least fifteen times. She has paced and grunted. She has sat and stood. She has twiddled and spun in a circle. Watching her at times, I feel like a dolt. I feel as if her frustration is at our stupidity, certainly not at her own. She is clear. She knows what happened. She needs us to listen. She needs us to understand. She needs, most desperately, to be believed.

Before she leaves the room, she gallops up to the two-way mirror and gazes at herself in the glass. I bring my nose right up to the cool glass. Though she is just gazing into the mirror, it seems she actually looks directly in my eyes and pauses for what feels like an eternity for this child. I know she cannot see me. I see something in the eyes of Eva McConnaughay that I have seen in Emma. It is not so much a vacancy as it is a deep longing. She rolls her eyes up into their sockets and flutters her lids, as if the stimulus is overwhelming. Her interpreter takes her hand and gently leads her out of the room for a snack.

This child is able to describe sexual events that any other six-year-old could not. In a small, private Sunday school in another state, she describes being taken to use the bathroom by her teacher while all her other schoolmates are lolling at the ocean's edge during a Sunday outing. She describes having "sex." Again, she tells the world that he loves her. He will love her always. It is his job to help her into a fresh set of clothes.

As she signs and it is translated, I see in my mind's eye the opportunity that an adult would have with this little girl. I think of her lanky, pristine, little-girl body, the smoothness of her skin, the texture of her feathery tresses. She is perfect prey—she cannot speak, no one would believe her.

After some feeble excuse, I leave the room. I cannot watch. I leave the building so that I can smell the air. I walk laps around the courtyard. I feel like Eva as she spins in circles. I walk so that I know that I am there. I need to know that I am in the world. I hear the traffic and feel the sun as it warms the top of my head. I can smell my hair. I know that I am here, somewhere.

Days later, after locating the teacher in another state, he is brought to Colorado for an interview. I watch the police interview of Eva's Sunday school teacher. Again, I watch behind a mirror. I am tipped back on a chair with my bare feet holding up the wall. The muscles behind my eyes feel swollen, and the small of my back feels as if it will give way. My exhaustion has me somewhat giddy. Thankfully, I am alone.

When Nathan Nelgrace is brought into the room, he is noticeably agitated. I find that my eyes go directly to his penis, then to his hands, and finally stop at his mouth. I envision him unzipping his pants and stroking his erect penis as he changes Eva into a fresh set of clothes. The thought rockets from my mind the moment I feel my body register her fear. The moment I see that child's face in my mind's eye, her gaping mouth and the thick, erect penis, I fold. At that instant, my anxiety surges up through my chest and I whip around, thinking that someone is in the room with me. I am alone. I move my chair so that the back of my head does not square with the door. My hideous paranoia clings like skin to my thoughts. I fear, alone in that stuffy, tiny crypt, that someone is going to come in and blow the back of my head off.

I can articulate his denial because the script is so etched in my brain. I listen to him talk about his work with the church, in particular special-needs populations, for over twenty years, his commitment and his compassion. I hear him pontificate on the need to advocate for and better represent vulnerable populations. I see the rings of sweat soak the fabric of his shirt underneath his armpits. As he speaks, his eyes move from his hands to the floor. I notice his wedding band. He never mentions Eva's name. He righteously wants to know who could do such a thing to a child. He has no idea on earth why this child would implicate him. There is always another person present when he has charge of a young girl. His mouth is parched as he reaches for water. His hands shake as he begins to pour. Kindly, the detective does not skip a beat—he pretends he does not notice a thing.

I think of Eva's statement that he loves her, that she is his girl-friend. Again, I find my head in my hands. I see her naked loins as he changes her clothing, slipping on her panties, and touching the creases of her labia. I am sick.

As with Emma, my plea fell on deaf ears. I knew the day I watched Eva and the day I watched her teacher's interview her that they would not prosecute the case. I could hear the lament. I went anyway. I presented the case with all that I had seen and heard and felt.

I am sitting at a long oval conference table as attorneys, advocates, and social workers file into the room. I have Eva's file in front of me. I am flipping though the pages so that I don't have to make small talk. The detective and I present what I believe to be a tight, detailed case. I taste my conviction and defensiveness. I feel my self-neglect and my doggedness. I am weary.

As I present the evidence in the case and how convincing I believed Eva's disclosure to be, I look around the room. A woman sitting at the table has her eyes closed. She is napping. Others are nodding in agreement, with compassion and concern. A young man is looking at his watch. I feel myself losing the battle. I wonder how it would feel to my client if I took a snooze during a treatment session. The woman opens her eyes; they are bloody around the rims. I wonder if she is a survivor of incest. Had I been one, I would probably drift off as well.

I try to woo them. I know how to compel people. I sprinkle every sexual detail that I can muster. I sketch my portrait of Eva the same way that I had done with Emma. I bow, I scrape, and I grovel. Then I hear the words that feel as if a yellow jacket has landed a hard sting to my cheek—the sting that I cannot bear to deliver to the mother of Eva.

"She will not be a credible witness. We cannot put her up on the stand. There are problems with the unique way in which this child signs. It is not a traditional signing technique. The research is troubling. What if her interpreter is skewing or distorting the information? What if the interpreter is also a survivor? How do her issues come into play? The defense will have a heyday with this."

I rise from my chair in midsentence and collect my case file. My abruptness slows down everyone's speech. I stand at the head of the table and thank them for their time. If one more person tells me why we can't prosecute this case, I think I will wretch. One woman says, "This sounds like a really hard case, Holly." I nod.

As I exit, I tap the shoulder of the woman who couldn't keep her eyes open. I get very close to her ear and whisper, "How was your nap?" I never look back.

I have parked several blocks from the meeting place. I walk through an alley of hyacinth-blue hibiscus trees in full blossom. I pull back a bloom and look into its crimson center. Merged, they are the color of Eva's satiny bow. I think about the lady who said that this must be hard. I think that I cannot do this anymore. I cannot continue to advocate for children without justice. I cannot look one more Meredith McConnaughay in the eye and promise that I will fight for her daughter.

My heart aches. I slip off my sandals and walk across the sumptuous front yard of a sprawling Victorian. Every blade of grass is the same size, as if a devoted manicurist snipped each blade in uniform perfection. As my feet wade through the velvety green, I see my footprints in the grass. Sometimes the universe takes better care of its lawns than its children.

*   *   *   *   *   *   *

"C-o-c-c-c-k s-u-u-u-c-c-k!" Emma bellows. "N-o-o c-o-c-c-c-k s-u-u-u-c-c-k in nina!" There is utter pandemonium, and they have cleared out the classroom. The teachers, paraprofessionals, and social workers are all clamoring at once, and I cannot calm them. When Emma got to school this morning, she was stark naked under her coat. She proceeded to wrap herself in blue crepe paper, like a mummy. She taped her own mouth. She grabbed at the teachers' breasts and rubbed her vagina. She stuck her finger inside of her vagina and she smelled it.

We interview her at school. By then she has been dressed. She is sixteen. She sits at a table with hundreds of sheets of blank paper and she paints. She paints all day without a pause. She draws penises, vaginas, scrotums, and breasts. They are her mother and her father and a man named Todd. "Cock suck!" she screams.

I am watching her. Her teachers are soothing her. At sixteen, she is terribly overweight and unkempt. She still has the round full face and the oily hair. It is still Emma. I have a law enforcement officer brought to the school. Emma is flipping through drawings at an ungodly pace. All the same. Genitalia. Amazing paintings, detailed.

Over the years, this has been her vehicle of communication. She paints. All the paintings are sexual. Her medium is brightly colored poster paint—blue, red, and green, with blue being her favorite color. All of the paintings involve her father, her mother, and a man named Todd. She is sitting with me, and although she knows my face, she is frightened.

As she fades from frenzy to exhaustion, she grabs my wrist. Holding on to it as if I were the last being on earth, she grasps with the right and paints with the left.

Her painting is a big heart. Inside the heart are two eyes, a nose, and a mouth. The mouth is frowning, and she draws tears flowing down the cheeks of the heart. She lifts both her feet and plants them in my lap. I am frightened that she will kick me. She pulls back her toes to show me the picture of the crying heart she has drawn on the soles of her feet. "Sad soul!" she cries. "Sad soul!"

My sorrow and my woe are overwhelming. I feel the bands of muscle around my chest contract. I look at her with such sadness and I start to cry. "Sad soul," she says to me. "Sad soul," I reply. It is a muted whisper.

I remember her smelling my hair when she was four. I remember her kiss. My eyes take in the moon shape of her face, streaming with tears. She turns away. At this juncture, I am cognizant of what I must do to deliver Emma to her sanctum. As I relate the story of the last twelve years to the judge, my mind quietly leaves my body. It's as if there is nobody at home.

The jingle of the phone in the middle of the night portends death. It always has, somewhere in my mind. My heart settles as I hear the familiar voice of the on-call worker on the end of the wire. In my haze I can hear the din of a police station. She has a four-year-old child who has disclosed sexual abuse by her daddy. He rubs his bare penis against her belly to make it erect. She gives me the child's name, which is unfamiliar. I walk her through the protocol. "If the mother is protective, suspend contact with the father and I will take care of it on Monday." She apologizes over and over again for waking me. I tell her that I am sorry that she is with a cop at one o'clock in the morning on a Saturday night, dealing with incest.

"Don't forget to look at the moon before you sleep tonight— it's stunning! It looks like a huge, pregnant belly suspended on black velvet!" I want to leave her with a lovely thought. We hang up, and I know that the next few hours are a wash until I can tire my mind again. The name of the child has evaporated from my memory.

I am out in my flower garden at six in the morning, stroking all my beautiful lilies as they open their long, throaty petals to the morning light. I am soaking the earth with water, fully aware that the heat of this summer morning bodes a scorching day. With the night's intrusion tucked deep in a recess, I load up my children and their shiny red wagon and head to Teller Farm for a walk.

Teller Farm is an expanse of acreage that meanders and twists around streams and enormous cottonwoods. My eyes take in

Longs Peak and the majesty of the Continental Divide. The tips of the peaks are frosted in white. I put my babies in the wagon as we begin our search for the great blue heron. He is always tucked among the grasses by a shady stream whose bed is carpeted with emerald green moss.

We round a lovely bend to my favorite wall of lilac trees in full bloom. It is an enormous cresting wave of colors—cobalt, jouvence, and mulberry. The last hedge hangs down in an arch, its branches laden with sensual puffs of periwinkle blooms whose scent dizzies one's senses. As the wagon pauses under the canopy of violet, my son's little arm reaches high enough to pluck off a blossom. Scurrying out of the wagon, he presents me with his treasure. Unable to secure the flowers in my own hair, we tuck it in the hair tie of his sister's blond ringlets. She giggles with glee as she puts her tiny hand to her head to touch this bobbing blossom. Back in the wagon, we head toward a maze of cornfields to cut across the farmland. Gazing back, I scan their faces, trying in vain to keep them somewhat shaded. The plume on my daughter's head rocks rhythmically as we cross the gravelly terrain.

I look back at my children again. I am suddenly overcome. I am gripped as my breath quickens and my palms begin a profuse sweat. A familiar yet foreboding tingle permeates my entire torso, settling into my stomach. I begin a descent into panic as my vision begins to blur and the blood courses up from my neck, slamming against the inside of my head. I pull the wagon over into the shade and put my head between my thighs so that I will not vomit or faint. I take air in and out of my body, hoping it will quell my fear. I feel my daughter's hand on my back. I am drenched in sweat. I look up to tell her that Mommy doesn't feel well. As I lift my head, my angst consumes me as I watch my fingers tuck the loose strands of her hair behind her ears.

It is the sprig of lilac in her hair and her cascading ringlets that rocket my memory. The sprig of lilac has awakened the visual of the satin bow in Eva McConnaughay's hair. My body remembers before my mind. It has been so many years. I pull my daughter into my lap while my son discovers a ladybug on a nearby blade of grass. As I let my eyes settle on the blossom, I remember the name of the child from the night before. I feel as if it was always there. The moment the worker told me, I stopped listening. Nelgrace. Rachel Nelgrace. An unusual name; I would not have forgotten it. Nathan Nelgrace must have had a child. I compute quickly in my head that it has been almost six years. Astounded by my epiphany, I feel fleeting elation eclipsed by sadness.

*   *   *   *   *   *   *

Susan's office is like a womb. It is in the attic of a historic mansion in Boulder. It has a small crescent window that faces the east. The west-facing window makes me feel as if my fingertips could touch the Flatirons. There is always a small vase full of delicate tea roses, housed on a Tibetan prayer table. It makes me want to kneel in reverence. There is a Turkish rug on the floor whose primitive design is etched in a tiny corner of my brain. There are flecks of crimson in the weave that I always mistake for blood. My heart bleeds in this room.

Her office is situated on the fourth floor, and there are times when I feel that I will fall to my knees at the building's arched entrance and crawl like a baby up each step, waiting to catch my breath at each landing. It is at times like those that I dread the ascent—my mind and my heart resist opening. Other times, in jubilance, I fly up those steps, taking two at a time, intoxicated by a glimmer of epiphany or self-awareness that may liberate me.

I am lying on her couch, with a soft velvet pillow over my face. I do that when I am ashamed of a feeling or fearful of a judgment that is always a fantasy far worse than reality will ever bear.

I fell in love with her healing hand a long time ago. I fell in love with her grace and her compassion. I fell in love with the fact that I could tell her every secret there was to tell about me. I always expected to feel shame; instead, I felt acceptance and understanding.

"I am having the same dream. It is the telephone dream. I am at a phone. I am dialing home and I can't remember the number, and once I get the connection, no one can hear me. I am screaming into the phone, and there is nothing but dead air. I have no voice. I am not being heard." She is silent.

I rise and move toward the window. I feel like Emma and Eva. I want to twiddle. I want to rock. I want to repeatedly open and close the window shades. "Emma's father was never prosecuted. Eva's teacher walked away. They refused to reopen her case because she does not have language. I am trying to let go. I did the best that I could do, but I am enraged."

I lie back down on the couch and put the pillow over my face again. I feel crazy. I wonder why this won't go away. Someone told me a long time ago that there will be children like this. There will be times when I will leave an interview and know that a child is being sexually violated, and there will be nothing I can do. It will gnaw at me. It will infiltrate my dreams. It will split my heart asunder. I will have to walk away. She looks at her clock.

On my descent down my four flights, something in me feels lifted. As I push open the doors to the air, the fragrances of spring hit my skin, and I realize that I need to be done. Perhaps it is simply saying out loud what aches. Perhaps for Emma and Eva, knowing that they tried to tell is sufficient. I want them to know that I heard, yet on some level this is more for me than it is for them. And I realize that sometimes I am just a vehicle, a conduit for the utterance to move from the child to the universe. And I need to sit with that, and it needs simply to be okay. For now, I have done all that I can do.

9
CHAPTER

Falling from Grace

Lena is curled up in a chair in the corner of my office looking like a discontented pussycat. She is too plump to demurely coil her body in the chair. Her taut legs are tentatively tucked under her body, periodically slipping off the chair. As long as I have known her, Lena has unsuccessfully attempted to pour her zaftig body into a size five. My eyes are fastened to the gapping crevice between the third and fourth buttons of her dress. Her breasts pull so tightly, I fear that they will launch a button directly across the room, and what an embarrassment we would have then.

As it stands, neither of us has ever been so leary of the other before. She nervously pops out one of her contacts because her eye is irritated. As she focuses in my direction, one eye is blue and the other is green. I tilt my vision and fix my gaze on the blue eye. That is the true color of Lena's eyes. Nervously, she brushes a few strands of salt-and-pepper hair from her brow.

I have always been aware that I can become enamored with people without truly knowing them. There is usually some aspect of a person that captivates and lures me—I float blindly into some web, fighting my instinct, seduced by all that is irreverent and unhallowed. This is true of Lena. Over the years she has worked with me, I have fallen for her loyalty and her devotion. I have been awed at her perseverance and envious of her undying love for her family. Her laughter is lithe yet devious. When she opens her mouth to laugh, I think of my grandmother. They are missing the same back tooth on the right side. I am intrigued with the tattoo of the serpent that coils around her left ankle. At the age of forty-nine, she is an accomplished social worker, with a lengthy list of accolades attached to her name. This chameleon-eyed woman has ensnared and bewitched me. I have been under her spell. I am soon to be awakened.

As we sit in awkward silence together, we are joined by the unspeakable. At this moment, it would be my preference, as I believe it would be hers, to vanish in the air like a quick puff of smoke. Lena fidgets, methodically peeling the ruby lacquer off her nails. She will not meet my gaze.

Earlier this morning, an investigator for the Department popped through my door unannounced. One thing I know for certain—this is not good news. She asks me what I know about the child care arrangement for Lena's granddaughter. Questions are fired off in rapid succession. I want to stop her, fully aware that one of Lena's co-workers is sitting directly across from me in my office and is privy to this inquiry, which is leading somewhere unpleasant. She seems unaware and not the least bit concerned. Her perfect auburn ponytail, fastened by a black velvet bow, is pulled so tightly that her eyes are stretched to the side of her head. Her ice-blue eyes query me over bifocals perched on the tip of her nose and held in place by sheer magic. She asks me if I have any idea why Lena would have her granddaughter in day care with the department covering the expense. "It has to be a mistake, some sort of mix-up," I reply. My retort must sound so confident and assured that she is skeptical, and I quickly surmise that she questions my role as a potential co-conspirator of sorts.

On my way to the Child and Family Advocacy Center, I am trying to read the intake report at the stoplights. I am a master at reading as I drive from one meeting to the next. I dare myself. I have yet to rear-end anyone. I can peruse an incest report minutes before I walk into the room with a child. Today, I have lost my footing. I am distracted. I am disturbed by her inquiry. I do not believe that Lena would be capable of bilking the department. In my twenty-year history at the department, this has never happened. I assure myself that it is an innocent error. Not Lena. Not wonderful, perfect, unassuming Lena. My denial drops down like a weighty velvet theater curtain; not a pinhole of light streams through. My mind is closed.

I am perusing a report about an eleven-year-old girl whose stepfather gets off on fondling her breasts each and every morning before she leaves for school. It is a feeling of knowing that something unique and remarkable has pierced your psyche, yet the demands of the day sweep you along in a current that flows in only one direction. There is no turning back.

Behind the two-way mirrors, I am putting a tape inside the VCR to record my interview. The room is pitch black, and I am precariously perched atop a chair to insert the tape. As I turn to face the mirror, I am nose to nose with Elizabeth Ross, my eleven-year-old interviewee, who is preening in front of the glass. I back up instantly, fearful that she will see me. She is gesturing in front of the mirror. I sit down on the desk and drink her in. She is meticulously examining a microscopic skin eruption in the undulating divot of her chin. Her face is several inches from the glass. I am poised on the edge of the desk, knowing that she is waiting for me. She is enchanting in an ethereal type of way. There is not a single crease on her skin. Her face is embryonic— fine and unformed. Her skin is translucent, like rice paper. You can actually see the intricate map of violet veins underneath her skin. The lids of her eyes look like the rib of an insect's wing. Her flaxen hair reaches the small of her back. The ends look as if they have been dipped in white paint. As I am appreciating her pristine youth, my fingers find their way across my aging worry lines, burrowed deep in the crevices of my forehead. When I look at this lovely eleven-year-old, I feel crinkly and depleted. I feel conspicuous around preteens, as if my maternal uncoolness will be an immediate deterrent. Elizabeth contains the complicated admixture of surface vulnerability coupled with a sense of power and bravado, which to me seems a contradiction.

I slide off the edge of the desk and enter the room. I switch gears as rapidly as one moves from fifth into overdrive. She sizes me up, and I feel self-conscious. I want to bare my pearly whites and ask her if I have spinach in between my teeth, just to break the tension and quell the hysteria that is seeping out my ears—a hysteria that comes of my newfound knowledge of Lena, in addition to Elizabeth's revelations.

I reel in this impulse. In exchange, I simply introduce myself. She asks me if I am Greek "or something." Her question is attached to her commentary on my hair and the olive color of my skin. "Italian and Jewish," I say. She says that she has always wanted to have really dark skin. She says she hates her "whiteness." She describes herself as "ghostly." I tell her that I have always longed for straight blond hair, and instead I ended up with this wild dark mane. She laughs. I have passed the test so far. It is hit-and-miss. Elizabeth's body begins to settle as she gracefully loops her legs, Indian-style, on the large, overstuffed couch. Her gams tuck neatly, without effort. Lena wafts across my mind's eye. Elizabeth wears the signature layered look of many young girls. She is wearing at least four layers of clothing on the top part of her body. It looks like a camisole, a T-shirt, a sweatshirt, and then a light jacket. This is not an unfamiliar uniform for preadolescent survivors.

Elizabeth informs me that for the past six months, prior to hopping on the bus for school, her stepfather rouses her from sleep by lifting her bedsheets and fondling her breasts. She feigns sleep and often wears a sweatshirt to bed in an attempt to ward off his touch. It is to no avail. His monologue is always the same; "I love you. You are my little slut." She is terrified of this man and is fearful that she will urinate in the bed when she hears her bedroom door open in the morning. Her mother is often asleep. In the last few weeks, his ritual has progressed. He will stand over her bed with an erect penis and masturbate, ejaculating on her breasts. He forbids her to wash off the ejaculate before she goes to school. He tells her he wants her to wear it. This morning after she got to school she went directly into the girls' bathroom, dampened a paper towel, and slid into a stall to wash off her breasts. As she was doing this she began to vomit, and a teacher came in to help her, thinking she was ill.

As she is talking to me, I watch her anxiously slide her hands up inside the sleeves of her jacket. She makes little claws out of her fists and tucks them up inside her sleeve. It reminds me of the little mitts they put on my babies in the neonatal unit, so they would not scratch themselves. Her feet roll out from beneath her and she begins to knock her knees together. I have lost all visual contact with her. Her knees are flapping wildly and her arms look like flippers inside the sleeves of her jacket.

As I am formulating my next question, I notice that there is a stream of moisture rolling down her chest. She is crying without a sound. I assume that she has mastered this feat during her stepfather's visits. I break my rule of not touching children I am interviewing. I scoot my chair directly across from her and place my hand on her arm. Ever so quietly, as if in slow motion, she gently places her head in my lap and begins to heave, again without sound. I have never seen this. I am speechless. I stroke her silky locks away from her face. As I do this, I motion to the cop behind the two-way mirror to stop the tape.

I cannot bear to have people see this; to have people gawk at her pain, to be aroused by the salacious detail of her disclosure. I myself cannot bear being observed. I am fearful that I will fall into a heap, covering her body with my own. We will meld. The warmth of her tears is damp on my stockings. She is a deluge of tears. A veritable floodgate has been flung open, right in my lap.

I wrap a wing around her. As I stroke her head, I practice saying nothing. I believe I need a lap. I desperately want to deconstruct. This child is shattered. I find that I do not know what to do next. This is not an unfamiliar place for me to arrive at. There are times when I hear the graphic detail of a child's abuse and am absolutely nonplussed. I am unable to formulate any retort whatsoever. I become somewhat mute. I am paralyzed by my own ineptitude. I sit absolutely still without moving. I look down at the profile of her face. Her unblinking eyes are in a trance. Her breathing is steady. Her fingers grip the outer thigh of my right leg. I pet her like I would a dog that had come to rest his head on my lap. My mind reaches out to Lena. My denial snaps shut on my thoughts. I reroute myself.

Ms. Ross, Elizabeth's mother, is sitting at the kitchen table with an advocate. Her index finger methodically traces the rim of her teacup. She has enormous black eyes. The rims look like they have been bleeding. They look tender to the touch. I lock my gaze with hers and recite in detail each nuance of her daughter's disclosure. I enunciate the sexual detail. I wrap my tongue around those words, hoping to galvanize her, to startle her out of her seemingly hypnotic affect. I detest my insensitivity and my cruelty. I want to jolt her. I want to slap her with my newfound knowledge.

I want to rouse her. She has been sleeping. As I am speaking the words that any parent would shudder at hearing, she lowers her head, like a sack of marbles, into the palms of her hands. I watch a small artery pulsing rapidly on the side of her neck. I am thinking about what it would be like to amplify the sound of the blood, hissing and slamming through that vein. I rest my hand on her shoulder. She lifts her head and looks directly at me. I am prepping myself for the classic lament of denial. Instead, she says something that I am totally unprepared for. Her eyes look maniacal. The pupils are as large as black olives. "Where have I been?" This is clearly a rhetorical question. She slowly enunciates her lament like a prayer or a mantra.

"Where have I been?"

"Where do you think you have been?" I ask. I never hear her answer. I have nothing to say to this woman. Her absence is unforgivable.

My emotional absence is equally appalling. I left the moment this child's head found its home in my lap. The actual physical touch of her warm, heavy mind on my knees is more than I can bear. When I come skin to skin with a child, sometimes I am unsure of where they leave off and I begin. Oftentimes, I focus on the crescent-shaped moons on my fingernails to find my way home. These are my hands; these are my uneven nails and ragged cuticles. These hands are rowed by a stack of Burmese rubies and diamonds that are mine; looking at these sparkling jewels, I see the circles of my marriage, the honor of my three babies signified by three blood-red rubies, ten tiny sparkling gems to signify ten tumultuous years. These hands belong to me. I desperately need to come home to myself.

As I am gathering my belongings, Elizabeth summons me to ask me a question in confidence. She is still in the interviewing room and is exhaling her sweet breath on the mirror, writing her name in script. She dots the *i* in her name with a heart. This is the little-girl part of her that I ache for. She turns to me and tells me she is fearful of facing her mother. I assure her as best I can that her mother is searching her soul for the source of her absence and unavailability. I am sending this message to the heavens, hoping that I have not been duped. I am trying to convince myself, as I know she is. She must. Her world, otherwise, would be shattered.

Elizabeth continues to write on the mirror, avoiding my eyes. She asks me if I know whether or not she will continue to grow breasts. I am shocked and utterly confused by this question. At this instant, not understanding her question, I respond, "I wonder why you ask." She is worried that her stepfather's semen is like a pesticide that has annihilated her breasts, and they will no longer be able to thrive and grow. "You see" she explains, "I just have these little bumps . . . they began to show when he started coming into my room . . . " At this moment in time, my mind has a harnessed explosion, and I want to kick this man's ass to China and then back again. I hate what he has done to this child. I feel as though I could spit.

I put my hand on her cheek and I tell her that there is nothing that will keep her body from growing. I tell her that she is beautiful and bright, and that the semen from her stepdad's penis is like spit and tears, nothing more, nothing less. She will grow beautiful long legs, long lustrous flaxen hair, and lovely womanly breasts. I tell her that she did the right thing by telling. I tell her that I believe her. I tell her that if tonight, or tomorrow, or any other time she has any other worries, all she needs to do is to call. She looks deeply into me, so deeply that I want to flee.

Junctures such as these are for me, without hesitation, the most disturbing. I can guarantee this child nothing. When I send daughters home with their mothers, I literally pray for compassion and nurturance. I want these mothers to be gentle with their children. I want them to say that they are sorry and that they will now keep their daughters safe. I want them to take a stand. I want them not to fold. I want them to reach deeply into their souls and honor the utter preciousness of their children. I want them to discard their partners. I want them to embrace their daughters into their very being.

Elizabeth and her mother are brought back together like aged adhesive. The staticlike current between them is fizzling. It is dangerous and unsettling. I can give them my guidance and give them back to each other; the rest belongs to them.

When I leave the Advocacy Center that evening, I decide to walk home instead of driving. I am a mile from the center and am desperate for oxygen and for the celestial bodies to guide my way. My mind skips between Elizabeth and Lena. I think about my husband and my daughters. I think about their delicate unformed breasts. My thoughts begin to spin out. I recite a piece of poetry the entire way home to keep my mind still:

> maggie and milly and molly and may
> went down to the beach (to play one day)
>
> and maggie discovered a shell that sang
> so sweetly she couldn't remember her troubles, and

milly befriended a stranded star
whose rays five languid fingers were;

and molly was chased by a horrible thing
which raced sideways while blowing bubbles; and

may came home with a smooth round stone
as small as a world and as large as alone.

For whatever we lose (like a you or a me)
it's always ourselves we find at the sea.

Since I have been a little girl, whenever I am frightened, I recite rhymes and poetry in my head. The harping refrain is like a soothing melody, like an elixir in my veins; otherwise, the tape in my mind will keep going, and I will combust.

The night is black and brisk. There are certain zigs and zags in the path that make my heart race. There are the geese that float around the pond. There is the stone bench tucked beneath the willows. As I get closer to the deer pond, I begin a sprint home. I can see the light from my dining room window and I want to cry. When I open the front door, my chicks waddle out, one by one, throwing their arms around my waist. I smell their beautiful heads, which is intoxicating. My eldest is glued to the television, for which at times I am grateful. It is now that I must mindfully, and ever so consciously; close the door on my day.

The following morning I wake with my heart scrambling up my throat. I can barely find air. I slip out the door before my children rouse. I must get to my office as soon as possible. Oddly, I find that this familiar cinder-block space of mine brings me some strange solace, particularly when a crisis is brewing. I find that when I am there, my sense of being out of control is somewhat lessened. I have lived in this approximately 150 square feet for the past twenty years. I have gazed at the same seasonal faces of the north ridge of the first Flatiron. It is a mighty beautiful sliver of a view. My cinder-block closet is a mural of my children's artwork, their photos, and their ceramic love vessels filled with paperclips and doodads. The shelves are packed with books on incest as well as mountainous volumes of child welfare policy and protocol. There are almost always fresh flowers on my desk. I cannot bear being without color and aliveness—I already feel as if I am suffocating.

I am leafing through a detailed file of a four-year-old girl in a nearby day care center. Special-circumstances child care is a service available to families, particularly when this service will prevent out-of-home placement in cases of abuse or neglect. This child has been incested by her stepfather. To ease her mother's burden, child care has been provided.

A tentative knock sounds at my door. Before I can respond, the door opens a crack. It is Lena. My heart melts when I see her, as always. She is visibly rattled as we look at the case file together. I remember this case because the mother has a name strikingly similar to Lena's, both first and last, without the hyphen in between the parts of the last name. My eyes scan the demographics on the computer printout. "Lena!" I burst out. " This woman lives down the street from you! She has a granddaughter born on the same day as yours! Lena! This is uncanny!"

I can feel Lena's breath on my shoulder. She is standing up behind me perusing the file. Her breathing is staccato. She replies, "Isn't it amazing!"

My face is within inches of hers. Denial is a powerful engine. I have yet to compute the inference. All that I have believed about Lena must remain intact. Should it be a sham, the architectural design of my own truth will begin to fragment. Our gazes are fixed. I am scanning her face like one would scan a fetus in a sonogram. I am looking for the fluttering twinkle. I am looking for the heartbeat. I believe her. This is some unearthly coincidence. This is the explanation for this misunderstanding. She leaves my office. I have not an inkling of the implications of my own denial.

Within the hour, my supervisor and the personnel director summon me into her office. They inform me that they have just asked for Lena's keys and have put her on leave. I am shocked and numb. They have thoroughly checked out the child care facility. The child in question is Lena's granddaughter. She has been utilizing these services at the expense of this other family. The day care identifies Lena as the legal guardian of the child—as the grandmother. I am mute. They instruct me to have no contact with Lena or anyone else with regard to this matter.

I leave the office and walk back to my own. I put on my coat and grab my keys. I feel like I am sleepwalking. I am slipping on my gloves as I walk down the hall to leave the building. I reroute myself and walk to Lena's office. The door is closed. I walk in without knocking. I shut the door quickly behind me. Lena looks like an automaton. She has no color and no heartbeat. She is gathering some of her belongings, and she whispers, "Holly, they never let me tell my part . . . " I place my gloved hands on her face. I look at her, studying the detail of her face. The creases in her jowl and above her brow are familiar and soft. I say, "Lena, you must go home and tell your family the whole truth." I tell her, "I love you, no matter what." I find that an interesting thing to say. I must know in my core that this is my goodbye to Lena. I can feel the heat from her cheeks through the worn leather of my gloves. I turn and leave. I had become the guardian of the secret, the secret of Lena's imminent demise, perhaps even my own: a poignant irony for a woman who manages incest.

I return to work that afternoon to find two plump Thanksgiving turkeys perched on my desk, a donation from a local grocer in the spirit of giving, for families that are without. They are tagged with household numbers and addresses. I am told that these are to be delivered to two of Lena's families, the story being that Lena has gone home ill. I leave an hour early so that I can make my delivery and get home before dark. I am flooded with emotion that I have neatly compartmentalized in an effort to fulfill my duty of delivering the turkeys. I place both birds in the backseat of my car.

As I am pulling out of the parking lot, I am struck with sadness. I have always known Lena to be vigilant of families in need. She has always been the first to get a new washer for a family, a new muffler, a kitchen table, or mattresses so that children will not need to sleep on the floors. This has been her strength, her sensitivity to the indigent.

Services for incestuous families are no different than services for neglectful families or families that have survived child fatalities or domestic violence. We reach deeply into the coffers to provide them with amenities that might reduce the stress of their lives, even minutely. We know that a new washer will not heal the ravages of incest. Perhaps when we unzip the horrors of these families, when we work to eliminate the dysfunction, we must assuage our own guilt by giving a gift—to deflect, to diffuse our own internal fear and repugnance.

I have lived in Boulder for over twenty years. I keep driving around the same loop and realize that I must have the wrong address. I call back to the office to confirm. It is the right address. I am feeling irritated. There is no house attached to this address. I try the next home. I am driving in circles. I am light-headed and exhausted. It is growing dark. I look in my backseat and curse the fucking turkeys, those two big fat birds nestled together like a pair of lovers. I feel my hysteria mounting. I can't find the second address either. I find myself in a cul de sac in a snug little neighborhood.

I see a man pulling into his drive—coming home from work, I suspect. I get out of my car and walk toward the man. My legs feel like jelly. He is kind and approachable. I show him the address. He has lived there for six years and there is no such address on his street. I thank him and get back into my car. At this point, my car smells like raw poultry. I want a cigarette, something I do only a few times a year. It is my closet vice. I rest my head on the steering wheel and start to cry. I want to go home. I head north. I am wiping my tears and my nose on my leather gloves. They are soft and warm and smell so familiar. I drop the turkeys at the homeless shelter. The staff at the shelter is overwhelmed by the faux generosity of the department. I depart quickly.

I drive by my office and stop in to call home. I walk down the hall to Lena's office and flick on the light. The office smells like Lena. I sit down in her chair. I look at the photos of her family and her friends, babies and grandchildren. There are dried roses in a vase and mementos from a festive occasion. There is a small ceramic dish from Siena, where she vacationed this summer. I open the top drawer of her desk. It is crammed with pens and pencils, nail polish, hand cream, loose change, hair barrettes . . . I lay my head back on her chair and stare at the ceiling. I wonder what she is thinking at this very moment. I wonder if she feels shame. I wonder whom she will talk to. I wonder what she has shared with her family. I wonder how she got here. How will I keep my silence? I rock myself back and forth in her chair. My body suddenly screams. I feel it coming. My hands begin to tremble and sweat. I can feel my heart rate begin to quicken.

I take some deep breaths and focus my eyes on the photo in the calendar. It is a photo of a baby nestled in a teacup. The baby is chubby and round. It has a fluffy pink peony covering its head. I think about the bathing cap I had when I was a little girl. I loved the one with the gaudy magenta blossom that looked as if it was growing out of my brain. I begin my verses in my head to ward off this menacing panic. It slams me with such momentum that I cannot contain it. I feel it in my belly. I have merely touched the surface.

I begin to read through the infamous file about the four-year-old child who lives down the street from Lena. The guardian of these children is very depressed. She is experiencing financial difficulties since her husband lost his job. She cannot afford child care. I feel my day's food roiling around in my stomach. I feel as if I will vomit. It is Lena! There is no woman with a similar name who lives two doors away. I continue to read, and it is if I am reading her diary. I close the case file and ever so quietly pull out the drawer where she keeps her files. I cannot feel myself breathe. I pull out fifteen files and methodically leaf through them. I am stunned. Tiny vessels in my brain feel like detonating. I feel as if I will faint. Instantaneously, I remember the turkeys. I am frantically rummaging through the files. I am hyperventilating. There are no families! These cases are contrived. They are created. They are fictionalized. There is a photo of Lena in a black evening dress, a scarlet rose tucked into her silvery hair, looking down at me from her bulletin board. I roar, "Who the fuck are you?"

My mind is flooding I cannot even string together a logical thought. I pick up the phone to call my husband and can't remember my phone number. I keep reversing the digits. I am beside myself. I open up my wallet and flip open my checkbook. There is my phone number. I finally reach my husband. I am babbling and somewhat incoherent. He keeps asking me to slow down. I can hear his agitation, but my thoughts are moving faster than my mouth can formulate the sentences. I know that I am scaring him. I am scaring myself. I can hear him fumbling for his keys. I can think his thoughts for him. He is thinking that I am unsafe. He is cajoling me.

He is trying to get me to compose my thoughts so that he can figure a way to get to me and keep me on the phone. He is wondering who will come stay with the kids so that he can retrieve his wife, shovel up the pieces, and carry her neatly home. I stop talking and he gets very nervous. "I am fine," I say. "Really, I am having a momentary breakdown. I can't believe this! I am a fool."

He lures me home. I must recite every landmark, every traffic light, to guide my trip. I parrot the luminary celestial constellations: the Big and Little Dipper, Orion, Cassiopeia, the Seven Sisters. I find my way home. I fall into bed, unable to speak.

The next morning I carry the fifteen cases across the courtyard to the administrator's office. I can see her head in her window bobbing up and down on the phone. There are two enormous blue spruce trees outside of her office. They are majestic in stature and grace. I knock gently on her door and enter. She is still on the phone but motions me to sit. I feel as if I am in the principal's office. I don't know what to do with my roving feet. She hangs up her call and sits across from me. My voice is quivering. I feel as if I am eight years old. I push the files toward her. "These are not real."

She queries me, confused. I repeat, "They are fake, fictitious, make-believe, pretend. They are pretense, false, phony. They are a sham." She is taciturn. She quietly sizes me up with her oval cobalt eyes. She is looking at my neck, my clavicle. I protectively place an open hand across my throat. I am waiting for her response. My eyes start to tear. I imagine the rims of my eyes the color of coho salmon. I slowly lower my forehead into the palms of my hands. The minute the heat of my head hits my hands, I utter, "Where have I been?"

I am Ms. Ross. I am no different from my client. At any given time, I am the perpetrator, the victim, and the nonoffending spouse. I am the triad, collapsed and merged. How did I let this happen? Where was I? I explain to her my discovery. The turkeys without a home; my ransacking of Lena's office; my contacting the school district only to find that there are no such children registered anywhere. She is silent. Her eyes begin to smile. Her quick mind is moving through the various scenarios. She is in awe of Lena's craftiness, her acumen, and the cunning design for her sinister plot. I begin to outline what I believe to be the far-reaching implications of her embezzlement. I am sitting there, fully aware that I must step gingerly in my exchange with my superior. I must be methodical and meticulous. I cannot skip a beat. I must convince her that I will be instrumental in unraveling this secret. I am cognizant that I must cautiously navigate this uncharted terrain. Most importantly, I must absolutely signal to her that I will buffer her against the embarrassment that would otherwise befall our agency. As any dutiful daughter would, I assume full responsibility. In vain, I attempt to cushion the reputation of the department, hoping it will remain unpunctured and intact. I will take the fall, and I know it.

The following morning I am sitting with personnel directors and police detectives. My body is ill. Friends of Lena are present at a large conference table. They have brought in envelopes filled with cash. The bills are crisp and green, the type of bills one needs to peel apart. They would like to reimburse the department in any way they can. The breath of one woman is rancid. Her mouth is dry and frightened. I rise to open a window. I avoid meeting anyone's gaze. I am afraid I will fold. I wonder if people would do this for me. It is an act of both pride and humiliation. They want to right Lena's wrong. If they pay back the money, it will go away. If we deliver a turkey or replace a car muffler, incest will vanish. They speak eloquently and pleadingly on behalf of their friend, on the hardships of raising her grandchildren. They speak about all that she has contributed to the protection of children. After they have left the room and I have escorted them to the lobby, one man pleads with me to save Lena's job. I lift both my arms and see that my hands are cupped, holding only air. I am holding all that is unspoken and unknown. I am holding all that is out of my control. I am holding nothing. I imagine the ache of a mother who opens her arms to a stillborn child. There is nothing to fill the emptiness.

I am wondering where the money came from for Lena to take her family on a European vacation last August. The farthest I could get was to a tiny corner in the southwestern part of Colorado. I am curious about the new dining room furniture that was recently delivered to her home. How about the skin treatment to smooth her aging skin? As my mind reels with questions, I tally up her spending. Memories of Lena's expenditures are itemizing themselves as fast as I can scan her life. As her home filled with grand objects, what were friends and family thinking? They loved her. They believed her. They trusted her. She had served the department with such humility and grace. Her duplicity was unfathomable. I feared for the sanity of her loved ones when they became fully aware of her crime. I feared for her grandchildren. I feared for myself.

The scaffolding of my identity was sure to come crashing down. I sat in the conference room alone after they left. My heart ached for these people; a woman I no longer knew. I thought about Ms. Ross and her daughter, Elizabeth. I thought about incest and its insidious dynamic. I felt as if I too had been sleeping, and though Lena continuously left an astounding trail of cues, I never once pursued them. I did not want to—or could not—face my own frailties, which would simultaneously be uncovered.

I had never attended to the daily drivel of paperwork. In fact, I had ignored it and often filled my recycle box with unread memos that meant nothing to the client but meant everything to the almighty system. I remember a therapist once said to me, "When you spend more time with paper and less with the human spirit, then your time is done." My peers all knew this about me. I wore my deficit with a shameless kind of pride. I did not know any other way to admit to my failure. Lena knew this about me. She knew that I would never decipher a crimp in a case opening or a computerized entry that had been tampered with. She played me masterfully, like the fool that I was with regard to bureaucracy. She took my failing and ran with it.

I felt so much like the mother of a violated child who could not and would not face her truth. All the cues that I had been given; all the times my mind had closed and wandered without listening. The times that I did venture down the path with Lena, to query her about inconsistencies, she firmly closed the door. Relieved and in denial, I made my own exit . . . one more child I could not protect.

My denial about Lena and her deception was a mechanism for survival around my denial of my own inadequacies and short-comings as a supervisor of an incest team and all that it entails.

It is exceptionally rare for a client to thank a caseworker for services rendered. Our clients do not ever invite us into their lives. We are there because they, as parents, have failed to protect their children. Mothers have immersed their babies in scalding water. Fathers have landed a ferocious blow to the solar plexus of their tiny son for some minuscule infraction. Uncles have used their nephews or nieces for a perverse sexual pleasure. We are there not by invitation but rather by legal mandate. Every holiday season enables us to collapse the hierarchical nature of our roles and enter our client's homes with gifts and generosity. Social services has a program every Christmas where our families are adopted by corporations, private businesses, or citizens in the community who wish to sponsor a family in need. Each family member is able to fill out a list of items needed: winter coats and hats, books, kitchenware, a new washer or dryer, bed linens, a vacuum cleaner, whatever. While the donors are anonymous, the social workers are the people who, several days before Christmas, load up their cars and deliver gifts to the families they serve. It is a very pleasing experience, where animosity and anger melt.

Three days before Christmas I am brought to an office that is probably twice the size of mine. In this office are the gifts that

Lena has requested for her families and their children. I walk in, and my pulse begins to race. I feel truly enraged. There are probably upward of three hundred beautifully wrapped gifts. Citizens in our community spent weeks shopping and then wrapping presents for these fifteen families. There are hand-decorated Christmas cards, sparkling ribbons, and bows. They are addressed to illusory children. These gifts were purchased by generous, giving people. I must open every gift, decipher its contents and assign it to a child who meets its criteria. This task is unwieldy.

As I gingerly unfold the wrapping, I am struck by the fact that these gifts were selected by Lena for her family and for herself. Each family request has a sordid tale of children sleeping on cardboard, hence two beautiful twin mattresses replete with linens and matching comforter. Or the family, recovering from a near fatal car accident in which the mother was left mangled and would benefit from weekly massage. All for Lena and her family. I unwrapped, examined, reassigned, and rewrapped each and every gift. It took me two whole days. Each gift found a hungry child or family. The last gift was a home computer; finding a suitable home took a bit of time. I am sitting with this computer at my feet. I want to retch. Her greed and her devious cunning are inexplicable. What need of hers was not being met? Where had this gluttony come from?

I am thinking about how all those items tell the story of Lena. This room, once crammed to the gills with one woman's needs and desires, is now empty. There are a few stray pieces of ribbon and paper. I feel a deep sense of shame. This gift program is very special. I made certain, to the best of my abilities out of my own guilt and failing, that this program would not sink with its abuser.

There was nothing in this room for Elizabeth Ross. There was not one gift that I felt would ease her pain. There was not one item that would soothe her anguish or mend the innocence that was extinguished by her stepfather. On my way home that night I stopped by her house. Her lovely face lit up as she opened the door. I noticed she was wearing one layer. I had nothing in my hands for her. No gift. I barely had words. She fixed me a steaming cup of tea and we just talked. She was light and young. Things with her mom were better. She felt relieved. She was sleeping without interruption. She rambled about friends and school and Christmas vacation. She was animated, and her cheeks were flushed. There was an aliveness in her face that I had not previously seen. The transparency of her being was formed. Before I left, she asked me when I would be back. I flipped a satiny strand of blond hair from her shoulder. "Whenever you would like," I said. She reached out her arms to hug me, an eleven-year-old's hug that made me cry the minute I stepped out into the cold night. That embrace was worth more than all the gifts in that other room combined.

It is Christmas Eve, midnight mass. I am standing next to my mother, who is more at peace in her holiness than anywhere else on earth. Whenever I am in a house of worship, there are tears that pool themselves in the back of my throat. I have never quite understood this; all I know is that there is a strong sense of community around me and somehow I never feel I belong. I can hear my mother's voice as she sings a hymn. I am restless and misplaced. I close my eyes and pray for myself. I ask my angels to help me find my way. I ask them to provide me some respite from my mind so that I can celebrate the season with my own children. I slip my hand into my mother's warm hand. It is aged and so beautifully familiar. I slide off her huge marquise diamond wedding ring and put it on my marriage finger. The slivers of light that dance around the gem mesmerize me. My mother is irritated because I am not paying attention. I ask her if the mass is almost done. She quiets me as I spin the diamond around on my finger.

At the end of the sermon, my mother embraces me and kisses my cheek. In her very holiest of tones, she tells me that I must forgive Lena. "No fucking way!" I blurt out, a bit too loud. With that she takes her thumb and her first finger and pinches my arm. She twists a piece of flesh through my coat with such delight. She rolls her eyes up to the heavens and does a quick "In the name of the Father, the Son, the Holy Ghost . . . "

We are walking out of the church. "Ma," I say, "I will forgive Lena when I am good and ready, and I am no where near ready." She goes on pontificating about forgiveness and anger and God giving you as much as you can handle. I am burrowing my body deep into her shearling coat. It is frigid outside, and I don't want her to slip. I use a quip my oldest daughter uses on me: "Besides, Ma, you are not the boss of me! I'm forty-two. I know when I need to forgive people."

"I *am* the boss of you," she replies. "I am your mother." I pull her closer.

I remember the night Elizabeth Ross and her mother left the Advocacy Center. When her mother tried to place her arm around her daughter's shoulder, Elizabeth recoiled and scurried ahead, like a sand crab scooting across the ocean floor when it senses danger. I am a dutiful daughter, obedient and servile. I have swallowed a bellyful of rage and deceit to protect my mothers, but most importantly to protect myself.

Lena's sin became my shame. I carried it as I would a cancer whose tentacles burrowed deeply into my very spirit. For close to a year I could not lift my head and look colleagues directly in the eye without wondering what they were thinking. I knew their relief at the fact that it was I who had been deceived, not they. *I* had been duped. *I* had been bamboozled. *I* was disgraced and dishonored. One colleague told me that I deserved what I got. Another hoped that this situation would enable me to look deeply into myself for some very important answers. I was easily the pocket for everyone's blame. Lena had been arrested, and I had been placed on a corrective action, my reputation forever compromised.

*   *   *   *   *   *   *

On Ting's table one afternoon, I felt my hot tears run a perfect line into the channel of my ears. They soaked the pillow and would not end. I asked Ting, through my sadness, if there was a point on the body where he could place a needle for my shame. If he could just find that microscopic meridian and puncture my shame with the needle's head, I could perhaps release myself. I was half expecting a long, bellowing sigh, but he closed his eyes and I heard his melodic Chinese-accented, "Yes, yes." He gently placed his long, beautiful fingers over my slightly fevered forehead, and I willingly surrendered the beads of my shame into the palm of his hand.

Spank Me: On Sex and the Unthinkable

I fall in love easily. I always have. I fall in love with people and their passion. I fall in love with ideas, particularly those that nudge my irreverence. I fall in love with fabric, rich in texture and in weave. I fall in love with art that brings me crashing to my knees because it awakens a mysterious, unutterable desire. I fall in love with music, especially when its erotic rhythms hail from the Portuguese. I fall in love with foreigners, whose languages slide off their tongues with effortless romanticism. I fall in love with a certain summer light that descends right before dusk and paints the landscape with surreal, almost edible color. I fall in love with smells, especially exotic floral blends that fade throughout the day and meld with the scent of my skin. I fall in love with the song of the lark and the echo of a flute played deep in a canyon. I fall for the softness of the skin on the nape of my son's neck and the luscious scent of my daughter's hair. And at times in my life, I have fallen in love with the manner in which people have fallen for me. Unwittingly, I cannot help myself.

In my calling, I have fallen in love with a purpose and a mission and a need to push the river as far as it will go. I am smitten by all that I learn about myself, most oddly by my frailties and weaknesses, which at times seem bleak and unsalvageable. I am a dizzy fool for all that can transform the self.

Yet as we all know, love can fail us, love can send us spiraling down an abyss, but most importantly, love, when it is done well, with honesty, respect, and compassion, can sustain us forever, and possibly longer than that.

I cannot read about incest until after nine-thirty in the morning. My senses are simply insulted by the suggestion of such atrocity. Most mornings I feel my way through the darkness and pee with my eyes closed. I navigate with my feet so that I won't wake my slumbering children—no lights, little rustling, just a teakettle on the stove and a steeping bag of herbs. I begin the ritual of packing lunches and placing a love note in each lunch box. When my children open their lunches at school they can see my scrolling penmanship dribble off their missives. There is always a heart, and a barrage of *X*'s and *O*'s that bleed onto the texture of their napkins. I want them to take my love through the day with them. I'm sure it soothes me more that it does them. There are times in my life when I spend more time with children at work than I do with my own. Something is not right in that.

My daughter situates herself every morning on the countertop in my bathroom while I dab on the last finish and touches of my face—a wisp of mascara and Rose Reflect for my lips. All the while, she runs commentary on the crow's feet that stretch like tentacles from the corners of each eye. She is vigilant about new strands of gray that uncoil from some deep root in my scalp. I am humming to myself in my head. There is a certain juncture in motherhood where one's child no longer finds them the center of the universe, no longer the most breathtaking beauty on the earth. This is a sad day. As I turn around and lift her off the sink, she plants a luscious, loving smooch on my mouth so that the pink transfers from my lips to hers. My day has begun.

I take a circuitous route to my office some mornings, dawdling and lengthening the quarter of an hour I have before venturing into a new day of twisted eroticism and perversion. As I turn onto the Diagonal, which will spill me out into Boulder, my eyes scan the foothills and the Flatirons. After living here for over twenty years, that vision still takes my breath away. It settles me into my morning. In the spring, the Flatirons wear a sumptuous wash of Nile-green velvet, in the winter they are majestic, dusted with a powder of confection.

I leave my office door wide open. I have never trusted what is behind a closed door. I turn on my muted desk lamp. As usual, there are a number of reports on my chair. I have a mailbox as well as a space cleared off on my desk for paper; still, my people are conditioned to leave their reports on the chair. I will never miss incest on the chair. I will always be forced to retrieve those referrals and to hold them in my hands. I will have to read them. This is my responsibility. It is my job to assess every referral for incest in Boulder County.

When I first began managing this program I read word for word each and every referral. Now I scan for jurisdiction and the residence of the alleged offender. I am looking to see if the child is safe and what type of response time is warranted. This morning there are a number of referrals that came in the night before. I grab my teacup and head for the kitchen area in search of hot water. I am lolling and resisting, and I know it. Each inconsequential ritual is a prerequisite for my day.

I have had the same ceramic mug for over twenty years. It is titled "Le Lapin." The cup is anointed with a merging of carefully etched bunny rabbits. When one looks closely enough, one can see that they are involved in various sexual acts. Bunnies mounting each other from the rear, bunnies loving on each others bodies, bunnies with their snoots in the crotches of their fellow cottontails. This cup was a gift before I joined the Boulder County Sexual Abuse Team. It was a sign—the gods must have known. Nonetheless, that cup is like my binky. I am frantic if I leave it in another office. If it broke, I would dissolve. There is something sweet in their exhibitionistic, orgiastic trysts. It reminds me, as I need to be reminded, that sex is sweet. It is playful, it is a rush, and it is sultry, desirous, and hot. Its liquid passion is what oils the most creative, artistic endeavors of the human mind.

Sex has always intrigued me. I have thought about it for as long as I have known about it. When I was a little girl, my parents would have parties where the grown-ups would sway to the velvety croon of Nat King Cole. While we craned our necks from the stairs, my brother and I would watch as the lights would dim and the bodies would melt into one another, and partners would be exchanged in what seemed a methodical fashion. Men's hands would move from the small of their partner's back and drop deftly down to their rears. Nuzzled into each other's necks, they would press their pelvises into each other, and like a fire, I could feel it in my own ten-year-old loins.

My first few years of work with incest were filled with a sense of awe and valor. I wanted desperately to puncture the dysfunction of incestuous dyads and reroute desire back into its appropriate bed. But it wasn't so much about sex as it was about intimacy, the recapitulation of historical trauma, and the need to master control over one's pain. The sexual vignettes that I would read were like snippets of erotica gone awry. I was riveted by the material; I was repulsed and intrigued. As an intimate team of colleagues, we staffed these referrals amongst ourselves. It fueled a prurient spark between us that was rarely uttered. The entire work arena was sexualized—from guttural humor to submerged flirtations, which periodically reared their heads in inappropriate venues. My body, at the beginning, hummed constantly with sexual titillation.

Each year chipped away at my innocence. Each day had me drifting down yet another meandering current of sexual aberration and debauchery. My sexual world as I had known it had split open like a melon—each seed sprouting a new revelation of sexual impropriety and heinous violation of the pristine bodies of our children. Soon, there was no sexual act that I had not heard of. There was not a single cognitive distortion or rationale on the part of a sex offender that was unique to my senses.

When Tonya Jones settled herself into my office one summer afternoon, I was startled by her poise and directness. She was a stunning young girl whose height defied her age; I would have guessed her at seventeen. She wore a simple summer halter dress and yellow thongs. She had a decal of smiling daisies tattooed to the nail of her big toe. The contrast of the white linen gauze against her ebony skin was striking. She was built like a leggy colt, somewhat wobbly and uncertain. Her equine head was regal, with its plaits tied together with white ribbon. She exuded an unusual admixture of reticence and sass, each jockeying for position. She settled her spindly legs underneath her bottom and fiddled with a nonexistent thread in the hem of her dress.

Only one other time in my career has a child sashayed into my office unannounced, yet with intention. It is a rarity that speaks to the integrity and unformed self-reliance birthing within their growing spirits. This impresses me, and it always throws me for a loop. Tonya was forthcoming with a squeaky edge of restraint. She was afraid to go home this afternoon. When the school bell rang, she decided to come here to Social Services instead of busing it home. A friend had told her about our agency, a friend whom a family member had abused. Tonya's father was Jamaican and her mother was Caucasian. She lived with her aunt and uncle while her parents were relocating to Colorado.

It was hot last night and she could not sleep. She came out to the living room and lay on the couch underneath the ceiling fan. She was wearing a billowy chemise that belonged to her aunt. She does not wear panties when she sleeps. As she was falling back to sleep, she was awakened by her uncle massaging the back of her neck. It felt so heavenly that she closed her eyes. He raised her chemise over her bare bottom and stroked the outside of her thigh. He bent down and kissed the back of her neck.

As she continues with her story I note that her demeanor is contained and her enormous dark eyes swallow my response. As she speaks, her elocution has a tiny hint of Jamaican and West Indian—it is liquidy and smooth. She runs her hands up around her throat and touches the back of her neck the way one would revisit a lover's touch. She is dreamy and precise.

"In some ways it felt so nice." She pauses waiting for my response. "I am ashamed," she says. Her chin drops down to her chest and I marvel at the perfection of the part in her hair. For a moment we are silent, and I think that she will tell me more. To quell my curiosity, I nudge her to see if there is a crescendo that has yet to be revealed. She fears her aunt will find out. She fears that she will not resist him if he returns. She looks at me and pointedly states that she is just fourteen and a man has never touched her before.

I calculated fourteen. Where was I when I was fourteen? Had I been touched? I remembered learning to French-kiss. I was up in Julie White's attic. I was telling her that I wanted to kiss Billy Christanson. Shy and ashamed, I had no idea how to French-kiss. She drew it on the chalkboard. The tongue inside the mouth. I was grossed out. She scooted closer to me on the dank, mildewed couch and French-kissed me. I got it. Girls know all the tricks.

Tonya's fingers, like her legs, are slender and never-ending. She gesticulates like one who is conducting an orchestra—long, sweeping motions in the shape of a backward **L**. There is something unreal about this child. She has an innate sensuality that would be difficult to resist. I am reeled into her vignette as if I were watching a movie. She seems more fearful of her newfound murmurings than of a sexual violation. I dutifully secure her safety with a friend of the family until I can reach her parents.

While relieved, Tonya finds it difficult to leave my office. She asks me questions that seem peripheral and like excess banter. She compliments the color of my pearly toenail polish.

"Is there something else you want to tell me, Tonya?" Her legs are wrapped like wisteria around the legs of a chair. She has a mystery about her that is precocious yet pristine. She chooses her words carefully. She wonders out loud to me if she has done something to seduce her uncle—if her laying her body under the fan on a hot summer night was somewhat of an invitation. She admits that she has thought about her uncle in that way. She says that he is very handsome and kind. Since she has come to Colorado, she has felt something between them. Her eyes fill with tears as her head tilts toward the ceiling. Like the Madonna, she lifts her face, praying that her pain will rise to the heavens.

I am talking about myself. A fledgling in this field, her question resonates with a discomfiting familiarity. I tell her in fledglingese that no one has the right to touch her body without her consent, especially a family member whom she trusts. She nods, trying to digest my words, yet knowing all the while I am miles from the issue. She closes her eyes and rests her head against the wall. I think about the issue of consent and how a child as young as this could not know anything about consent. I can do nothing to assuage her sense of responsibility other than to remind her that she is a child, not an adult.

She slowly rises from the chair and sits back down again. Confused, I ask her if she is ready to go.

"I undress with the door open so that he can watch me," she blurts out. "I pretend that I don't see him. I can feel his eyes watching me . . . " Her long, slender fingers cover her shame. I swallow a stringy strand of saliva and decide that I must carefully pick my words before I speak. I approach her and touch her hand; she grabs my left hand, which startles me. She begins to pray for forgiveness. Tears cascade from her eyes. She prays into the palm of my hand—it's as if she speaks in tongues. I cannot understand her. I put my right hand on the top of her hair and feel the heat as it billows off the top of her scalp. The warmth that radiates from her crown feels fevered and possessed. I imagine the heat of sex as I watch the beads of perspiration cling to her hairline. I think about holding her shame in my hand. It is slippery and wet from mucus and tears.

I ruminate that evening over Tonya and her uncle. Her dreamy dark eyes are a fixture in my mind's eye. I am troubled that she sees herself as a seductress, and yet there is something so powerfully sensual which drips from her being. How could he resist her?

I awaken in the middle of the night. The moon hangs in my window, creating a ribbon of light across my bed sheets. I can hear my husband's breathing, deep and masculine. The room is sweltering, and I inch away from his damp body. My mind replays the image of Tonya's lanky body as she disrobes with full awareness of her voyeur. To quell my own arousal, I quietly descend the stairs and let myself out the back door. The night air is not much cooler than the still air that hangs over my bed. I sit on the steps listening to the electric croon of the crickets. I remember the cicadas' hum in the summer as they clung to the soupy wetness of the East Coast air.

I have been here before. I have been to that place where the image in my mind and the senses in my body are completely engaged—where it is redundant and rehearsed, like a film loop that plays over and over again. Once a sexual vignette is a potential source of fantasy, I seize it and step into the body of the fantasy as if it were mine. I am troubled by my penchant. I wonder for the umpteenth time why I do this work. I wonder if I prey on the ill fate of others so that I myself will revel in my own sated self-satisfaction, which is nothing more than innuendo and suggestion. I imagine I feel the same as an offender, dirty and secretive, pathetic and feeble in my raunchy exploitation.

As I crawl back into bed, my husband in his stupor throws a leg over me. He pulls me like a spoon into him. I feel him press against me and I give way to my pleasure as my mind hooks into my day. I am caught, flailing at the end of line, like a slippery trout, with my mouth pierced by shame and obsession. I cannot get loose. I cannot free myself.

I wonder sometimes what it is called when a client presents in therapy with the same issue that has plagued the therapist for all his or her life. Sometimes I sit on the therapist's throne and think that it is I who should be paying my clients. Sometimes what they bring me is like gold. I think that they have come to teach me. That they are my vehicle for change. There have been times when I have visually and spiritually changed places. I am fascinated by this exchange. I love this when it happens—but it also shakes me to my roots and collapses the careful structure that has been created. It is like a swift kick in the pants when one is totally unprepared. It is the utmost in that which is endearingly human.

* * * * * * *

When Aiden found me, as a private practitioner in my own practice, she was coming off a year-long relationship with a teacher at her high school. The relationship, of course, was a secret; he loved her with all of his being. He wanted to leave his wife and marry her. They would have to wait, of course, until she turned eighteen.

I looked at her as she spoke. I felt my mind leave my body. I could not take my eyes off of her face. The claylike mask of makeup had been deftly painted on her face, much the way a geisha presents her snowy mask to the world. As she spoke, I thought of what it would be like to take a palate knife and peel off the layers of paint that had hardened. I thought about painters who reuse their canvases: rainbowed layers of expression, impulsive and unbridled, only to be rejected and covered up, judged by self as perhaps too revealing. I wondered what she knew about me.

Aiden was lovely, no doubt. I had seen this before, but not to this degree. I felt suddenly sleepy as I listened to her little-girl voice. I thought of the times when I have painted my own face to conceal and protect my intentions.

She wore her hair in a perfect French braid with little wisps of bangs that spoke of her innocence. Her jeans and her camisole were like skin, as if they had been painted onto her body. Her speech and her presentation were incongruous.

Her anger and her need for resolve were simmering. Over the weeks we had picked through the details of this relationship. We had looked at the utter violation and betrayal of trust. She did not love him. She wrote for him, poetry and prose, to please him, to please his senses. She loved the intrigue and the feeling of being special. There was a quality of being with him that felt like being fathered in a way that she had never been. She craved the attention. She knew of other students who had reported the same relationship with this teacher. Her individuality was extinguished with that knowledge. Her sense of being would periodically crumble.

Aiden and I traversed this landscape together for around six months. We located the teacher, who had moved to another state to work. Other students were interviewed, and we found a plethora of victims. She navigated though the criminal justice system to track him and finally to have him arrested.

As we skated on this thin ice, Aiden's transparency became far more fluid and clear. With each session, I began to see her skin more clearly. The eye definition and the outline of her lips stood alone without paint or adornment. Her days of self-hatred were apparent when she sketched and outlined her eyes with black eyeliner. The days that she honored herself and her need for duplicity, she was fresh-faced and real. She understood her intentions. She embraced her motivations.

One day, Aiden bounced into my office with the buoyancy and verve of a springy teen girl, alive and unfettered. I noticed a pale sprinkling of freckles across the bridge of her perfect nose and commented on how joyous and light she seemed. Her tennis shoes were untied, and she was less put together in a way that bodes freedom, not lunacy. She was bursting to ask me a question. I was prepared to answer some sordid detail of her case. Instead she fidgeted, drumming her long unpainted fingernails on the rubber soles of her shoes, the last vestiges of her faux self.

"In the last few months I have really wanted to ask you a personal question, but I have been afraid that you would get angry." I could feel my heart quicken with her suggestiveness and the unknowing boundary that could be easily trespassed. I wiped my sweaty palms on my skirt. She noticed.

I let her continue. "I think that you have had the same experience as me. I think that you were seduced by someone who was older than you, even a teacher." I cogitate quickly. I feel the constriction in my throat. I calmly place my hands underneath my thighs, as if I need to keep them firmly in place. I rise and open the window. She is right. It was a teacher. I must hold my secret.

"I wonder why you might think that, and why it would be important for you to know," I query.

She is settled and poised, and I am a wreck, as if she has seen straight through my soul.

"I found you by accident. I tried to get in to see another woman, but she had a waiting list. Someone suggested you. I believe that things happened serendipitously. I know that wherever you are led, it is for a reason. When I told you about my teacher, you guided me in this healing as if you were on the same path with me. Sometimes, when I couldn't finish a thought or a feeling, you could do it for me. One day, when I was talking to you about the sex we would have and where we would have it, it's like you knew. I didn't even need to tell you, and you didn't seem shocked."

Our session ended, and I never really answered her question. I fluffed it over with some abominable psychojargon, something I abhor. I tucked my own secrets deep into my therapist self, only to gyrate with anxiety for the next few days, until I could uncork my agitation in my own therapy session.

I lumber up the stairs to my therapist's office thinking about all the things that I could talk about other than my own history and the fact that we are not so different from our clients. What disturbs me most is my own transparency and my need to heal others while healing myself.

I begin my diatribe with angst and apprehension. I cross and uncross my ankles, which is a behavior that belongs to someone else. I have never done this before, and it is as if I am trying to crawl into someone else's skin.

"It wasn't so much her question as it was my need to put her on a path to healing and finish all my unfinished business through her experience. I could fix her, but I couldn't fix myself."

"Say more," my therapist urges.

"I realize that when we have damaged forays into sexuality in our history, we are always struggling in our lives to right those wounds. I understand how much we idolize and yearn for the love of our fathers. When there is little reciprocity, we seduce every father there is to seduce, hoping somewhere that we will find the lost love of our daddies." I am pacing the perimeter of the room, unable to shut up because I am near something, an epiphany. "I replay all the incestuous vignettes in my mind when I am sexual, and I don't know whether it is a result of the work or whether it's an integral part of who I am. The face of the father or the elder is never my own father's face, it's an anonymous person. Somehow I know I need to keep playing the tape. Sometimes the only way I can understand this atrocity is by assuming the persona—by trying on the dress. It doesn't shame me."

She nods quietly and lets me hear myself. Her timing is perfect.

I am shocked by what I have to say. I am shocked that I have said it out loud. It is my deepest, darkest secret. It is key in my understanding of my motivation behind the work and how I assimilate the poison. It is fundamental in my success. I recognize the craziness, and I weep for myself. I grieve my internal perversion. I am an aggregate. I am victim and perpetrator, combined. How will I reconcile? How long do I need to do this?

*   *   *   *   *   *   *

Victoria Valles always holds the sides of her head together when she talks about her father. She replays the scenario over and over again like a broken record. I don't stop her. I let her do it. All the while it infiltrates my being and seals off a piece of my vibrancy. The floor of my pelvis feels numb. Periodically she tries to speak and the words get stuck. She freezes inside herself and looks at me in sheer terror. Sounds fall out of her mouth in little puffs of strangulated air. Her hands move from her temples to her throat, as if touching her throat will mysteriously create language that has long been asleep. She looks as if she is suffocating. Her enormous gray eyes are arid and offended. She trusts that I can bring her out. I teeter on an edge, not certain whether I can. I never show her my fear. It lodges inside my throat like a strep infection that invades your perversely engorged tonsils, pressing off your airway.

Victoria Valles is eleven. Years ago her father held her hostage in her own bedroom. He pressed her passive frame to the mattress while she listened to her mother driving down the dirt driveway to go to the grocery. She believed her little brother was with her mother. Her father held a gun to her head and had her suck his penis. If she didn't suck hard enough, he would stick the barrel of the gun down her throat and make her suck the metal. He teased and threatened to pull the trigger. He would pull the barrel out and put his erect penis back into her mouth. The braces on her teeth would scrape against the shaft of his penis, and he was so enraged by the discomfort of this, he would pull out his penis and place the revolver up her vagina and cock the hammer of the gun. The sound was indescribable—something like a click. She has no idea where she went after that. None. No access. The very last thing she remembers is that she turned her face away from her father toward the south-facing window. She saw a tiger swallowtail sail across the powdery sky outside and the horrified eyes of her younger brother in the lower right-hand corner of the window. He was balanced on a wooden crate. Somewhere in his five-year-old mind he knew to pedal over to a neighbor's, a half a mile away. He saved her.

This story came to me the first year in my job. I listened to it over and over again. Every time I saw Victoria she would tell me her story. I would sit in my office or her bedroom or on a bench in the park and she would tell me the story. Before we could talk about anything else—school, family, friends—she would tell me, word for word, every nuance of this event. What she was wearing, the time of day, the sounds that she heard outside her window, the distinct smell of rancid whiskey on her father's breath, his excited breathing, her unbreathing. The small yellow rose in the right hand corner of the ceiling where the wallpaper was beginning to peel.

Today, the wallpaper is gone; her room is painted a lovely shade of lavender. Sometimes at night she looks up at that ceiling and can still see the rose. She remembers the musky, sweaty taste of his penis. She remembers a wiry pubic hair stuck on the underside of her tongue. She remembers making believe that she was someone else, any one else. She remembers wishing that she were a dog being put to sleep, dying a slow and peaceful death. She talks at length about the metallic taste of the metal and the clicking sound. *Click click click.* She remembers a bead of sweat from his brow dropping onto her tongue and her swallowing it. She remembers seeing her baby brother's eyes, and then they were gone. She remembers the sirens. She was sure he would kill both of them.

There were times when Victoria would tell me her story and I would feel as if it were an offering of sorts. As if she needed to be exorcised. I asked her once why she felt compelled to tell me over and over. She couldn't answer. It didn't matter. My being had become a receptacle for her horror. Every time she told me, I could only pray that it would lighten her being. That it was like peeling off a layer of charred skin that was dead and unsightly. A layer that had no use, that was no longer a protective, sheltering entity in her life.

One afternoon as she told her story, she held the sides of her head as if they would split like a well-worn garment. I held her and she stopped talking. All the terror that had accompanied the story seemed to float far away, and miraculously she fell asleep in my arms. It did not occur to me that her trauma had become mine. As she washed the poisons from her body, they began to cling to my soul.

Sexually violated children master the art of survival through a vast array of adaptive stratagems. Though they are difficult at times to digest, I honor their means as I do my own. I have a keen understanding of the need to hold one's head high and to define oneself absent of external judgment and internal shame. Like a recurring dream, like the chorus of a song, we repeat it over and over again, ad nauseum, until its power and punch has wilted and can no longer stand alone.

Victoria's story, like the thousands of stories that I have listened to over the years, travels like a debilitating virus through my bloodstream, attacking the very essence of my being. It is stealthy and virulent, breaking down the protective mechanisms of its host.

I am not unlike most individuals who survive sexual trauma. Countless times in my life, I have traversed a landscape, maneuvering myself through the wiles of seduction, enticement, and manipulation. I have wooed and beguiled to meet my own needs and to circumvent the desires of others. Sex is a powerful potion—a means to an end and a device for destruction. Its potency lies in the balance. Like my survivors, if I open my heart, I fear it will explode.

I still dream about the pistol going off inside Victoria's vagina. Only it is not her body, it is mine. I awaken in the night with a phantom ache in my pelvic floor. It has lasted now for twenty years. I always think of Victoria and wonder where she is.

Long ago, all that was secret and forbidden fueled my erotic engine. Now, in the middle of my life, the sensuous slope of Nefertiti's neck can entice my desires. I yearn for my sensuous, erotic self—my hope is that she is merely sleeping.

Sometimes, in my darkest hours, I make my rounds to the beds of my sleeping children, just to hear them breathe. Most nights, I slide my hand into my husband's hand, and he always, without fail, gives me a squeeze.

From Field to Administration

The high priest and priestess stand quietly at the altar. A lacy fabric covers their faces. My vision captures the shifting of their eyes as they speak to me from beneath their shrouds. The breath from their voices creates a billowing from underneath the fabric as they pontificate.

I am kneeling at their feet. The floor of the holy house is cold. On a long Mission table in front of me are twelve babies, each nestled in a wicker basket. Scenarios label the baskets. None of the infants is named. I am instructed to stand. I respond swiftly and dutifully.

"We have selected you to minister to all of these children. You must nurse them on demand, whenever they are hungry."

I am terrified by how cold and dispassionate their voices seem. As I open my mouth to speak, I begin to cry. "I cannot feed these babies. I do not have enough milk." I can feel the tingling sensation in my nipples as my milk lets down. I continue to speak. "I only want to feed *my own* children. These are not my babies. I need to feed *my* babies. For the last twenty years now I have protected *other* people's children. I need to protect *my own* children. If I feed these babies, I will waste away. There will be nothing left of me." I am sobbing. I fold my arms over my chest so that they will not see the milk dripping from my breasts. "Please find someone else for this job. I cannot do it."

"You have been chosen. These babies have been incested. They are yours."

I turn to the high priestess. "What about you? You can feed these babies. You have time."

She raises her cloak. Her breasts are wizened and shriveled. "I have no milk. I am dry," she spouts rather tersely.

I awaken from my dream unable to breathe. My hands find my breasts quickly, quelling the lifelike horror of my dream state. My breasts are familiar, twelve years after nursing babies. I slip out of my bedroom, quietly finding my way down to the kitchen in the dark. The winter moon dangles in the window, full and haloed by blue and pinkish rings.

I open the fridge and take out the milk. I pour a glass and bring it into the dining room. The wood floor is chilly so I tuck my bare feet under my nightgown. I am disturbed by my dream. I am more depleted now than I have ever been before.

Dreaming of my children is a beckoning harbinger that shatters my nerves. I move to the stairs and sit with my glass so that I can hear them breathing. There is not a drop left in my weary bones to give. The system is asking the unthinkable. They are stretching my soul so that I will die. For an agency that protects children, they do little to protect their own. After twenty years, incest belongs to me. I want to fling it into the ether and disengage from my entire being. I orbit alone with my expertise because no one else will touch it. I have become invisible, the way survivors of incest become hidden and unapparent.

My plea to my commanders must be inaudible; they pretend not to listen. I have social workers falling away like wounded animals, overwhelmed by the emotions of being endearingly human. I pray for a catastrophe that will open the eyes of those who sleep the dead, dreamless sleep of the righteous and holy, of the high priests and priestess.

In the late seventies the Boulder County Sexual Abuse Team was housed in a building on Alpine Avenue. The building had a spicy reputation as a sizzling house of ill repute. So fitting. At one point the building was bought by its neighboring hospital; it became a thrift store known as the Pink Door.

I came to work there after the brothel and after the Pink Door. I came in at a time when the Sexual Abuse Team was perceived as an exclusive group, dealing with the heinous and deplorable. There was an aura of the unknown. Because the work suggested an unusual area of expertise new to the field of social work, its members exuded the mystique of a deeper knowledge. Something we did in our calling was more important, more revered. In all honesty, the work set in motion a dynamic that to this day contains an interesting duality. For some, the thought of working with incest is despicable and undesirable. For others, it proves provocative and intriguing.

Unblessed by self-knowledge, we were drawn to a world of sexual unorthodoxy; and in some ways, the members of the Sexual Abuse Team, including myself, carried on its tradition of secrecy with panache and plumped-up bravado. We were slated for it. It was our domain.

Not unlike incest, the physical setting-apart of the team led to its intrigue, while at the same time, it created a sense of exclusivity that was isolating, and at times even dangerous. The individuals that went on to manage this program protected its members and its reputation the way a parent should protect an incested child—with apology, compassion, and the vigilance of one who never sleeps, lying in wait for the next assault.

We could only hope to slowly educate a community where people to this day believe that incest does not happen. While the community lauded the program and its clinicians, the will to survive the constant reminder of this atrocity in the face of denial would be a Sisyphean feat, laborious and futile.

I was so proud at twenty-six to say that I was a clinician on the Boulder County Sexual Abuse Team. But when I told people where I worked, I was met with a myriad of responses, not at all to my liking. The expressions on people's faces were ones of disbelief, oftentimes contempt, as if they wanted to start a row. On occasion I would find myself at a party sandwiched between the wall and a severely traumatized survivor recounting every torrid detail of his or her incest. It was inescapable.

The more intrusive the work became, the more I reached out to my colleagues. I found myself spending hours on the phone in the evening, processing a distasteful interaction with a collateral, or a hideous trial where my testimony was obliterated and I found myself shamed by my incompetence. The cases became more and more distressing. It absorbed and consumed me. It exhilarated and challenged me. I was different. It defined me. I was unique in my understanding of incest. It was in me the way something inhabits your soul—a temptation, a forbidden fruit. I could not extricate myself and had no desire to do so. It would destroy me or it would leaven me. It was anybody's guess. It soon felt out of my control.

I loved the Morgal Bismark because it was the first restaurant in Boulder that clothed its tables with scrolls of white drawing paper and gave its patrons glasses of beautiful Crayolas to draw with. The walls of this small eatery were bordered with fabulous photos of the bicycle racers cruising the circuitous route of the Morgal Bismark bike race. The photos intrigued me, as the racers careened almost horizontal to the road, defying the laws of physics. Their speed created a blur of extraordinary light and color, as if one were looking through a camera lens doused by raindrops. My hands would sweat every time I looked at those photos.

On Monday evenings, we co-facilitated treatment groups for sex offenders and their spouses. The four of us who comprised the team would tuck into the Bismark while we talked about our groups and what we had planned for the evening.

I grabbed my favorite crayons from the glass that evening and began my limited repertoire of flowers, using fuchsia, periwinkle, and sea green. If I'd been feeling exceptionally snazzy, I'd have spruced up my drawing with gold and silver, because those crayons had flecks of something sparkly in them. Robert Plath was sitting across from me at the table, doodling and talking about his weekend. His shock of thick black hair hung in his face as he spoke. His fair skin flushed with color, as it always did when he was animated. He told us that on Sunday he had a special friend come over and surprise him with a home-cooked meal. The "special friend" was the mother of a child on his caseload. When he began to talk about her, my other two colleagues grew immediately silent, and I didn't get the gist until a few minutes later. They were both appalled at his disclosure and gently but firmly brought up every ethical slant they could think of. I distinctly remember the dialogue growing more passionate and heated as he wove himself in and out of his story, denying that there was a sexual component to the relationship but admitting that he was very attracted. I excused myself to go to the bathroom.

At home that evening, I lay in bed thinking about Robert and his involvement with his client. I wondered what it was he was doing. I thought about his loneliness and the fact that he had professed his attraction to me after I had been on the job a few weeks. I thought this peculiar. I remember the day he told me, pulling his face close to mine, his eyes closely spaced, narrow and long. I remember thinking to myself that he looked like an animal, a fox. "I find you really attractive. I hope that won't be a problem."

There was a way in which he said that to me which made me feel as if I had to appease him so as not to alienate him. He was quite a bit older and had been instrumental in my hiring. I dismissed the thought and closed my eyes that evening as I went to bed. I was in over my head.

The next morning I found Tara, my colleague, sitting in my chair in my office, looking exhausted and distressed. "I'm telling!" She blurted out her claim the way a child would when they wanted to get someone in trouble. My coat not yet unbuttoned, I sat in the client's chair, giving her the faux power we all assumed in this job of distorted sensibilities—a job where we were imbued with responsibilities that we doubted our right to have. We could question men and women on a hunch or on intuition. We could dismantle whole families with the understanding that we would challenge ourselves to put them back together. The responsibility was unwieldy, undoable.

"If you tell, he'll get fired." I heard my own words and shrank back in the chair.

"Why are you protecting him? He's sleeping with a client!" She was disgusted at my naiveté.

I had no idea why I was protecting him. My denial came down like a curtain on my brain, eclipsing logic or rational thinking. I felt sorry for him. I felt that he was lonely and that he needed to be loved. I knew it was a primitive, ludicrous response. I also knew then that the material we worked with at times necessitated hurling caution to the wind. It eroded our senses. It titillated and seduced us. It empowered us in ways that were venturesome but perilous. This I knew for certain: The woman he was involved with had entered our system because her daughter was incested by her husband. My colleague's need to rescue her and save her from herself and her reality was an overt abuse of power and further victimized her as the mother of a traumatized child. The roles were all a jumble—it was a serious breach that love had no role in at all.

It was not so much the sexual transgression that distressed me; it was more a question of what motivated him, what lured him to penetrate a very stayed convention. A therapist is never sexual with a client. That is the rule. An adult never sexually violates a child. My colleague pushed through a taboo, and somehow he could rationalize this behavior to himself and to the mother of this child, also a survivor of sexual abuse.

Incest happens with such frequency that it is no longer a taboo. The incest taboo in our country has become cloudy and obscure. The atrocity continues to permeate our culture.

As the days eked by I found myself flooded by conviction and contradiction. As with any sex offense, I found myself looking for the reason—the need for intimacy, the need to control and feel empowered, the unleashing of an intense subliminal rage that bleeds over into the violation of a sacred relationship. I found no answer.

We were a team of people whose sole purpose was to protect children from sexual violation by family members. Robert's transgression was a shame to all of us, to our credibility, to our integrity, to our reputations. It was like a vile secret that the community would soon be privy to. We were disgraced. And yet, how was it that we had taken on his shame? He had lured this woman into a relationship. His presence was like vapor. And we, the survivors of this system, were left to answer to our community and to ourselves.

And so we told. As dutiful members of a potentially disturbed system, we did what we believed was right. I watched as he was escorted out of his office into the personnel office. I listened to the familiar strutting rhythm of his heels clicking against the tile floor as he was led into that office. The door created suction as it closed, as if he was to be sucked into a vortex and would never return. He was done. Finito.

And that was exactly what transpired. Later he was led out of the building, where he handed an administrator his identification and his keys. My heart flapping wildly in my chest cavity, I could only imagine that this is a small piece of what children feel when they tell a family secret, especially a secret that is dark and sexual. And I wondered to myself why children do tell, what compels them to reveal their secret when there is so much that they risk and the gains are often accrued so long after the fact. It was with great sadness that this question took permanent residence in the crawl space of my mind.

The larger system could not make sense of the travesty that had been committed, both on the client who was violated and on the team that housed the secret. It needed to apprehend the offender and banish him. It simply moved on. It shrouded its liabilities by characterizing what happeded as a blip on the interior of a troubled social worker, as opposed to a blip on the interior of an entire system. The system inadvertently blames and pathologizes its people—it seemingly fails to protect those most in need of protection. How can our bodies and minds take on a daily assault of pain, violation and tragedy?

Someone is always left to clean up the rot in human services, particularly when the demise of a colleague is rapid and without discussion. The system muzzles its employees the way a family with a secret creates a tacit pact.

And so we sailed through our days drenched by confusion and grief. We skillfully placed this dirty secret in a tight compartment and processed it in private, in our dreams or behind closed doors to supervisors or colleagues. And we soon became adept at this skill, because the scenario repeated itself years later, when I was at the helm of the team and another individual left her marriage of twenty years and ran off with a client.

Clearly the Sexual Abuse Team enacted its anger and powerlessness through sexualizing. Whenever the system is squeezed, the social workers are the first to act out. Daily, the team is infused with sexual material. Daily, we open the valve to purge the toxicity, and in the process we attempt to keep sacred our own sexual selves. We attempt to separate our beds from the beds of our clients.

*   *   *   *   *   *

The teddy bear's body is badly tattered, in need of much repair. It is missing one cerulean glass eye, and the other is badly scratched. The remaining eye pops out like some ghoulish-looking carnival jester—one that is both frightening and intriguing to a child. After the eye dislodges, Lauren deftly presses it back into its socket. She does it as any veteran teddy bear owner would. Without even looking at the bear, she navigates with her hands. She is tender and loving toward her old comrade. He has seen her through many a storm.

"If Mo-Mo could talk, he could tell you all of the secrets. He has seen everything." She picks gently at the bear, smoothing his nonexistent fur, which has worn away to reveal the fabric precariously holding the interior of the bear together.

"He needs some mending, don't you think?"

She glances away toward the window. Her body is coiled, sinuous, like a venomous cobra. I am waiting to see the skin of her neck expand to form a flattened hood—something that will shield her shame.

She picks at the stuffing that oozes out of Mo-Mo's barren socket. I think of the people I have seen through the years who are missing an eye. The gruesome concave cavity is either sewn shut, with a bruised purplish-colored hue, or a glass eye is plopped in, rolling around in the socket dead and unseeing. People who are missing an eye rivet me. I wonder, in my perverse mind, how the eye was wounded—a poker, an auto accident, a stray chestnut flung from a slingshot in child's play? I wonder how such people see their world.

I rifle through my bag and pull out the ravages of a sewing kit. "Let's see if we can sew up some of Mo-Mo's seams so that his stuffing won't fall out. What do you think?"

Mo-Mo is tucked tautly in the crook of Lauren's elbow. She tightens her grip. I realize that asking her to let go of this bear is like asking her to release an appendage to me.

"He has to sit on my lap the whole time." Her voice is tiny and childlike. "I don't want him to be washed, either."

She lifts the bear toward my face slowly, and ever so cautiously places him under my nose. I move my face back tentatively. I smell the bear, which has a faint hint of something sweet, like chocolate on a child's hands, but its scent is also dank and smoky. Mo-Mo smells of urine.

"I think if we tried to wash Mo-Mo he might not survive. He's very fragile."

"Fragile," she echoes, her eyes fixed on my mouth. I watch as she scans my face for a hint of trust and compassion.

Lauren situates Mo-Mo on her lap and I begin to thread the needle. She rests her head on the back of the couch and closes her eyes while I prepare for the suturing of the bear. I make idle conversation. I want this young girl to emotionally stay with me. She will not disclose the incest with her father. I surmise that the only way that she will be able to talk with me is through the bear. If I fortify her "lovey," I will strengthen her in the process.

My eyes are failing me in midlife. I used to thread a needle for my mother in the blink of an eye. Now I hold the needle back from my face so that I can capture the tiny sliver of an opening in which to place the thread. I steady my quivering fingers. The dark thread slips through the eye of the needle on the first try. Maybe I have not lost my touch.

I kneel in front of Lauren and begin to sew the seam down Mo-Mo's back, beginning at the top of his head. While I am sewing, Lauren is talking to me about school and soccer and her best friend, Rochelle. I am listening and sewing as methodically as I possibly can. I am attempting to keep my seams straight. I am aware of my intentions. I want to ease her mind, and I want her to tell me what happened. She is engaged with this process, as she sees her bear being salvaged. She runs her hand along the seam of the bear's back. She is quiet as she turns the bear over, resting him on her knees. I ask her which part of the bear we should proceed with.

"Do his privates."

Her statement sears through me, and I teeter on my response. I say nothing as I begin to position the needle. I gently take one of the bear's legs and begin the mending. Lauren is bending over Mo-Mo. I part the floppy left leg the way I would clean a chicken, joining the threadbare remnants together. I am chattering away as I watch her right leg begin to gyrate, pumping up and down as if she were manipulating the pedal of an old Singer sewing machine. She gently rests her hand on my hand as I approach the gaping V between the stuffed animal's legs.

" I am ripped like that. I am torn . . . " She cannot finish her sentence. She speaks in a whisper, so tiny and diffused. I tuck a wisp of mahogany-colored hair behind her ear. I am on my knees in front of this child; she is balanced at the edge of the couch. Her eyes swallow my gaze in terror as I hear a soft trickle and smell the distinct odor of urine as it streams down her bare leg, out from her denim shorts. She tries to speak, to say something, but she is mute. Her mouth is agape. She drools hot saliva, which clings to her chin like a downy strand of webbing from a spider. Her eyes, in their ineffable horror, look far beyond me as she continues to urinate all over herself.

She clutches the bear as I hold the needle. Her breathing is shallow and tentative. I place my hands on her face and get her to breathe with me. I can feel my heart skittering around in my chest as I sense a familiar dread that grips my soul. I have her breathe while I soothe her. I tell her that she is frightened and that I understand why that is. I tell her that no one will know about her peeing on the couch. I know just what to do. Her color revisits her cheeks; a fierce burst of scarlet softens to faint rose. I pull my sweater over my head and I have her wrap it around her waist. I open all the windows in the room and lead her toward the door. I flip the cushion on the couch, tidy up the room, and we exit.

At times, I don't know what it is that compels me. I have flipped the cushion on that couch many times. I have hidden many a secret under those cushions. Most often, it is my fierce need to extinguish any suggestion of shame. I have never lost control of my bladder in front of anyone—not at the age of seventeen, like Lauren.

She follows me into the courtyard like a forlorn puppy, Mo-Mo secured tightly across her chest with both arms. I suggest that the warm summer air and the sun will dry her. We walk several blocks, and I buy her a cool drink. I hold the straw to her lips because she will not let go of the bear. I see people watching her, trying not to stare, riveted nonetheless and astonished at the beauty of her six-foot frame. Incongruous, with a tattered teddy bear and the glazed eyes of a somnambulist, she floats. On our walk back, she prompts me to channel all my queries through Mo-Mo. Dutifully, I surrender to this vehicle. We settle on a bench under the umbrella of a luxurious linden tree. As she sits on the park bench, permeated by sun and heat, the odor of the urine intensifies. I pretend not to notice.

"Mo-Mo, Lauren looks so sad. What worries her?"

Lauren puts the bear in front of her face so that I cannot see her. She begins to speak as if she was about six years old. Mo-Mo tells me that Lauren's daddy is a police officer and that he protects people from all the bad in the world. When she asks him for lunch money for school, he makes her show him her breasts. If she refuses, he takes her down into the basement, into a utility room where he can lock the door. He has her take off all her clothes and he looks at her body. He lays her down on a sheet and he puts a pillow over her head. He puts his penis inside of her and he has sex with her. He always wears his badge. When he is done, he turns her over and he puts his penis in her rear end. While he ejaculates, he whispers in her ear, "If you tell, no one will believe you, you cunt-faced whore! You filthy bitch!" He leaves her in the dark.

She listens as he unlocks the hook that fastens the door. She does not move until she hears him at the top landing of the stairs. She feels the iciness of the concrete floor. This began when she was six. She is now seventeen. She prays to God every night that he will be in the line of fire and that he will be gunned down. While he is lying in his own blood, she will squat and urinate on him; like a dog, she will piss all over his face as he lies dying.

My eyes are fixed on Mo-Mo's one glass eye. In the midst of this diatribe, it pops from the socket, as if nudged by some poltergeist. My heart leaps when this happens, its pace accelerating, spooked out of my mind on this glorious sun-dappled day. I am thinking that if Lauren extracts both of the bear's eyes, he will not be able to watch her when her father penetrates her. If she urinates on Mo-Mo, no one will want to come near her. Her father will stay away because of the stench.

Where is Mo-Mo when her father takes her to the basement? This towering beauty of a young woman, clutches a ragged, tattered toy as if it were the last vestiges of her control.

When she moves the bear away from her face, I see an expression that I have only been privy to a few times in my career. Her head is tilted to the side, a strand of hair catches a ray of sunlight, and its metallic coppery highlights glisten. Her bottom lip drips over her mouth, her eyes a hollow basin for her tears; she looks directly into my eyes and asks me if I still like her. Words burst like warm puffs of air from my lips. I cannot form a response. Then I ask her if I can hold her. I don't want her to see me cry.

She rests her head on my shoulder. I feel Mo-Mo between our tummies. I smell the rancid ammonia stench of her urine. I inhale it the way one would breathe in an abhorrent, noxious vapor, breathing shallowly, mostly through the mouth. She cries silently into my shoulder, and I think of all the times in my life that I have wanted to ask people if they still liked me, all the times that I have offended people or tried to apologize for who I was or who I was not. Such a primitive query—one that splits my heart open and reminds me of when I was a little girl, so unformed and uncertain, always self-deprecating, attempting to make amends for everything and anything so that people would not be displeased with me, so that I would not incur their wrath.

I lose myself in our embrace. I hold her the way she holds her bear. I don't want her to unravel and spill out. I want to sew her up, ensuring her a seamless garment where she will never again be poked, prodded, or split.

Back in the playroom, I close the door and begin to unzip the upholstery cover from the cushion, which I pull onto the floor. Underneath the cushion is a plethora of paraphernalia. Thousands of families and children have sat on this couch, where they have huddled and held each other, often for the last time. Hearts have been split asunder on this couch. There are pacifiers and crayons, and wrappers from treats and snacks—pieces of crackers and M&M's. There are playing cards and plastic baubles, probably worn by a little princess. There is a small race car and a dirty infant sock. Tucked in a seam under the rolled arm of the couch is a note, penned in a child's hand. It says, "Mommy, I love you. Take me home." I clutch the note the way Lauren did Mo-Mo. I think of the mother who could not fulfill her child's wish and tucked that missive far into an anonymous couch, creating an invisibility so that she would not feel her own failing, her own historic pain.

So many stains mar the slipcover of the couch that its original fabric is indistinct. There are vomit and tears and urine and ground-in food and mucus and feces. Each stain connects with a story, each more heart-wrenching than the next. The couch has hosted reunions and partings, goodbyes and hellos. It has been a small island of pain and joy, where relationships have collapsed and some perhaps have been healed. It is a monument to the unutterable pain of separation and joy of reunification between parent and child.

Overcome by the remnants of tattered lives I have found, I feel an abtruse sense of sadness. The fabric on the couch is threadbare, the seams are ripped; one arm displays yellow foam that has been plucked at and picked at by worried, frightened fingers. I have most certainly sat on this couch and unknowingly tugged at the stuffing. I realize that I am no different. I am horrified that our system allows this disgrace, both to its clients and its workers. This one piece of furniture is a foul, disgusting heap of degradation that will take years to replace. It is not only a message to our clients, but a clear communiqué to this family of social workers that we are unworthy—a truly startling revelation that speaks to this calling that I have chosen.

As I approach the window to close it, I see a bevy of landscapers planting perfect rows of fuchsia and lavender impatiens. The lawns of the building are beautifully groomed. The beds of smoothed river rock encircled by flagstone paths are impeccably landscaped. It is a sham. It is like incest. This couch is the reality of what transpires within this building.

Many things in life are lovely and unscathed on the outside. Their presentation to the world is duplicitous and contrived. Inside, no one would ever guess how our trauma and our sadness could be strung together, how inside these children there is a hollow cavern of shame and isolation.

It is merely a couch, I muse. How is it that I have become so enraged by this object? I think that I have become so deeply overlapped with my clients that I confuse myself with the system and its treatment of tattered spirits, and include myself with the tattered.

At computer training, I click on the icon for the supervisor. The image is of a handsome, broad-shouldered chap with a stately, clipped head and dark, mysterious glasses. Next to him is the icon of the client, a round startled face with a gaping mouth and strands of hair that sprout like blades of unruly weeds from a round head. Captivated, I stare at the screen and raise my hand, trying to get the attention of the trainer.

"Who designed these icons, please?"

She curtly waves past my question, as she finds it distracting and unimportant.

I cannot take my eyes off these icons. I look nothing like this cool, collected administrative person. And what about those shades? They suggest a guise—a deceptive, illusory, unavailable person. I recognize, with a somewhat irreverent satisfaction, that I strongly resemble the client. I relate more to the icon of the client, with my mouth in a perpetual O and my wild, unruly hair standing up on end. That administrative caricature is not me. I refuse to be that idiotic representation of the system. I shut down my computer.

On my route home I ponder what it is that disturbed me so. I detest my association with the upper echelon of a human-services department, even though that is specifically what I have chosen to do for the last sixteen years. What a sham I am.

Out in the farmlands, I drive past a shanty that leans westerly, probably a result of the fierce Colorado winds. Outside in the yard is an enormous regal willow tree whose canopy spans the whole front lawn. One branch supports a huge tire swing, holding the bodies of three squealing children. There are chickens running wild and a kitten sunning herself on the back of some old mangy mutt, fast asleep amidst the din.

Usually, I would wonder where the parent is. That's exactly where my mind would go. Today, I think that there is no such thing anymore as social work. It was an art that I was able to craft long ago, before the days of automation and bloodthirsty litigious lawsuits and ridiculously rigid boundaries between people. It was a time when a little went a long way. Families invited you into their homes, and they were thankful for the services that were provided for them. There was less hierarchy between caseworker and client. Goods were exchanged without the fear of reprimand.

As a caseworker, every Friday afternoon I drove to the eastern part of the county to supervise visitation between a father and his four children. Mr. Perez had sexually abused his niece while she was on a visit from her hometown in the Southwest. Because he had molested his niece, he could not have any unsupervised time with his own children.

Their home was down a dirt alley, sandwiched between two other tiny homes. It was cramped yet tidy. It was a shanty of sorts, held together by sheer pride and determination. It was held together by the will of Justina Perez, the mother of all the children.

Justina Perez was one of the kindest, most gracious women I have ever met. Her face was sculptured, with cheekbones so gracefully arched and elegant she reminded one of a saint. She was part Native American and part Latina. Her eyes were the shape and color of almonds. When she laughed, they disappeared behind her cheekbones. Her left front tooth was gold, a signature that she wore with beauty and grace.

She welcomed me into her home. She opened her door to me each and every Friday afternoon, and if I was the least bit late, she would scold me, wagging her index finger and giggling as she covered her sparkling front tooth with her bony hands. I think she was lonely in her life. Saddled with the care of four children and an alcoholic, philandering husband, I was a welcome relief. We always talked about things that were important to her—her children, money, having adequate clothing, food, and whether or not her house would fall down on her head. I would sit in her kitchen while her husband would spend time with the children. She was always making fresh tortillas for dinner. There was always a pot of beans and a fresh vegetable being washed in the sink.

Her oldest daughter, Magdalena, has hair as black as velvet; its ends just skim the slope of her preadolescent rear. As soon as she hears my car crackling up the dirt drive, she flies out the screen door, helping me in with my bags, wondering what I have brought. Today, Mario, her younger brother, spit his gum on the grass, and when she put her head down some of it had attached itself to the strands of her hair; she asks if I know what to do. In my bag, I have two shimmering green sequined barrettes for her hair. I have T-shirts and shorts for her brothers, and a pair of hot-pink plastic thongs for her little sister. She wants to know what I have brought for her mother; I was able to finagle a twenty-five-dollar certificate for groceries. She looks dismayed. Hot and sticky, I open the door of my car, and she sees a package wrapped in soft blue tissue paper and gold ribbon. She reaches down.

"It's for your mother!" I gently spank her eager little fingers. She smiles the smile of a child who wants only to please her mama. "Let me get in the door. I'll help you with your hair, and we can give this to your mom."

Exuberant, she smashes through the door with the gift in hand, as if she herself had purchased it. Justina wipes her floured hands on her apron and graciously accepts the gift.

"This is from Magdalena and me. We talked about it last week." Magdalena throws a quizzical glance my way, and I wink. She proudly smiles and sits at the kitchen table with her mother as she opens the box.

Justina unlaces the ribbon like an eager little girl, rattling off in Spanish various and sundry admonishments. Inside the box are lotions and scents and a small bottle of fire-engine-red nail polish for her toenails. She almost levitates off the floor. She giggles and covers her tooth out of nervousness. She grabs Magdalena and kisses her head. She walks toward me, and I am babbling something about every woman needing a bit of toenail polish in the summer, and she hugs me. She folds me into her delicate frame, and I think that we are two petite women who need this hug, right this minute, and that I love her. I can feel her shoulder blades, and I know she can feel mine. She is shy and unassuming and hardworking, a mama who protects her brood like a hawk. I feel as if I want to cry.

I spend the next hour trimming the gum out of Magdalena's hair and adorning those silky tresses with two shimmering barrettes. Anna is proudly flapping around in her flip-flops, and the boys look handsome and crisp in their T-shirts. We talk Justina into painting her toenails while I finish preparing the beans. I have learned to refry beans from Justina Perez. At the end of the visit, she folds four beautiful tortillas in foil and places them in my hands. They are warm and delicious. I covet them the way she does her girlish delights. I drive home, eyeing the tortillas at the stoplights, ravenous.

This is social work—the exchange that is so endearingly human, so sweet, and so simple. There is no giver and no receiver. There is simply respect, compassion, and love.

*   *   *   *   *   *   *

After the birth of my twins, my husband presented me with a gift—three strands of pearls held together by a ruby clasp. The strands were a tribute to my three beautiful children. The ruby was the blood and the passion that would forever bind us. I wear these pearls on very special occasions. The feel of them against my skin is lustrous and silky; they are always cool to the touch.

Tonight, I fondle the pearls between my fingers the way my Grandma LaRiccia would pray on her rosary. Often, I bring the ruby to my lips. I am present to accept my award at the Circle of Honor. It is for county employees who have served the community for over eighteen years. I loathe these events more that I care to say. I am here because I want my check.

There are easily hundreds of people in this room. I am sitting at a table with employees from public works, the land use, and the county attorney office. Next to me is my husband. I can feel my martini begin to warm me and settle my agitation. I am bantering with these unknown folks and their spouses, thankful for my husband's ease with people he does not know. I cup my hand as the pearls fall against my palm, like eggs in a warm nest.

I recall hearing a rumor this morning that the person responsible for presenting the award to me tonight feels rattled and vexed at the prospect of crafting a short narrative of my accomplishments during my many years of service with the county. My soul is immediately stung. In my mind, I review the laundry list of my accolades.

I have worked here for 20 years. For the last 16 years, I have managed the Sexual Abuse Team for Boulder County. My research has been published numerous times. I have created at least three cutting-edge programs to serve this population; the county awarded one program. In 1992, the Sexual Abuse Team was the recipient of the Distinguished Service Award from our district attorney. I have serviced more incestuous families than I would like to remember. I have run this program with dwindling funds and staff. The hearts and souls of my people are held together by their sheer commitment and tenacity.

I am aware that in the last 20 years, the sharpness of my tongue and my need to push the confines of my work environment have caused deep consternation and distress among my administrators. I have fallen from grace like an angel that has tumbled from the heavens. I have given voice when the safe choice would have been to remain silent.

I never hear what is said about me that evening. Sitting at the table, I am sure that my heels are too high and I will trip going up to the stage. An administrator of public works is presenting an award to one of his staff, a man who has worked for eighteen years clearing snow off the streets of Boulder in the wee hours of the morning after a storm. His man gleams with pride as he listens to his boss talk about his commitment, his warmth, and his love of the county and the safety of his citizens. He even tells hilarious stories about the artful way that he clears the snow—in zigs and zags so that it glistens just so in the morning light.

I think that this boss loves this guy, and that this guy loves his work, and that he is proud to keep the streets of Boulder County clean and safe. There is such a human exchange and heartfelt thanks in his words. The boss takes the guy in a bear hug and squeezes the hell out of him, and I feel the stingy salt of tears in the back of my throat. No one has ever spoken about me in public that way. No superior of mine has ever lauded my inner spirit and my accomplishments with such aplomb.

I empty the last mouthful of gin into my mouth. I am next to receive my award. I hear my name, but I never hear the words. I am embraced by the woman who presents my award. As I ease back from her body, I feel a resistance. I feel caught. I look down to see that a strand of my pearls is caught between the legs of a rooster pin that she is wearing. It is a pointy, hammered-metal folk-art rooster, with some plumes of color sticking out of his head. But there we are, inches apart, unable to unhook. People are starting to titter, and the county commissioners behind me are laughing out loud. We are fumbling, trying not to break the strand. I am inches from her face, and there are two thoughts that come to mind—she is stuck with me, and I with her. For a fleeting moment, I think of planting a big, luscious kiss on her lips. Luckily, my hysteria passes. She removes her pin and I hop off the stage, spending the next fifteen minutes untangling the pearls from her rooster.

For days we avoid one another, but the story trickles through the grapevine, fast and furious. A colleague of mine finds joy in such a happening. She says to me, "Only you . . . it could only have been you."

We finally bump into each other and are able to laugh about our entanglement. She tells me that the employees and bosses at Rocky Flats are only allowed to shake hands; there is never an embrace. I think that it is because all the employees at Rocky Flats are doused in radioactive materials; they are all contaminated—that's why they cannot touch.

I tell her that there are worse people she could be stuck with— I am really not all that bad. Her cool, azulene eyes take me in— my entire body, from head to toe and back again. She smiles and turns on her heels, headed for the powder room to check her hair and her face.

Pockets of Compassion . . . When Mine Are Empty

There is a woman sitting across the room on a couch. She has her notebook open and is copiously jotting down notes, even in the margins of the paper. Interestingly, she twists and turns the lined composition paper so that she uses up every bit. Along the blue margin, she doodles a vine of delicate flowers, beginning at the bottom and lacing them up to the tippy-top of the page.

My speech is a bit clipped tonight as I try emotionally to disengage from my audience, which is a couple dozen graduate students. They are here to learn about compassion fatigue and how it insidiously weaves itself throughout the fibers of our being, especially when treating incest.

As is often the case, there are expressions of distress and discomfort; there are also the empathic souls who nod as they listen to me. One woman has her eyes closed. Most are a tad squirmy. Some are delicately balanced on the edge of their couches or chairs, with their legs entwined like clematis up a garden trellis. There is a man with a round, full tummy, lounging on some pillows on the floor. He reminds one of a pasha as he runs his fingers through his gnarly beard.

My fantasy is that some people are making their grocery lists. Some are balancing their checkbooks. Some are thinking about the seemingly insignificant spat they had with a lover or a friend that sadly took on a life of its own. One man is cleaning out the links in his watchband with the point of an unfurled paper clip. I would imagine that some folks are thinking that they would rather be anywhere else on earth. I am wondering if I have enough gas in my tank to make it home.

What is it about me that always lets that fuel indicator slip precariously to the red line? What is it? Is it really that I want to sputter to a dead halt on some windy dirt back road, where all there is to be seen for miles around are neatly planted rows of corn? Is it that I tempt myself, or I tempt the gods? Is it that I really want to lose my way? Perhaps it is that this is my life—always heading toward empty, never quite full, wanting to drop in the middle of Goshen and start my life anew.

And then it happens, as it always does: Someone in the room begins to cry. It is the woman sitting across from me on the couch. Her shoulders close around her chest like a bird that pulls in its wings for shelter from the cold. Her chin falls with the weight of her sorrow down to the beautiful shallow divot in her neck. Long wispy strands of black and silver hair shield her cheeks and her eyes, and she begins to heave, silently and deeply, from a place inside her that I will never know.

Her colleagues notice and are frozen in their responses. Mr. Pasha props his heavy frame up on his elbows. He adjusts his specs out of nervousness. Most people look away, as if turning their heads will magically dry up her tears.

This is always a fascinating juncture. We are well equipped to deal with a tearful child, but when it comes to a colleague in a room with other clinicians, the judgment roils around in our brains, either chastising or celebrating the palpability of such raw, unadulterated emotion. Some of us like to be held when we cry, and some of us need to be untouched—we need the aloneness of our sadness. Some of us long for the warmth of a hand making contact with our hand; it is the skin to skin touch that soothes us. Some of us begin to tear up because our own loss rests right beneath our exterior. And some of us are rankled and exasperated by such a flagrant show of emotion. "Buck up!" we say. "Stiff upper lip!" and all that. I feel envy at the accessibility of such sadness. Mine is so intractable, stubborn, and unruly. It backs up in my throat. My sorrow is stymied and suffocated. I no longer know how to feel it, and I feel such envy for the woman who sits with her head down, sobbing. I want to cry like her. I want to feel like her.

Gingerly, I make my way around the room, behind the couch where she sits, crumpled and ashamed like a lifeless doll. I wager the risk as I always do, and I place both hands on her heaving shoulders as I continue my diatribe, never missing a beat.

Her skin feels fevered. I stroke the strands of her long, lush hair, and she allows me. She takes my hand and she holds it with both of her hands, and she brings my hand to her cheek. My speech never stops. The breathing in the room resumes as the pasha relaxes his body into his mound of cushions.

I make my way around the circle and resume my place in my chair. My lady's head is raised, and the man sitting to her right is offering her a tissue. He gives her the tissue and gently places an arm around her shoulder. She folds into his embrace and settles there for the rest of the evening. From her safe haven she asks me pointedly and brazenly, "How do you keep doing this year after year, 20 years now? It's sick! It's crazy! Aren't you angry? I can barely hear my clients anymore. I can't stand all the ugliness and all the pain." She pauses for a breath, and I am pleased that her passion is pinking up. "Don't you feel like there is a perpetrator behind every door? How is it that you have not gone crazy? Tell me what it is you do. What is your secret?"

There is a torrent of emotion that rushes from her voice. I realize, as I always do when asked this question, that I do not know the answer. There is no recipe for resiliency. Yes, I have felt crazy. And yes, when I drop my daughter or my son off for a sleepover at a friend's whose family I am not that familiar with, I leave with the sinking feeling of "what if?" And I go home that night and wonder if there is a sibling or a parent who will steal into my child's slumber and touch or stroke my child, who will awaken with voiceless terror, and I will not be there. I think of all those things and more. Often, I take myself to a maniacal edge of fear so that I may find my way back again. If I could recount the thousands of perverse thoughts that have lodged themselves in the crawl spaces of my mind, people would be astonished.

With dignity and self-assurance I tell these clinicians that I entered into psychotherapy when I began this work, and I have never left. I find that it is an island of safety where I can say out loud all that I fear and all that I wish for. I talk about therapy like preventative maintenance—like a tune-up. I think about pushing my tank to empty.

I tell them stories of all my blunders. I tell them about Lena and the turkeys and the fictitious families, and could anything be more shameful? I talk about shooting from my hip and losing my footing and not knowing. I talk about trusting my intuition and letting that be a barometer for my sense of the world at times. I talk about how sometimes my dreams help me get unstuck when I am entrenched with a family, a child, or the almighty system. I confess to my sins as a manager of a team of clinicians: my murky boundaries, my own neediness, and the poverty of spirit I feel at times. I tell them of my love for my children and how, in part, I pursue my calling on their behalf. And that sometimes I think that if I keep doing this, God will protect my children, and He will be good to me, and that I will go to heaven despite the fact that my clients have told me that I will burn in hell and I have believed them. In reality, I know that everything in our world is random and impermanent.

The room begins to soften, laughing with me and at me. I tell them that, most importantly, they must find the nuggets of gold in the work. That what we as clinicians see in abusive families is baby steps, and that those are to be celebrated. I tell them that they must release the outcome of their work to the universe—that attachment to the outcome of each case, each family, and each child will kill them. I tell them what I tell my children: "Do your best, and release the rest to the heavens. Be kind and respectful of others, and know that it could always be you." I tell them about a cop who cried and said that he felt as if all his life in law enforcement was like "holding back the ocean with a rake."

And lastly, I tell them the story of a pastor who was giving last rites to a parishioner dying of AIDS. He sat with this dying man and kept looking at his watch—inside his head he was wishing that the man would just die, just hurry up and die. And it wasn't because he wished that the man would no longer suffer from such a dread disease; it was that he did not want to miss the eight o'clock movie that he had hoped to see all week. I remember covering my mouth when he said it. He said it was such a profane thought, coming from one of God's servants. I kissed him and I told him that it was one of the most humane thoughts that anyone had ever shared with me. I told him that I loved it.

And the night closes with that last vignette. There is no magic bullet. "Be kind to yourselves." I bow my head and thank them. I excuse myself and say goodnight.

It is familiar and discomfiting when people feel that I have the magic bullet. I do not. My therapist can attest to that. I do not think that being in this area of work for 20 years is a testimony to sound mental health or sanctity. Perhaps I will not know who I am without my work. Perhaps it is simply that I will know who I am, and that, in and of itself, frightens me.

When I come home at the end of the day, I greet my children and my husband, and I kiss every one of them. I ask them all about their day, and sometimes I don't even listen to the response, but just pretend I do. I have all the responses down, replete with animation, and all the packaged facial expressions, but my spirit is empty and needs to be refilled.

Of late, I have taken to cleaning the kitchen sink. Cleaning is a very yin thing to do. I am methodical as I scrub. Sometimes my daughter will hoist herself onto the counter and tell me about her day or the most recent indignity inflicted upon her by her brother, faux tears and all. She indulges my scouring. Pinching together her nostrils as the odor of cleansers stings her sensitive little button nose, she spills our her day, uninterrupted. Often, I have yet to take my coat off. Sometimes, I don't even lift my sunglasses from my face. Tacitly and without hesitation, my husband clears a path for me, like one who is heading toward the basin for a well-deserved retch. He indulges my obsession. It only takes about ten minutes, and it soothes some part of me that I could never even put words to. Trying to explain this ritual would certainly compromise its intentions. I begin with the white enamel of the sink, using a mixture of vinegar and bleach and a sea foam sponge—shining the chrome faucets, running the disposal, and spraying all the debris down the drain. Finished, done, finito. My evening can begin.

My rituals have been quite different over the years. They change depending on my level of stress, my bank account, and what my day has seen. I have wandered through bookstores, settling into an overstuffed chair that swallows my anguish as I leaf through some dazzling fashion magazine. There is a small wine library whose merlots and Bordeaux have the loveliest labels and most delicious-sounding names. There is a papery in town where the back room has reams of beautifully displayed handmade papers. I have never seen anything like it. Sheets of individualized paper float along a wall, each one beckoning to be touched, inspected, and held to the sunlight that filters through the front window. There is a heavenly, almost ethereal paper with the transparency of a moth's wing, randomly speckled with flecks of color, like confetti—one would buy a sheet and never do anything with it but observe. They are remarkable. Some of the paper has fibers of gold silk. The paper is like hair and skin, unique and unreplicated.

Then there are always shoes. My vice. I wander till the cows came home. The smell of leather and suede is intoxicating. Any shoe that suggests a slipper or a flat, with virtually no heel, appeals to my senses. Gone are my days of stilettos.

At times I have driven to a breathtaking pocket of scenery where Spruce Street meets Highland Avenue. The view from this park bench in the spring and in the fall steals the breath. The colors against the sky and the mountains are surreal. The vision has a photographic clarity seldom seen by the human eye. It is a secret hidden spot where I can stretch out in the summer and smell the cedar of the bench and feel the sun on my cheeks. It is a space where I can breathe, cry, and simply rest my eyes and my mind before I journey home.

I believe this is a piece of resiliency for me. The space created between sadness and anguish and the return to my home must be deftly crafted in order for my spirit to again find its buoyancy and elasticity. There is a property in physics in which a material resumes its original shape or position after being bent, stretched, compressed, mangled, or mutilated, where it is re-created or transformed into something of greater substance and durability.

If I were asked to draft a time line of my career on the Sexual Abuse Team, I could do it in an instant, and I would cry the whole way through. I could celebrate my joys and my accomplishments; I would certainly feel the encumbrances of my blunders and misfortunes. Most importantly, when I have fallen deeply into the darkness, I can still taste and smell and see and feel the glimmers of light. I know the children, the families, and the lives that have nudged my sodden body to the surface when I have felt the water saturate my lungs. I know each and every one as if I touched their beautiful faces yesterday. Somehow, whenever I feel as if I am done, something or someone appears, like a shaman in a dream, to bring me back to my purpose and my intentions.

When the terrain has been the bleakest, each and every time, my heart has been miraculously opened and my spirit has found its way back home.

On Wednesdays, I screen. It is the job hated most in child protection. There is something that I enjoy about it. To screen means to receive all new reports of abuse and neglect. Perhaps I like to screen because it is a way of wedging oneself between the deliverer and the deliveree. You are simply the conduit, there to receive the information and pass it on. You do not have to absorb as much; it is fleeting and less cumbersome. It is, simply, the facts.

I am taking a call from a school psychologist in a middle school who is attempting the find the point person for a day-treatment staffing. Her voice is soft and liquidy. We are talking and I am checking on the computer to see who the caseworker is for both of these boys. It is about nine-thirty in the morning, and I feel rested and, for some odd reason, revitalized. There are mornings when I get to work and feel focused and with purpose. My morning has unfolded in its predictable manner. All my children got to school without a hitch, and I had a few minutes to stroll the perimeter of my property to uncover the first hints of spring.

I sit with my ankles crossed, legs on the top of the desk, lacing a Bic pen through the French knot in my hair. Sometimes, at the end of the day, I forget about the pen and find it at night when I loosen my heavy mane. The first blooms of a coral crabapple, like pink marzipan, light the tips of the branches outside my window. The woman is describing the boys, and I am thinking about where to refer her. There is a pause in our dialogue when the tone changes, and she stops. It is abrupt and breathy.

"Can I ask you your name, please?"

"Yes. My name is Holly." She is silent, and I have begun to wonder if I have lost my connection when, suddenly and inquisitively, she continues.

"Is this Holly Smith?"

"Yes."

This is not an unusual question, as I have overlapped with hundreds of agencies and clinicians over the years. In a very small, soft voice she says, "You were the caseworker for my son, Garrett Graham Hart. You were pregnant."

My body bolts upright when she says this. I know who she is. I can see her in my mind's eye. I can see her eyes, cerulean blue with light green around the pupil; lips tilted up at the corners when she smiles; and the whitest, most beautiful teeth. "Genevieve? Genevieve Graham? Is this you?"

Her voice responds in kind to my recognition. "I knew it was you. I knew your voice. It's as if I spoke to you yesterday, and it's been thirteen years."

This is one of those uncanny overlaps of destiny. I tell her that I am astonished that this is she, and that I answered the phone, and that she could tell from my voice who I was. I tell her that not even two nights ago, I was lying in bed thinking of her little boy, wondering where he was.

"How is your guy? How has he been?"

I am expecting what every person expects—a chronology of events: school, sports, friendships. Garret was a tall, lanky, beautiful blond boy with a crooked smile and a delicate, almost shy presentation to the world. I can almost feel his little hand as he used to slip it in mine; tightening the grip, we would squeeze back and forth like a current when we crossed the street to meet his father for visits every Friday afternoon. His hands were so fragile, smooth, and warm—like my son's, whose hands I love to hold.

But her response is silent. There is air between the wire and Genevieve, stale and punctuated, and I feel my breath get speedy. I feel light-headed and I am gripped. I fear what she will tell me, and I have the urge to temporarily put her on hold, forever, so that she won't tell me something that I could not bear to hear.

Her voice comes across the wire, fractured. She tells me that her son "passed away" two months ago. I hear myself gasp. I hear a voice that is mine but feels as if it belongs to another person in another time.

"Oh, Genevieve. I am so sorry. What happened? Was he ill?"

Please tell he was ill. Please tell me it was some random disease that claimed him. I could listen to that. I could listen to the clang of impermanence. I hear a high-pitched sound go off in my ear while my left eye starts to twitch.

Her speech is slow and tight. She desperately tries not to cry. She tells me that he was just turning seventeen. He was at a party with some friends, and a girl at the party had had an argument with her boyfriend, who had stormed out of the party. That evening she reported to the police that she was sexually assaulted by three boys at the party, one being Garrett. Within twenty-four hours she had recanted her story, but before the police could reach Garrett to inform him, he had shot himself.

The ring in my ears starts a hum in my brain, and I feel a well of horror spitting out of my mouth and my eyes. I explode with tears. I am telling her that I am so sorry and that it is unbearable to hear. She is crying and trying to soothe me. She is telling me that he was a wonderful boy; that he did well in school, he had a job and good friends, he had a girlfriend he loved, and that twice a week he came to her house and picked her up and took her to dinner. She told me he had worked hard to heal from the incest with his father, and he had.

"He is very tender and compassionate," she explains. "He is so respected by his friends and the congregation at his church . . . "

She moves in and out of present tense. She speaks to me as if he is alive, and I am confused. I think he lives inside her. I hear myself expressing my sorrow like a record that is skipping. I feel that I want to see her. I want to touch her. I want her to hold me. I feel very small. I remember the squeeze of her son's hand. I don't know how to soothe myself.

At the end of our conversation we decide that we will meet. She tells me that she remembers how overjoyed I was to tell her of my pregnancy. She remembers that her son wanted to feel my belly, which was still flat. She remembers that he put his ear to my belly, listening for the baby. She remembers that he told me that if it was a girl, I should name her Daisy. He was bent on that name. She tells me that I would never know how much I had helped her little boy, that with my work and my persistence, his father had faded away, and that this fading away had needed to happen.

I cannot keep listening to her. I feel inundated and submerged. I tell her that I feel it was a blessing that we have found each other again, and perhaps there is a reason for this. We say goodbye.

All this time I can see people passing through the screening room, half listening and half avoiding. People ask after me. I cannot reiterate the story. It is too warm. I ask to leave for an hour.

I find my way to Lolita's, a quaint hippylike bodega that sells single French cigarettes. I purchase just one and amble up to the bench on Spruce Street. There is a bit of a bite in the air, and I feel chilled. I think that I cannot do this anymore. I think that I am too sad. I think that most of my day I feel sadness, and I take it and I package it up in a neat compartment, and someday that compartment will explode, and I will be remnants and parts; my heart will be still, and I will no longer be.

Garrett Graham Hart used to put his shoes in the oven before he had visits with his father. He would put his little sneakers in the oven and turn the oven on so that they would catch on fire, and he would not have to visit his father because, of course, he would not have his shoes to wear. That visual has never left me. Nor has the visual of Daniel Hart kicking his pregnant wife down the stairs because his steak was too rare. Nor has the visual of him sucking his five-year-old son's penis.

I never even smoke my cigarette. I huddle on the bench in a thin linen blazer, hoping to keep out the wind. I watch the clouds scoot across the sky. One looks like a fiery dragon with a sinuous, vaporous tongue that disappears behind a snow-capped peak. I cry. I weep the kind of tears that feel as if they will never end. I weep tears that have lived inside of me for far too long.

I didn't have a Daisy. I had a Lily. I had a David, and I had an Olivia.

Standing at the kitchen sink one summer's eve, I watch my children playing tag and hide-and-seek out in the field. There are tiny purple flowers that blanket the grass as far as the eye can see. They are wild, persistent weeds that I love and care to think of as flowers. I am finishing up the last dishes of a wonderful meal. When I bought this old farmhouse, I knew that I would spend a lot of time looking out my kitchen window. The view would be important. This is the evening summer light that one lives for. Every color is darker and richer. The ribbon of light across the field catches a wash of violet against the blond and chestnut hues of my children's hair.

I watch as my eldest traverses the field with calculated agility and grace. She tiptoes through the flowers toward the kitchen window as she balances a small object, the size of a fist, on the top of her head. With such delicate concentration, she moves toward the window, stepping into my flowerbed so that her face meets mine through the glass of the window. She places a finger to her lips, signaling me to be still and silent. When she comes into full view, atop her glistening hair is an exquisite tiger swallowtail. This stunning vision fills my heart and stops my breath. Her sumptuous green eyes come down to half-mast as her lashes flutter, trying to stifle a breath or a giggle. She is astonished at her good fortune—a breathtaking butterfly finds itself adrift on her soft, silken tresses and rests there. Its wings open and close as if in slow motion, as if every movement to and fro is a breath.

I watch the butterfly as it crawls up her head. Its glorious oranges and yellows are iridescent, like silk or the sheen of velvet. Its midnight black outline, with a dusting of royal blue powder, glistens on its antenna. I am riveted as it inches around her head, and she barely lets forth a breath. Her sheer delight at this ravishing insect, like an adornment on her head, spills forth from her eyes, as if she has been chosen. She inches toward the glass and places her lips on the pane. I lean over the sink and place my lips against hers, through the cool glass. And as would be with her nature, she has mastered yet another feat, a kiss with a butterfly balanced on her crown.

She steps down from the flowerbed and walks back toward the field to join her brother and sister. She tempts fate with a lilting skip, knowing full well she may certainly lose her precious sojourner to the heavens. Miraculously, the butterfly stays put. I muse that she looks like a wood nymph encircled by her fairies, out there in the field.

As the sky begins to don its cloak of blue, I finish my last dish. Out in the field the children watch in awe as the butterfly gracefully ascends toward the heavens. I watch them wave and blow kisses. Dishrag in hand, I wander out to the porch and make a wish on the evening star.